27 JU

20 JAN

26

Three
Essays

LEONARDO
DESCARTES
MAX WEBER

Other works available in English translation

Three Essays

LEONARDO

DESCARTES

MAX WEBER

Karl Jaspers

TRANSLATED BY RALPH MANHEIM

A HELEN AND KURT WOLFF BOOK
HARCOURT, BRACE & WORLD, INC.
NEW YORK

Acknowledgment is made for permission to use the quotations from *The Philosophical Works of Descartes,* translated by Elizabeth S. Haldane and G. R. T. Ross. Reprinted with the permission of Cambridge University Press.

Contents

v

Leonardo

as Philosopher

Introduction

Leonardo has left us a few marvelous paintings in a poor state of preservation, notably the *Mona Lisa* and the *Last Supper,* a self-portrait whose authenticity is doubted, but which all who have seen it remember as the face of one of the world's unique great men, and thousands of pages of notes and sketches. In addition we have the reports of contemporaries and his influence on other painters, who echoed his ideas in their works. The barest glimpse of Leonardo can still be gained from the ruins and fragments of his painting, from his daily notes, and from his influence on others.

Leonardo is famous as the *universal genius* who could do everything, as the *artist* who inaugurated the classical art of Italy, but whose tragedy it was that he failed to complete many of his great projects. Since Vasari it has been generally held that he squandered his talents and is consequently inferior to Raphael and Michelangelo, who were artists in their whole being and completed innumerable great works.

He is famous as a scientist. He has been called the founder of modern science. But this has been questioned on the ground that he did not use the methods of the mathematical sciences in his investigations, that the similarities between certain of his formulations and the principles of the future science are misleading, that most of the machines he designed were products of his visual imagination and could not have been built, that his application of mathematics is very limited and nowhere commensurate with the scientific acumen of Galileo.

He has less frequently been called a *philosopher,* an allegation that others have resolutely denied, arguing that he was lacking in the power to construct systematic ideas and concepts, that his numerous references to philosophy are without cohesion, and that he did not share in the continuity of the philosophical tradition.

It has been asked: was Leonardo essentially an artist or a scientist, or a philosopher, or something that cannot be subsumed under any of these established categories of intellectual endeavor? Leonardo became a mythical figure, the incarnation of mysteriousness.

Historians of art, of the sciences, of philosophy, have communicated the results of intensive investigations. From Goethe to Jacob Burckhardt and down to our contemporaries, men have tried to state what has moved them in Leonardo, to recall what has been forgotten, to restore what has been lost, to reveal the hidden.

I shall attempt to give an account of Leonardo's philosophizing, describing first the character of his thinking, then its content, and its reflection in the painter's way of life. Finally we shall look into Leonardo's particular greatness, which perhaps transcends the distinction between artist, scientist, and philosopher.

I
The character of his thinking

1. Leonardo's thinking—and this is its distinctive feature—is based entirely on the eye and the hand. What has existence for him must be visible; what he knows must be brought forth by the hand.

Leonardo praises the eye. It is less deceptive than the other senses. It reflects all the works of nature. Only through the eye can the beauty of the world be enjoyed, and solely for the sake of this vision is the soul content to be confined in its human dungeon. The loss of sight leaves the soul in a dark prison, without hope of ever again beholding the sun, the light of the whole world. Thus there is no man who would not rather lose the senses of hearing and smell than that of vision.

Goethe describes the consequences of this identification with the eye. Because Leonardo's "grasp of nature was directly visual, because his thinking was grounded in the phenomenon itself, he hit upon the truth without detours." "As clarity and discernment of the eye belong to the realm of intellect, so our artist was in complete possession of clarity and intelligence."

But what the eye perceives becomes clear only when the hand creatively reproduces it. In dissecting an organism, the hand thinks in movements without words, and it does the same in drawing from nature or in projecting a design of the imagination, which creates what nature had not produced before. This thinking, not in concepts, but in lines, forms, and figures, is vision and action combined.

The ancients disparaged painters as artisans. Leonardo reversed this judgment. In his view, nothing that arises in the mind through contemplation can attain perfection without a manual operation. The "theory of painting" leads to the "activity" of painting, which is superior to the mere theory. Thus Leonardo's thinking—and he himself looked upon it as thinking—was at once vision and action; it was thinking vision, vision made manifest by the work of the hand.

But the eye and the hand achieve knowledge neither by passively looking at things nor by blindly manipulating them. The visible becomes truly visible only through thinking action. This thinking action consists of two steps.

With the help of *mathematics* it creates and finds structure in the fluid chaos of sensation. It is mathematics that first makes possible an exact vision of things. "No human investigation can be called science unless it operates by way of mathematical representation." Leonardo has in mind a concrete, visual mathematics. By mathematics he understands all order and law accessible to the eye.

But for Leonardo mathematical insight into the orders of reality is not yet a knowledge of the real. It must be accompanied by a penetration into the particular, into the endless detail of real perception. Consequently he criticizes impatience and the passion for abbreviation. Men, he laments, wish to grasp the mind of God, which encompasses the universe; but they behave as if they did not have time enough to acquire a thorough knowledge of a single detail such as the human body. He himself, as Hegel said of him, went into such details "with almost morbid thoroughness."

For Leonardo the visible is known only through the tension between ordering structure and endless particularity. He never strays into fantasy. He always shows visually what he thinks, and he always thinks what he sees. Amid all the richness of his sensuous visions, he remains sober. He does not strive for special powers with which to contemplate the supersensory, but lives entirely in the real world; within it he preserves human proportions and remains a man speaking in terms intelligible to man.

Leonardo insists on perceptibility as the condition of certainty. Without the eye and the hand, nothing would exist for him. For something to be, it must be visible and tangible. All "things are doubtful that defy the senses—for example, the nature of God and the soul, concerning which men dispute endlessly."

2. But Leonardo has more than this in mind. He does not content himself with the tangible and the visible. His philosophizing is far removed from ordinary empiricism and sensualism. Everything that can exist for us, he believes, is in some sense reproducible, not only the external nature that already exists, but also and above all the ideas that emerge in the mind, the potential reality. Knowledge is not random reproduction (comparable, for example, to our photography), but a bringing forth of what the mind sees. It ranges from the drawing of possible machines conceived by the technical imagination to the painting which manifests the invisible in the visible, and includes an awareness of the symbolic character of all visible things. The imagination opens up accesses to being, for which the artist creates visible figures; it is only through the truth of these visible things that being becomes truth.

Leonardo speaks of visible surfaces. What does not become surface does not exist. But in the surface we must see the ground; we must learn to see through the sensuous surface to its asensory origin. The origin speaks in the surface, it can, as it were, be grasped, but not by the mere senses.

From the standpoint of method, this is the crux of Leonardo's thinking. Everything that is real passes through the senses. But what the eye and the ear perceive is itself spiritual when seen in the right way. Within the sensory world we are always soaring above the sensory world, but not into a realm beyond the senses. And conversely: in order to exist for us, the spiritual must become surface.

Throughout his *Treatise on Painting* Leonardo speaks of the spiritual in the sensuous, of number, form, and reason in the concrete world. It is in this light that he treats perspective, proportion, the elementary laws of movement, the structure of organisms, the expression of constant character traits in the structure of faces and bodies, and of momentary passions in gestures, and so on. But these insights, which comprise Leonardo's "science of painting," are by no means the ultimate secret of the spiritual. Leonardo does more than he says; of this he was aware, as he shows in occasional propositions, though he never states it systematically.

If it is true that his few pictures produce a unique effect on us, what is its source? The smile, the charm, the landscape as the background of man's being—are these in themselves the essential? Do these pictures affect us as they do because every last brushstroke is a product not only of intuitive creation but also of thought? Or because they matured in the lucidity of a philosophical consciousness? Do Leonardo's search for the true nature of being, his investigations in the universe, enter into the content of his pictures? Perhaps an indication is provided by two celebrated and fundamental features of his painting—his composition, which made him the founder of so-called classical art, and his use of chiaroscuro.

Pictures in which every detail throbs with life, but in which the whole is a unity thoroughly composed and in which nothing exists haphazardly for itself—this came as a revelation to his contemporaries and opened up a new world of art. Leonardo made a discovery which in essence could never be repeated. He found a cipher for the unitary order of the cosmos. In so doing, he achieved a classical perfection in which formula and convention had not yet made their appearance, the sublime and ceremonious, the pompous and decorative are still absent. But for Leonardo this cipher of perfection is only a part of his work, a step, not the conclusion.

Chiaroscuro seems to be the exact counterpart of this perfection of form. Hegel called it a magic of colored illusion, in which objects evaporate. The deepest shadows are suffused with light and rise by way of imperceptible transitions to the brightest radiance; nowhere is there a harsh dividing line. Objects dissolve in an objectless play of reflected illusions, which blend into other illusions, becoming so spiritualized that they verge on the realm of music. What Hegel intimates with these words was first discovered by Leonardo. It operates like a cipher of that which makes all objects transparent; with the pure surface of the most fugitive object it opens up a dimension that would be hidden by a solid bodily representation. What Correggio carried further and allowed to get lost in sensuous enchantment, what Rembrandt embodied through another unique metaphysics, has its beginning in Leonardo, as a new way of making visible the invisible—through the process of thought.

The character of spirituality in Leonardo's creative intention is also manifested in his attitude toward his work. He no doubt intended to finish his works, but with him completion was not an ultimate aim or criterion. The purpose of his visual thinking transcends the finished work.

It is no accident that Leonardo was not satisfied with any of his works. He was unable to complete his paintings, because his intention went beyond the limits of the work. In the *Last Supper*—it is believed—neither Judas nor Christ was finished. Goethe formulated an old explanation: "He was unable to complete either the betrayer or the God-man, because they are both mere concepts that are not seen with the eyes." A higher meaning strives to make itself visible, but the visible work is not adequate to it. The essential expresses itself in something that shatters the limits of visibility or in an incompleteness that leaves the solutions open. In this indeterminate visibility the invisible speaks, but it can no longer be seen. We glimpse a transcendence which nevertheless remains hidden; the incorporeal in the corporeal speaks to us. The work as it stands says more than any perfection. Even in the seeming perfection of Leonardo's finished work there is something that points beyond it. Leonardo himself never formulates any such idea. But this interpretation seems to explain why he was never satisfied with his finished work.

Then there are the sketches and experiments in which Leonardo did not even strive for perfection. He took ugliness for his subject, depicted real and possible deviations and abnormalities. He did sketches of cosmic events impossible to visualize, pictures of the end of the world, or of rainstorms. His head was full of chimeras, said Castiglione when the aged Leonardo was in Rome.

It is hard to speak of individual pictures. A Frenchman has said that all those who speak of the *Mona Lisa* lose their reason. The open eyes under the high forehead, the barely suggested smile, the quietness of her attitude, the aristocratic negligence of the folded hands have made spirituality visible in the corporeal figure of this woman. It seems likely that in the ephemeral person Leonardo perceived the eternal idea of nobility, which he identified with human reason. In her there is no coquetry, no seduction, no social mask, but only the serene aloofness of the soul. In lucid awareness she combines heart and mind, love and thought, and maintains the tension between them. Leonardo saw the dignity of woman, of which her sexuality is only one component. This spirituality in the corporeal is beyond understanding; it transcends everything that Leonardo was able to teach in the *Treatise on Painting*.

In Leonardo the clearest visibility takes on a dreamlike quality because it points to essential reality. His objects are not vague; they are sharply defined but transparent. He knows no degrees of reality, no cosmic hierarchy as in the medieval view of the world, but the one reality, which *is* the Encompassing and *in* the Encompassing. But he knows different kinds of vision, namely, the blind vision for which a reality without transparence is everything, and the true vision, for which all the things of the senses become spiritual, as though the invisible were the true reality.

3. The problem is thousands of years old. Because art must be sensuous and can be spiritual, there is a sharp dividing line between the art which, for all the splendor of its artistry, is confined to the world of the senses, and the art that is the language of transcendence. With all its magnificence the art of pure visibility seems insubstantial beside the art which discloses the invisible; the impulse to enrich life pales before the attraction of eternity, the vital-

ization of the spiritual before the spiritualization of the
living flesh.

Accordingly, philosophy, from Plato to Augustine to
Kierkegaard, has claimed the authority to judge art, music,
and poetry for the good and evil in them. The mere thinker
who examines works of art and takes a critical attitude toward them consults a philosophical authority in the artist
or poet himself.

Leonardo did not speak with the clarity of those great
philosophers. But he shared in their struggle for the spiritualization of the sensuous. Sensuous reality is indispensable; without it there would be nothing but empty
abstraction. The spiritual is the essential; it must not be
engulfed by vital impulses, by the passions, by the sensuous
figures in which it appears, for then there would be nothing
but an intoxication of the senses and a reality without
transparence. Nothing is real unless it enters into the realm
of the senses. But the sensuous as such, the purely sensuous,
is empty.

Leonardo may be regarded as one of those artists who
have most astoundingly expressed the corporeity of the
spiritual and the spirituality of the corporeal.

How did he accomplish this? A number of his remarks
throw light on the matter. "Unfortunate is the master whose
work is in advance of his judgment. Only one whose judgment towers above his work can move toward perfection in
art." But according to Leonardo this judgment which
guides artistic creation has two stages. First there is the
judgment which unconsciously deludes itself. Then there is
a judgment concerning this judgment.

Leonardo describes the first kind of judgment. The
artist's own *physis* involuntarily reproduces itself in the
figures, gestures, movements of the work. "For the soul,

master of the body, is itself one and the same as your judgment, and delights in works which resemble that judgment which it created by constituting your body." "This
judgment is so powerful that it guides the artist's hand
and causes him to repeat himself."

But this living soul, which in equal measure constructs
the artist's body and guides his work, governs the creation
of the work only until "it becomes our own judgment."
This true, "own" judgment sees through the other unconscious judgment. It comes to itself by constant listening to
the judgments of others, by the practice of different styles,
whereby it achieves harmony with all other judgments and
rises above them.

Where the artist's own *physis* erupts blindly through
its judgment and then remains captive to its individual
vital essence, the result is works determined solely by the
artist's nature. If this painter is "a fool," his paintings (in
narrative cycles, for example) "are without coherence and
conciseness; the figures take no account of their function,
one looks in this direction, the other in that, as though in
a dream. Thus every psychic and bodily state represented
in the picture follows the nature of the painter." But
if the painter's judgment is superior to his work and to
the judgment of his *physis,* he is enabled to give proper
guidance to his work.

In other words: the artist is master of his work as the
thinker is master of his thoughts. He exercises this power
by reflection. His judgment penetrates to every ramifica-
tion of what his creative mind and his hand produce. This
accounts for the length of time Leonardo spent on his
works. Such judgment did not impede his creativeness, but
stimulated and purified it. It was not the ruin of his work
(like the artist's thoughts in Balzac's story about the un-

known masterpiece), but its element. Leonardo's creative power increased with the power of his reflection. His work is the opposite of blind activity. The inexhaustible spell of Leonardo's pictures may well stem from this unity of thought and artistic ability, from Leonardo's fundamental attitude—all art and more than art—which placed him above his work and enabled him, thanks to his imagination, to express what cannot be said in words or formulated in terms of ideas or perceived by a passive looking at things, but attains conscious presence through thinking vision.

4. Leonardo's vision, this perception of the spiritual in the corporeal, helps us to understand the nature of his science and the attitude that governed his scientific investigation. Leonardo is rightly regarded as one of the creators of modern science. But in what sense?

A. For him, to know is to *reproduce*. In drawing and painting, in the fashioning of tools and technical devices, in scientific experiments, the work of the hand and the eye is at every stage bound up with, and completed in, visual reproduction.

The human body, says Leonardo the anatomist, cannot be represented in words alone. "For the more closely you describe it, the more you will confuse the reader. Consequently, you must picture as well as describe." In Leonardo's anatomical studies the drawing almost crowds out the text. He analyzes and clarifies his ideas in the act of drawing. With Leonardo, drawing became a method of investigation in the morphological sciences. Anatomists, botanists, geologists revere him as a master. He created the visual thinking that develops from drawing.

The objection has been raised that knowledge and vision are two different things, that to see is not to know, that clear form is a question of aesthetic judgment and not a scientific finding. This is not so. In all morphology the draftsman works under the guidance of the scientist, the scientist himself works as a draftsman. This visualization, to be sure, cannot discover any natural law requiring measurement, experiment, formula. But it opens up a characteristic field of knowledge, which is first discerned in the image, though like all science it requires language for explanation.

Leonardo has also been criticized for identifying graphic reproduction and art. It is argued that scientific drawing represents facts, while art creates a vision, that scientific drawing deals in empirical reality, whereas the essence of art is to convey meaning. Leonardo is himself aware of the difference: painting, he says, derives its power, first from following nature, then from outdoing nature through creation. In both cases knowledge is embodied in a formative activity. The anatomical draftsman does not photograph; he abstracts and constructs the essential. But in so doing he does not invent; he finds what is already there, whereas the artist, working with what he finds, arrives at something new. The dividing line is fluid, as may be gathered from Leonardo's physiognomic sketches and the drawings of horses in which he varies their movements ad infinitum.

B. Knowledge is based on *sense perception.* "All knowledge is futile," says Leonardo, "that is not born of sense perception, the mother of all certainty, and that does not end in visible experiment." He denies that "there is truth in sciences which from beginning to end remain in the mind, chiefly because in such purely intellectual processes experiment has no place, for without experiment nothing can be known with certainty." Thus knowledge does not reside in passive looking on, but in activity. The passive man is a mere parrot, the inventor is active. The inventor is the mediator between nature and man.

C. As a modern scientist, Leonardo strove for *certainty*. A reliable insight that stands up to inquiry is invaluable as such. "So contemptible is falsehood that, even were it to praise the works of God, it offends against His divinity; so excellent is the truth that it lends nobility to the most trifling things that it praises. Thus the truth, even when it deals with base and insignificant things, is infinitely superior to all sophistries and falsehoods concerning the highest and most sublime problems of the intellect."

D. Modern science is *universal*. The striving for universality is dominant in Leonardo. All reality is worth knowing. The range of his interests was unlimited. Whatever exists, let it be seen and known.

E. In its consciousness of *progressing* toward the infinite, in its eagerness for discovery, modern science is open to the new and free from traditional opinions. Imbued with this striving, Leonardo passed from a grandiose but closed and unreal world into a world that is open to reality. For him realities were no longer examples confirming what was already fully known; they demanded to be examined in themselves and known in every detail. Rejecting authoritarian total knowledge, he moved forward, searching and finding. He reduced the old metaphysical abstractions to means of expression, useful for the formulation of his thoughts, but without validity in themselves.

Reproduction, reliance on sense perception, the striving for compelling certainty and universality—these impulses characterize Leonardo as a modern scientist. But when we look into the actual content of his science, limitations will become apparent.

1. Leonardo's discoveries, especially in anatomy, botany, and geology, are not guided by a constructive theory in the modern sense, but spring from an optical view of things, guided by an all-embracing cosmic consciousness.

Thus in describing the human form, he aspires to "reveal the nature and habits of men." In his projected work on anatomy, he announces his intention of showing the development of the organism from conception to uterine growth, from the one-year-old child to the adult man or woman. Then he would proceed to represent the basic states of existence in bodily terms: joy in the different ways of laughing, suffering in the different ways of crying, combat "with different movements bearing witness to killing, flight, fear, boldness, and homicidal frenzy," the exertion involved in pulling, pushing, carrying, holding, supporting. Modern anatomists admire the precision, fidelity, and clarity of his anatomical drawings, but are disappointed at the absence of all the principles of modern anatomy: the idea of comparative anatomy or of a system taking in the animals and plants, fundamental plans underlying the structure of the organisms, the basic vital functions. They are amazed that Leonardo should have drawn the structure of the heart correctly even in detail, but clung to Galen's conception of the movement of the blood despite its incompatibility with his own anatomical findings. Leonardo seems to stop where observation requires an encompassing conceptual view to lead it to new observations. Observation is guided by observation and not by a motivating abstraction. Though he employs many traditional concepts, such as "natural motion" and "center of the world," he does not think them through systematically, but employs them inconsistently to express his observations, and not for their own sake.

2. Leonardo writes: "Let no one read me who is not a mathematician according to my principles"; and "mechanics is the paradise of the mathematical sciences." "The instrumental or mathematical science," he says, "is most noble and extremely useful." Why? Because "by means of it, all living bodies that move perform their activities."

On the strength of such statements, Leonardo has been regarded as one of the founders of modern mathematical science. But this view is not tenable, unless it is merely taken to mean that the general interest of the Renaissance in mathematics, its passion for technical contrivances, and the activity of the workshops created favorable conditions for the subsequent growth of the exact sciences.

Leonardo, it is true, speaks a good deal of mathematics. We have many mathematical drawings from his hand. But one cannot help noting how small a part mathematics played in his actual investigations of nature. In speaking of mathematics we may have in mind pure mathematics as a discipline of the constructive mind, dependent on nothing but its own evidence; mathematical science, in which mathematics goes hand in hand with observation; and finally, the mere calculation involved in technology. Leonardo made no original contribution in any of these departments.

It may be asked whether Leonardo understood the nature of mathematics. For practical purposes, in any case, it meant no more to him than the geometry that added clarity and precision to his diagrams, or than utilitarian arithmetic. Leonardo's thinking was often geometrical, more rarely arithmetical, because even arithmetic is less visual.

We must not look for the spirit of mathematical science in Leonardo. He was unfamiliar with the rigorous method of the scientist who elaborates a mathematical construction, interprets its consequences, and verifies it by experiment. Such procedure alone would have placed him in the community of true mathematical scientists, who advance into the infinite by secured stages. To him mathematics was merely an instrument for the exact representation of observation, never a means of pressing beyond observation and, by reducing experience to a minimum of measurements, of penetrating the world that has opened to mathematical science. For Leonardo the visual image remained the essential; thinking as he did, he could never have reduced it to the rank of a mere point of reference. In the visible world he sought for an invisible which expresses itself precisely in a qualitative abundance of forms. He did not look for physical laws, which cannot be represented graphically, but expressed only in quantitative or formal mathematical symbols. On the contrary, his investigations were a series of quick raids—he made discovery on discovery by observation and graphic representation, but failed to follow them through. He did not go beyond the visible to derive the process of the invisible and verify his theory by measurements. Radically committed to observation, he could not go beyond it. By their universal character certain of his statements seem to anticipate principles of mathematical science. In Leonardo the worlds of Newton and of Goethe had not yet parted. But in him the prevailing spirit was that of Goethe, not of Galileo or Newton.

For Leonardo, mathematics and mechanics remained a world of the visual and tangible, of what can be made in space with the hands, either directly or with the help of machines. He studied the mechanics of the body as he studied the mechanics of machinery. Both are functions of all-embracing life. In the light of the subsequent separation between mechanics and biology, Leonardo's conception is ambiguous.

In considering the priority he accorded to what is visual and alive, it is simple to say that Leonardo was not a modern scientist. But when we consider the implications of his mechanical view of the life process and the conception of the organism as a machine which, in the period beginning with Descartes, was to obstruct all true biological knowledge and inquiry, we must condemn Leonardo as a precursor of this fallacy. Leonardo was not yet aware of any contradiction between mechanism and vitalism. To him mechanism was a means of visualizing the structure of motion, not a general theory of process.

Thus Leonardo may be identified with the spirit of modern science, but not of mathematical science. Yet it should be remembered that mathematical science is only one component, and not the determining factor in the grandiose edifice of modern science.

Leonardo's modern scientific attitude is attested by his hostility to magic, to belief in spirits, and to all the opinions which spring from imagination uncontrolled by critical observation. He insists on reality. And what is real must come to us through the senses, the eye, through verified experience.

Leonardo attacks the prevailing belief in spirits. There are no such things as disembodied beings in space. In the realm of the elements, there is nothing without a body. "The spirit has no voice. There cannot be any sound without a movement or percussion of the air. But there cannot be a movement of the air when there is no instrument. Nowhere is there an instrument without body. Since this is so, a spirit can have neither voice nor form nor force. And if a spirit were to take on a body, it could not pass through a closed door." Spirits are an impossibility. Neither they, nor the human magicians, who lift enormous weights, provoke storms and rain, transform other men into cats and wolves, can ever have existed. For if they had existed, they would have been more powerful than any army, they could have destroyed any fleet by stirring up tempests; they would inevitably have become the masters over all nations. Hidden treasures and jewels would have been visible to them. They would have flown through the air in all directions, from one end of the universe to the other. If such an art existed among men, why did they not preserve it? Moreover, if it had existed, how can it be that the world still endures? For there are many who would destroy God and the whole world to satisfy a single one of their desires.

Leonardo attacked the makers of gold. He praised the alchemists for the useful things they invented; but in trying to make gold they are led into error by an insane avidity for gain. Nature alone produces the elements. From them man produces an infinite number of compounds. He cannot produce the simple original substances. No alchemist has ever succeeded in artificially producing the least of the things that can only be made by nature, not to mention gold which is in truth begotten by the sun.

He assails the speculative chimeras, the hair-splitting and delusions of those who babble about sublime and mysterious things. "Will you take refuge in miracles and write that you have knowledge of things which are inaccessible to the human mind and of which there is no demonstrable specimen in nature?"

In opposition to magicians, alchemists, and speculative visionaries, Leonardo advises his readers to confine

themselves to what is within their reach. Men should not
waste their powers on futilities in disregard of the actual
possibilities. Let them hold on to the things of nature, instead of attempting the superhuman, dig for gold in the
mines instead of ruining themselves trying to make it. For
"nature avenges herself, so it seems, on those who try to
work miracles; they will possess less in the end than other
men, who are more prudent." Such will be the lot "for all
eternity of the alchemists, the would-be creators of gold
and silver, and of those supreme fools, the necromancers
and magicians."

To sum up: Leonardo's scientific endeavor brought
forth numerous genuine discoveries in the empirical world,
but each remained isolated, he did not integrate them into
a guiding scientific theory. He arrived at discoveries
through empirical mechanics, the morphological conception of organisms through practical manual operations. His
fundamental attitude, however, was not a theory, but an
all-pervading view of nature as a living totality.

II
The content of his thinking
(metaphysics)

A conceptual system of the world as a whole was alien
to Leonardo's thinking. He took up every possibility of
thought, but none became an assumption with him. With
every observation he began all over again. The infinite
detail of natural phenomena served him as a guide in the
contemplation of the All, which is represented and perceived in every particular. To him, observation was not

merely a means of confirming his opinions; he approached things without bias, experimenting, playing, as it were, with ideas and images, without fear of contradictions. He lived in the world as a whole, but he experienced it only in the particular. The scientific discoveries that he left behind him were mere by-products of his quest.

1. The cosmos is not only mechanism; it is all-pervading life. The earth as a whole is also a living organism. Its flesh is the soil, its bones the strata of rocks, its blood the water in the veins. The ebb and flow of the sea are its breathing. Its body heat is provided by fire. The seat of its life is the fire that erupts in curative springs, sulphur pits, and volcanoes.

The world is a *unity*. From this unity derive principles such as: each thing tries to maintain itself in being, but each thing strives to be whole, to escape its incompleteness. Mechanical principles also point to this unity: nature carries out every action in the shortest way. Once the cause is given, the effect occurs in the shortest possible way. The earth is moved from its position by the weight of a little bird that settles on it.

The core of all things is *energy*. When a wave in the surf breaks against the beach, dies down, and is carried onward by the next wave, when the power of a stream enters into a whirlpool that nothing can resist, when horsemen do battle and horses in endless formal variations disclose untrammeled power, when the emotions speak in the faces and gestures of men, they all bear witness to the same thing: motion springing from energy. Leonardo's energy was nothing like the concept of latter-day physics. He dimly anticipates such concepts, but only as partial aspects of the total energy which he calls an "invisible power," a "supersensory power," a "spiritual, incorporeal power."

Leonardo describes energy. This invisible force has its source in living bodies. From them it is transferred to inanimate bodies and gives them an appearance of life. Without it nothing moves, no sound or tone is produced. Energy is infused in bodies by an external power, they are diverted from their natural state of rest. It is a wonderfully effective vital force, compelling all created things to change their shape and position. A body that is in its grasp has lost its freedom. Energy is in conflict with what it dominates. With overwhelming force it expels whatever resists it. Itself hard pressed, it overpowers all things. It is increased by resistance. But in this struggle it does not endure. The motion it induces does not last. It grows great in conflict, in peace it wastes away. The greater it is, the more quickly it consumes itself. Slowness makes it strong, swiftness makes it weak. While compelling all things, it rushes with furious speed toward its own dissolution.

Leonardo speaks of this energy almost as though of a living being: it consumes itself involuntarily. It lives in necessity and dies in freedom. It is forever striving to lose and waste itself. It impetuously drives away whatever resists it; but at the same time it banishes what opposes its dissolution. In struggle it overcomes its cause, namely, resistance; it kills resistance but at the same time itself. As resistance increases, it becomes more powerful, but thereby runs headlong toward the death it desires. Its great force magnifies its drive toward death. But such a drive is paradoxical, for all things strive to escape death, and force itself is only such a striving.

In all phenomena Leonardo "sees" the power that he calls invisible. He sees it in the struggle between the energy of the spirit and the inertia of lifeless matter. As it increases in intensity, this struggle between life and death destroys life, but death is immediately surpassed by new life. Struggle itself is the restless, indestructible principle that transcends life and death.

The most magnificent thing in this world of forces is the *sun,* which Leonardo praised as Ikhnaton did before him and Goethe after him. In the whole cosmos, he says, I see no body that is greater and more powerful. Its light illumines all the heavenly bodies. All souls have their source in it, because the warmth in living creatures comes from the soul. There is no other source of warmth or light in the universe. He admonishes those who prefer the worship of men, or the worship of gods such as Jupiter, Saturn, and Mars, to that of the sun.

2. Our earthly world was not always as it is today, and someday it will end. Leonardo sees the world in process of drying out and burning: the air will be thinner and without moisture, the rivers will run dry, the soil will lose its fertility. The animals will starve. Man will take many measures to preserve himself, but in the end he will be doomed to die. The once fruitful earth will be barren and empty. And then the earth will be destroyed by the element of fire. Its surface will burn to ashes. Probably, says Leonardo, that will be the end of earthly nature.

Leonardo's prophecies are a product more of perception than of thought. He saw the past and future in the present. The fossils he collected showed him the life of a remote past, when there was ocean where now there are mountains. His famous exploration of a cave gives us a moving expression of what he looked for and how he looked: "Impelled by an ungovernable longing to behold the vast abundance of the varied and strange forms that nature has created . . . I came to the entrance of a large cave. Bending my back, my left hand clutching my knee and with my

right shading my lowered, contracted eyebrows, I peered
to see if there was anything to be distinguished, but the
deep darkness impeded my view. After I had been there
for some time, two feelings stirred within me: dread of the
gloomy, menacing cave and desire to find out whether there
was anything marvelous in it." Leonardo made his way in
and was lucky enough to find an enormous skeleton. At
once he saw it as a living creature: "O mighty, once living
instrument of constructive nature! Your great strength was
of no help to you; you too were compelled to leave your
tranquil life and obey the law which God and time impose
on creative nature. Of what avail were the branching, sturdy
dorsal fins with which you went your way, impetuously
dividing the salt waves with your breast in pursuit of your
prey. . . . Here you rest now, destroyed by time, at peace
in this narrow space, your bones, bared of skin and flesh,
forming an armor and a prop for the mountain on top of
you."

Leonardo described and depicted natural catastrophes,
the end of the world, the deluge. He perceived the primal
forces of the cosmos through their creative workings and
the destruction of their creation; he identified them with
the one all-embracing necessity. Some of his drawings suggest atomic explosions. But the incongruity of such a comparison shows once again the radical difference between
Leonardo's view of nature and modern mathematical science. For Leonardo the primal forces are the secret and
limit of all things; they are the destruction of nature by
nature, whose manifestations we perceive but not its forces.
For modern physics, by contrast, the primary forces are
knowable and largely known; they are invisible, unrepre-
sentable forces, accessible only to an unintuitive mathematics; dormant in matter, they have now been seized upon

by man and made available for his purposes. Leonardo's science is the mechanics of perceptible masses and at its limit a description of the rise and fall of the cosmos. Modern physics is the knowledge of the primary forces of matter and a technique making man the potential destroyer of the cosmos, or at least of the planet.

Leonardo represented the world process in his so-called "prophecies." His pictures of the future are mere extensions of the present, not datable predictions of definite events. Along similar lines, his "fables" express wonderment at the destinies of man, noting what is and asking questions, but making little attempt to answer them. Mingling metaphor and immediate observation, he builds up a view of existence by observing what happens in nature, what men do to animals, the customs and occupations of men.

At the sight of a donkey being beaten, Leonardo reflects: "O indifferent nature, why are you so unjust to your children? . . . I see your children given to others in bondage, without ever deriving any advantage for themselves, their services requited by the worst mistreatment, and nevertheless they devote their lives to the welfare of their tormentor."

Leonardo relates the ruthless acts of men to what they themselves suffer at the hands of nature. Of cannon: "From beneath the ground will come something that will deafen those nearby with its terrible roar, that will kill men with its breath and destroy cities and castles." Of firewood, lime kilns, and boiled fish: "The trees and shrubs of the far-flung woods will turn into ashes. . . . The earth will finally be made red by days of burning, and the rocks will be changed into ashes. . . . Creatures of the water will die in boiling water."

Hearing the cries of infants being swaddled, he writes: "O cities of the sea, I see your inhabitants, women as well as men, fettered by strangers who do not understand our language. And only in sobs and laments will you be able to vent your grief at your lost freedom, for those who fetter you will understand you no more than you understand them."

Watching ants, he thinks: "Many communities will hide in dark caves and sustain themselves and their families for many months in darkness"; considering the lot of the bees: "Many others will be robbed of their provisions and then be cruelly immersed and drowned by unreasoning men"; and of cows: "Their little children in countless numbers will be carried away to slaughter." And he concludes: "O divine justice, why dost thou not awaken?"

He describes the cruelty of men, which will show its full fury only in the future: "Then creatures will be seen on earth who fight one another unceasingly. . . . There will be no limit to their wickedness. And when they are glutted, they will satisfy their lusts by spreading death and suffering, affliction, fear, and terror among all living beings. In their boundless pride they will even try to storm the heavens, but the weight of their bodies will hold them down. Then there will remain nothing on earth, under the earth, or in the water, that they will not hunt down, ferret out, and destroy, and nothing that they will not carry away from one country to another." And again Leonardo concludes: "O earth, why dost thou not open? Why dost thou not fling them into the deep crevasses of thy giant chasms, and cease to offer heaven the sight of so cruel a monster?"

But Leonardo also sees smiling opportunities for man. The enthusiasm with which he set out to invent a flying machine is only the most striking instance of the hopes he attached to technical invention, both for its utility and for the new experience of the world it would open up. He envisaged the development of the mails and of other means of communication: "Men in countries far distant from one another will speak together and touch and embrace one another, although they are in different hemispheres, and they will understand each other's language."

But in times of calamity men will succumb to madness: "They will hear animals speak in human language. They will see a glittering light in the darkness. . . . They will appeal to statues of the saints, but the statues will not hear them. They will obtain no answer. They will beg mercy of him who has ears but does not hear. They will offer up candles to him who is blind and clamorously implore him who is mute." On the occasion of a funeral: "They will show the greatest honors to men who can know nothing of them." And Leonardo concludes: "O strange mankind! What madness has driven you to such a pass?"

Leonardo was aware of transience, even in what is seemingly most enduring; he saw the corrosion of all things, and saw the cosmic process as a series of catastrophes. What happens today will happen for ever; he saw each barely perceptible incident from the standpoint of the whole; the evil that was done before his eyes would come upon all men.

But Leonardo's cries of horror were more lamentation than accusation. They are not prophetic agitation, not calls to rebirth, not penitential sermons. He merely contemplates the natural process, comprehensible in part, but though visible incomprehensible as a whole, the process which brings forth the cruelty but also the splendor of every day. "It is so": that is the end of his horror.

3. It is strange when Leonardo, this always visual thinker, touches on the abstract. For it too must take on a kind of visibility.

He speaks of the fundamental form of happening as the envelope of things, and gains an intimation of *dialectic:* The forests will bring forth children who will help to kill them: the ax handle. A wall that harbors tiny seeds in its crevices will be destroyed by their roots. In growing, the power of nature devours itself.

The thrushes were glad that the owl had been caught, but through the lime-twig this same owl caused them to lose not only their freedom but their lives as well. Countries are glad when their overlords lose their freedom, although the consequence is defeat at the hands of their enemies, who deprive them of their freedom and often of their lives.

We produce the opposite of what we strive for. Man scrimps and saves for fear of poverty, in the illusory hope of someday enjoying the goods he has earned with so much hardship. The more you try to escape misfortune, the more miserable and uneasy you will be. In the belief that they are running away from horror, men race like madmen toward its boundless power. Many busy themselves trying to lessen it, but the more they take away from it, the greater it grows.

Leonardo speaks of time: "O time, devourer of things! Transforming them within you, you give new and different dwellings to the lives you have stolen." "O time, quick ravisher of created things, how many kings, how many peoples you have destroyed! What transformations of states and conditions have taken place!"

Time affects the work of nature and the work of man differently. What nature produces is always the same in kind. What men produce is forever changing, languages, for example: They "have always been infinitely different and must remain so, because of the innumerable centuries contained in infinite time."

Leonardo speaks of *nothingness*. It is distinguished from a vacuum. For a vacuum is divisible to infinity. Nothingness cannot be divided, because it cannot be less than it is. Of this nothingness he says: "It dwells in time, it stretches into the past and the future, it lays claim to all works past and those to come, but possesses nothing of the indivisible."

In another connection he says: In the realm of nature we find no nothingness, it is impossible and has no being. And yet: "Among the great things around us, the existence of nothingness is the greatest."

Let us sum up: in his reverence for the visible world Leonardo looks on nature as a secret which reveals itself to the investigator ad infinitum. This reverence finds its fulfillment through the eye, in thinking vision, in the determination to take account of everything that is visible or can be made so. It finds its fulfillment in the transparence of this visible world, in which all phenomena become metaphors and invisible forces become visible.

This view brings with it an infinite delight in appearance, but also an infinite sorrow over the way of the world. "Nature was for many a cruel stepmother and for some a kindly mother."

Why is this so? Leonardo provides no answer. Indeed, he seldom raises the question. When he occasionally does, when the tension between the expediency and the inexpedience, the beauty and the ugliness, the kindness and the cruelty of nature demands an interpretation, he utters the immemorial twofold answer as though in passing: "Nature is full of innumerable reasons that have not yet been brought within the range of experience. . . . Nothing is superfluous and nothing is lacking in any species of animal or in any product of nature." And as to the forbidding aspects: "The deficiency does not stem from nature but

from the means with which she creates," that is, matter.
This, however, is not Leonardo's thought, but a random
borrowing from ancient philosophy.

4. What is man's position in the universe? Is man or
nature pre-eminent? For Leonardo there is no pre-eminence. As microcosm, man seems to be raised to the level
of the totality, as a creative being he seems to outdo creative nature. But he is encompassed by nature, the All, as
the great power beside which he is as nothing.

Leonardo sees man as part of nature. But within nature he is a unique being; he is nature, he exists entirely
in and through nature, yet he is more than nature, because
he is free to rise or fall. Leonardo sees both the greatness
and the littleness of man.

"Man is distinguished from the animals, but only in
the extraordinary. He is a divine being. For where nature
stops creating forms, man begins, with nature's help, to
make innumerable forms from the things of nature. For
beings whose behavior is as appropriate as that of animals,
such forms are not necessary. Consequently the animals are
without any such striving."

But Leonardo warns: "O man, what do you think of
your way of being? Are you really as clever as you suppose?" Man is a strangely powerless and powerful being,
powerless in the presence of nature as a whole, powerful
in respect of himself. That is his way and his hope. "You
can have neither a greater nor a smaller dominion than that
over yourself."

But Leonardo saw how many pervert man's potentialities and fail to live up to them. "Few men are displeased
with their vices. Many hate their fathers and all those
who reprove them for their vices. Neither object lessons
nor human counsel make any impression on them." In con-

gratulating his brother on the birth of a son, Leonardo went so far as to write: "You were glad to have created an active enemy, who will strive for freedom with all his might, and find it only with your death."

Utterly contemptible are "crude men with an evil way of life. They do not deserve so magnificent an instrument as the human body, but only a bag that takes in and excretes food. They are only a passage for food, and have nothing in common with the human race but their shape and voice; and in all other respects they are far inferior to animals."

In view of men's crimes, he adjures them: "If one man be found virtuous and good, do not cast him out, but treat him with respect; do not compel him to seek refuge from your persecutions in deserts, caves, and other lonely places. If such a man be found, show him honor; for such men are like gods on earth for us."

5. *Death* comes to all living things. Man alone knows this and bears death in mind. In his affirmation of life, Leonardo is always aware of death.

One animal lives by the death of another. Why is this so? "Delighting in the creation of ever new lives and forms . . . nature creates far more swiftly than time destroys. Therefore she has decreed that many animals should serve as food for others. But since this is not enough, she often sends down pestilential vapors on accumulations and herds of animals, and above all on human beings who increase very rapidly. . . . Thus for the sake of constant increase, the earth strives to lose a part of its life."

This tendency, objectively a necessary factor in life, has its subjective counterpart in a death urge. "As a moth is drawn to light, so man always hopes and yearns to find his way back to primal chaos. With unflagging desire he

eagerly looks forward to each new spring, each new sum-
mer, the new months, the new years, thinking that the
things he longs for come too slowly, and unaware that he
is longing for his dissolution. But this ardent desire is the
quintessential spirit of the elements, which, imprisoned in
the life of the human body, always desires to return to its
source."

The cosmic urge of the elements is present in the
drives of men.

But what reality has death? It is and it is not. Its being
is similar to that of sleep. "What is it that men passionately
yearn for, but do not know when they possess it? It is
sleep." "Every evil leaves affliction in the memory, except
the greatest evil, namely death, and this extinguishes memory along with life."

Knowing the law of nature, Leonardo lived serenely
and loved life. "Expecting to learn how to live, I learned
how to die." "As a day well spent brings happy sleep, so
a life well spent brings happy death."

Even the thought of an egg being eaten reminds him
of the invaluable gift of life: "Ah, to how many it will not
be given to be born." When ambitious men foolishly "content themselves neither with the gift of life nor with the
beauty of the world," that is their punishment for embit-
tering their own lives.

6. What is the position of Leonardo's thinking in the
history of philosophy?

Leonardo does not construct a system of metaphysics.
If we were to derive a system from his thoughts, it might
be roughly as follows: in the creation of the world art and
knowledge were one. God created everything in forms, and
ordered everything according to measure, number, and
weight. Mathematics is at the source of creation, the Creator

is a mathematician, but this in the widest sense, encompassing all formation, order, and law.

Cognitive man, the microcosm, repeats Creation in his cognition and carries it on in his own creation. His knowledge is itself form, it copies the forms of nature and brings forth new forms. Thus the work of the artist is not naturalistic reproduction of the contingent, but the form in which nature lives and is apprehended in its essence. The man who creates through knowledge penetrates to the foundation of the world, the revelation of which is essentially one with artistic creation.

Because Leonardo perceives the source in the manifold phenomena of the world, two things which are otherwise separate remain one in Leonardo's vision. From the standpoint of specialized, exact science or of art for art's sake, confusion reigns in Leonardo. For him morphological observation is inseparable from causal interpretation, mathematical mechanics from meaning and purpose, and beauty from symbolism. Thus every work becomes at once knowledge of an object, expression of a mood, and, by the infinite resonance of its meaning, metaphor.

But what of Leonardo's Christian paintings? The subject matter of his masterpieces, *The Last Supper,* the sketch for the *Adoration of the Kings,* the *Virgin of the Grotto,* the *Madonna and Child with St. Anne,* is Christian. Of this Leonardo, who seems to reflect on everything, does not say a word. To paint Christian subjects was as natural as the performance of Church rites at birth and death. Actually, Leonardo employed these themes as vehicles: for the expression of motherly love, feminine beatitude, the impact of emotion on men of different character, and as an excuse for a composition based on gestures of adoration.

In Leonardo many traditional philosophical ideas

meet. The sources of his ideas have been studied in detail.

Western metaphysics can be broken down into several great historical types. In Leonardo we find elements of the Aristotelian cosmos with its degrees of motion, more of the Stoic cosmos as a rational totality of forces, a few ideas from the materialistic philosophy of Democritus and Lucretius, next to nothing of the Platonic division between world and transcendence, and very little of the Neoplatonic spirit, except in so far as it is implicit in the Stoic conception of the animated world.

Leonardo lived in no system, but used them all only as means of expression. He did not subsume phenomena under categories already presumed to be known, but investigated them and allowed them to open up new realms of knowledge. This fundamental attitude—to accept no knowledge as complete but restlessly to pursue every particular reality; to delight in observation, and look upon all things with serenity—this reverence for the visible world is what distinguishes Leonardo from all ancient and Christian metaphysicians.

III

The life of the painter as a cognitive form of being

Leonardo was conscious of his life as a magnificent form of being.

1. Many writers have called attention to the sociological situation of the artist in the Renaissance. Like other men, the artist was dependent, in so far as he required the support of the powerful, on princes, cities, and the Church.

But an able artist was sought after. He alone possessed freedom along with his dependence, for he was at home everywhere and able and willing to move about. He was in a position to see and know the world. His arts were his letters of nobility. He acquired proficiency in science, invention, building, the arts, and personal skills, from riding to the playing of musical instruments. He built canals and war machines, planned ingenious festivities, created works of art which brought world fame to his city as well as himself. He became *l'uomo universale*. He lived as a prince among princes.

This was true of Leonardo. In applying for a post, he was obliged to laud his abilities, as in his famous letter to Lodovico il Moro in 1482. In his nine points, the greatest stress is laid on his accomplishments as a military engineer; only one point has to do with his peacetime accomplishments as an architect, hydraulic engineer, sculptor, and painter. To be sure, he too suffered great disappointments. "The Medici," he notes, "made me great and ruined me." He served Lodovico il Moro for sixteen years. When this prince was overthrown by the French, Leonardo wrote: "The Duke has lost his city, his property, and his freedom, he has completed none of his works." A few years later he went to work for Lodovico's adversary, the King of France; in between he served Cesare Borgia and his native city of Florence. Leonardo gained and maintained his freedom.

Leonardo conceived the artist's sovereign way of life as an ideal, which he also fulfilled. He made great demands on the profession of painter, and formulated them more fully and clearly than anyone else. He planned literary works which would instruct painters in the knowledge that concerned them. This knowledge was by its very nature encyclopedic. If these books had been finished, they would have amounted to a new form of medieval *speculum,* a genre with which he was thoroughly familiar. But he conceived his encyclopedia in an entirely different and new sense, as a tool for painters considered as men of all-embracing science, and as a manual of original scientific investigation, to which he wished to lead painters. The painter's way of life was his great theme.

2. The true painter is *universal.* He "who does not take equal pleasure in all the things that are contained in painting is not universal." He "who is not a universal master, able to depict every kind and quality of form, cannot be a good painter." There is "no greatness in studying a single theme all one's life and achieving a certain perfection in it. Since painting embraces all the things that nature produces, all those which result from the fortuitous action of man, and finally, everything that can be understood with the eye," "that man is a wretched master who is proficient at making only one figure," "a nude, a head, garments, animals, landscapes."

Universal painting of this kind is based on *knowledge.* Practice without knowledge is like navigation without helm or compass. Consequently, "practice should be based on sound theory," and the painter should "study with rule and order." "For one who knows it is easy to become universal."

Leonardo praises activity as such. "You must exert yourself," "the mind languishes without exercise." "Fortune helps only those who bestir themselves." But this activity must have its measure in the man. "Man deserves praise or blame only for the things which it is in his power to do or leave undone." "Do not strive for the impossible."

Activity is the main thing. "Death rather than weariness." "A life well spent is long." "He who is fastened to a star does not turn back."

But it is *love,* and not mere empty industry and con-
scientiousness, that permits a man to soar in his action. "To
learn to know the admirable things of nature, that is the
way to love the architect, that great inventor. Great love
springs from great knowledge of the beloved object." The
lover is moved by the thing he loves, but if "what he loves
is base, the lover becomes base." False love leads down-
ward. "In the beginning one resists more easily than at
the end." "Intellectual passion drives out sensuality."

Neither knowledge, nor a skillful hand, nor industry,
nor universality, nor love, can produce anything by itself.
The essential is *imagination,* which is always original.
"Never should a painter imitate the manner of another;
for in respect of art he will be termed not a child but a
grandchild of nature."

Strange phenomena suggest to Leonardo how inven-
tiveness can be stimulated: "If you look at walls spotted
with all sorts of stains or at rocks of various composition,
or at ashes in the fire, or at clouds or mud, you will discover wonderful inventions in them, landscapes and fantastic things such as devils, human heads, animals, battles,
cliffs, oceans, clouds, or woods." But he goes on at once to
warn the reader: this vision is still nothing. "It is exactly
as with the sound of bells, in whose ringing you may intro-
duce any name or word you can imagine. But although
such stains give you inventions, they do not teach you to
complete anything whatsoever."

Work on the basis of knowledge, and the judgment
which precedes each work and makes critical decisions—
these two make possible the activity of the painter whose
imagination has given him forms.

3. How does a painter live with other men? He will
inevitably suffer: "No perfect talent without great suffer-

ing." He should learn "patience in the presence of great vexations." If the vexations increase, you must multiply your patience, "just as you put on more clothes when the cold becomes more intense. Then vexations will no longer hurt you."

A painter needs solitude. Then he can consider undisturbed what he sees and consult with himself; thus he becomes "like a mirror." "If you are all alone, you belong entirely to yourself. But if you are with even one companion, you belong only half to yourself."

But such solitude, necessary for reflection and inspiration, does not occupy all the painter's time. Leonardo insists on companionship: it is better to draw in the company of others than alone. Rivalry acts as a spur. You learn from those who work more ably than you. Praise encourages. Since we delude ourselves so readily about our own accomplishments, it is good "to listen willingly to what your adversaries say of your work; hate is more powerful than love." Thus we should not refuse to hear the opinion of anyone.

In friendship Leonardo demands magnanimity: "Blame your friend privately, praise him in public." But emulation should never cease: "Pitiful is the pupil who does not outdo his master."

4. Leonardo's high ideal of the painter's existence is based on the importance of painting as an instrument of knowledge. In the manner of the traditional disputes about the relative merits of the active and the contemplative life, or of the humanities and medicine, Leonardo compares painting and poetry and accords the higher rank to painting.

Poetry is painting that is heard and not seen, painting is poetry that is seen. Poetry is blind painting, painting is mute poetry. Poetry treats of moral philosophy, painting encompasses natural philosophy. Poetry describes the activities of the mind, painting shows what the mind effects by movements of the body.

The pre-eminence of painting is evident for Leonardo. Painting is as far removed from poetry as the body from its shadow. Painting has the thing itself, it presents the works of nature to the intellect and feeling; poetry has only words. Hence if poetry is to convey an impression of reality, it must be complemented by the imagination.

Only painting can fully represent reality. It "extends to the surfaces, colors, and figures of all the things created by nature." Thought, to be sure, penetrates to the inside of bodies, conceives their intrinsic forces. But it is not saturated with such truth as the painter brings forth. For in his own being he apprehends the first truth of bodies. The eye is less deluded than the intellect.

Painting is science, it is the source of sciences, and it goes beyond science.

It is based on geometry and arithmetic. It invented perspective. Through perspective it instructs astronomers, it shows geometry how to form figures, instructs engineers and builders of machines.

It studies bodies according to their structure and movement, so becoming anatomy, zoology, botany, and geology. It "concerns itself with works human and divine, all those which are contained by a surface, that is, contours of their own."

It invented the signs used in writing.

It is more than a doctrine. It is an art. It not only studies but also produces. The scope of what the painter brings to knowledge by making it visible is all-embracing. "The painter is master over the worlds of reality and dream." "He outdoes nature. For the productions of nature

are finite in number, but the works which the eye commands the hand to execute are infinite, as the painter shows
by inventing innumerable forms of animals, shrubs, trees,
and situations." "If a painter wishes to perceive beauties
that move him to love, he is lord and God over them. If he
yearns for inhabited regions or deserts, if he wishes to see
valleys, or large expanses from mountain peaks, or the
horizon of the sea, he has all these at his command. Everything there is in the universe, in reality or in the imagination—all this he has first in his mind and then in his hands."

Painting is more satisfying, because it shows the exact
portrait of the object that is loved; it arouses the senses
more easily than poetry.

Painting is communicable to all; its language is equally
comprehensible to the Greek, Latin, or German, while
poetry is bound up with a particular language.

Painting is a more noble art; ability to paint cannot
be acquired by all. Its works cannot be reproduced in many
copies like books. Essentially literature garners up wares
that have been made by other artisans. When a poet tries
to speak of astrology, he steals from the astrologer, of philosophy, from the philosopher.

If some of Leonardo's formulations verge on the absurd, it is only because he allowed the richness of the visual
world, which he actively knew, to blunt his feeling for the
rest.

As a result he himself was unaware of the value of his
writing, though he composed the clearest expositions and
magnificent poetic passages. According to Goethe, it was
Leonardo's lucid and rational visual view of the world that
enabled him to paint also with words, setting before our
eyes the violent movements of complicated happenings
such as battles or storms.

It also followed that he did not revise his written texts, that he preserved all the stages of expression, from the haphazard and inane to the perfect formulation, nowhere striving for perfection; that he made no attempt at order or disciplined construction and did not go beyond the spontaneity of immediate diction.

Leonardo did not despise poetry, he merely placed it in a lower rank than painting. But a very different tone becomes audible in his angry attack on men of letters. Their high claims are absurd, their criticism infuriating. They find fault with inventors, because they themselves have never succeeded in inventing anything. They cite the authority of writers for their opinions, exercising not so much their intelligence as their memory. They deck themselves out with other people's accomplishments. They call painting a mechanical art. They look down on painters, because they are not scholars. But anyone who looks down on painting loves neither philosophy nor nature.

Leonardo carried on a memorable struggle. The wordless world of the eye, painting as a language of the visible, combats intellectual discourse as the abstract language of writing and speech. Experience is opposed to book learning. Active creation in concrete works is opposed to the derived character of the language of words. In his whole being, this man who gained knowledge through action, who created with his hands, despised the existence of the writer alienated from life.

Most painters do not write. Their lives are not long enough to complete their own work. And painting itself does not disclose itself and its ultimate intention in words. "Like the excellent works of nature, painting ennobles itself by its own resources, without the help of any other tongue."

But Leonardo took it upon himself to write. He believed that in general writers "can gain no insight into the science of painting," but that his own precepts were different, since they were "derived not so much from the words of others as from experience."

IV
Characterization of Leonardo

We have considered Leonardo's method (to penetrate to the spirit within the body by means of the eye and hand), his view of the world (the cosmos of forces), and his form of existence (the life of the painter, who gains knowledge through vision). Now let us go back to our initial question: in what sense was Leonardo a philosopher?

1. If Leonardo is taken as one of the founders of modern mathematical science, it is an easy matter to refute this contention and so seemingly discredit the whole of his scientific endeavor. If Leonardo is taken as a universal modern scientist, it can be shown that admirable as his discoveries in anatomy, geology, botany may be, they have been superseded in practice and are of purely historical interest. If he is taken as a painter, his greatness is unassailable, but here again it may be argued that his work itself is fragmentary, and that its author is more of a celebrity than a continuously active stimulus. Thus he is known chiefly as a historical figure, as one of the pioneers of classical art, as merely one—and not necessarily the greatest—among many great artists.

But in one respect we discern a unique greatness which is more than historical: in the being itself, who was the source of all this scientific and artistic creation and whom it served: the personal embodiment of a philosophical existence and knowledge of the world.

Here the scientist, the technician, the artist are one, and in this unity no one factor is dominant. It is not Leonardo's intention but the interest of posterity which singles out one as the essential—usually the artist. We may call this unity Leonardo the philosopher, if by philosophy we mean not a category of science, not a doctrine, but a universal knowledge which gains awareness of itself as a whole and takes itself in hand, hence as a form of human existence which embraces knowledge. In art, science, painting, architecture, and at the same time above them is situated a spiritual area, into which they all lead; they are not self-sufficient. Such a philosophy gains historical weight where it becomes communicable as a whole in existence, work, and thought. Leonardo is a philosopher in the same sense as Goethe.

There are several poet philosophers. Leonardo was the only artist philosopher of a high order. In him art became the organon of philosophy, because he not only carried on the activity of the artist as an instrument of knowledge but also made it an object of reflection. This distinguishes him essentially from such great metaphysical artists as Michelangelo and Rembrandt. But he is also distinguished from those who are explicitly termed philosophers by his method of philosophizing. Because art was the organon of his philosophy, Leonardo's philosophical medium was not so much rational logic and systematic conceptual construction as a concrete philosophical logic and a conscious way of life.

What Leonardo was and did demonstrates: First, that philosophy remains poor and incomplete without some-

thing that is more than thought, that first gives body to
ideas, something that is created in art and poetry, and that
this must become an organon of philosophical insight. Secondly: Leonardo's life and work bear witness to the authority which everywhere, and also in art, sees the alternative and decides between good and evil, true and false, substantial and empty, salutary and unsalutary. For art, like all
other realizations, is an element of believing existence and
as such subject to this Platonic judgment. What we speak of
here is something fundamentally different from what con-
noisseurs of art call quality. For spiritual creation can be
Luciferian, high in "quality" and worthless in its enchantment, beguiling men into irresponsible aesthetic enjoyment, admirable and terrifying.

2. Where unity of the whole becomes intellectual reality and is aware of itself as such, philosophy is present.
Great philosophers of the nineteenth century believed the
division of spiritual life into provinces such as art, literature,
science, and religion to be fundamental. The tangible existence of works of art, works of literature, scientific findings,
religions, made this classification convincing, and it became
so deeply ingrained by habit that we have great difficulty
in shaking it off.

Applied to Leonardo, such a view carries the following
implications: He is famous for his paintings, much less for
his scarcely known literary work, still less for his scientific
findings, which seem to be mere curiosities, amazing us by
their anticipation of future discoveries. From this standpoint, his science appears to be a mere secondary activity,
without any real relation to his art. We can be interested in
one without necessarily being interested in the other. Leonardo's many-sidedness is not the many-sidedness of a unity

that lies in the nature of things, but the regrettable dispersion of an overversatile talent.

A proper appreciation of Leonardo is possible only if we understand the limited bearing of such a division of cultural spheres into art, literature, science, and technology. Then his painting, writing, and scientific endeavor point to a whole, which precedes all divisions and cannot be subsumed under them. In an existence such as his all the varied activities and states of being spring from a center and are directed toward a goal. This existence was a mode of being, of seeing, of loving, of experiencing sadness or joy, of perceiving reality and objectively communicating this perception. It is the unity which this man seeks as a living reality, which he himself becomes and represents.

When we try to grasp this unity, the historical reality that is present in this one man coincides with the objective problem that we are trying to clarify by a universal concept. One cannot understand a historical man on the strength of a concept. But we can attempt to know the reality in accordance with its universal principle.

On this point, I wish to say only the following: all these separate fields tend toward futility when they isolate themselves, when specialization becomes separation, when correctness within each autonomous field is taken for the truth, when each field, setting itself up as an absolute, lays claim to dominance. Then science, art, religion, love, politics, economics, each proclaims its independent law as an ultimate, against which there is no appeal. But the higher authority, which springs from the Encompassing, which imposes its measures on each of these domains and at the same time enables it to remain meaningful and in contact with the source, is not just another particular; it cannot

be apprehended directly and objectively, but only by way
of those separate fields. All of them derive their meaning
from the source, which is one.

Yet the fulfillment of this totality is impossible for
men. The more powerfully and profoundly it strives for
expression in a human being, the more drastically it is
bound to fail, and this failure itself manifests the truth.
But this never happens without ambiguity; it cannot be
compellingly demonstrated.

3. Leonardo has been much criticized. It has been said
that his whole existence was contingent subjectivity; that
he failed to keep his promises and disappointed his em-
ployers; that his work was at the mercy of moods; that he
kept turning to new occupations and never finished anything; that his scientific methods were without logical structure, hence subjective and contingent like everything else
about him.

The facts on which these reproaches are based are incontestable. But the way in which they are stated and interpreted in reference to Leonardo's character strikes me as
utterly mistaken.

This much is certain: Leonardo's work is fragmentary.
There are few finished works of art from his hand, and
it is doubted whether even these were really completed. He
was an indefatigable worker—witness the abundance of
manuscripts and drawings he left behind him. But he never
completed a book, neither the anatomy which was far ad-
vanced, including hundreds of drawings, nor the projected
work on geology and cosmography, nor the encyclopedia
for artists, which he seems to have planned. The *Treatise
on Painting* was compiled after his death and the title did
not originate with Leonardo. As for the countless projects
of buildings, city plans, canalization, military engines, and

contrivances of all sorts, it is certain that few if any were ever executed.

The question is: why did he leave his work unfinished?

The explanation that his moods led him to disperse himself is refuted by the persistence and meticulousness shown in the work he actually performed. If he neverthe-less left his work unfinished, it was because the attraction of other, related tasks made him set aside the work in hand, though always meaning to go back to it. He considered his work as a totality and held that everything he did must be subordinated to that totality. But the whole was so enor-mous that it could not have been fitted into the life of any one man.

This whole was knowledge of the world. But this was a new kind of knowledge which by its very nature could not be completed: Leonardo's aim was not a rational schema of the universe, but knowledge growing from concrete perception. This was the modern scientific attitude, as opposed to all dogmatism. Consequently, every field de-manded specialization. In everything he undertook Leo-nardo became a specialist. But how could any one man complete the task that has occupied the Western mind for centuries and is still far from concluded? He could not content himself with any special field, because what con-cerned him was the world as a whole; but only specializa-tion offered real access to the whole. His superhuman effort to specialize in everything in a single lifetime was doomed to failure. He would fling himself wholeheartedly into a single field and soon set it aside, going on to something else but meaning to go back.

Another reason why Leonardo could not achieve total knowledge of the world by his innumerable specialized endeavors was that empirical reality was not enough for him. He was captivated by the spiritual content of all reality. In order to manifest this content, it was necessary to design images in his mind, which his hand would fashion into reality in works of art. But since the spiritual can never be fully represented and since the idea is in advance of every work, no work of art can be adequate.

Filled with the striving for totality, Leonardo was assailed by new images demanding to be set down and by ideas springing from observation and clamoring to be formulated. Nearly always he saw an obscure relationship between these images and ideas and his total conception of the world; this meant that he had to take them up, that he could not abandon them. As a result, Leonardo's work, which achieved world fame on the basis of a few relatively completed examples, grew, like his entire visual thinking, from a vast field of project and experiment, without definite goal. His endeavor was a "working in prefigurations," as Gantner convincingly called it. Only in small part were these prefigurations projects that would attain their goal as finished works of art. They were not, like the sketches of other great artists, disciplined by their aims. Rather, they were a perpetual beginning, toward the translation into images of all things without exception. This accounts for the many projects which by their very nature defied completion, and for his daring attempts to make every mode of the invisible visible, often at the cost of failure. He did not see such failure as genuine failure, for he was convinced that everything could be made visible.

The fragmentary nature of his work with its abundance of projects in *statu nascendi* resulted also from the universality which finds all finished work inadequate. For in the context of a striving for total knowledge, which anticipates its fulfillment in prefigurations, the fully elaborated work, along with the satisfaction it confers, implies a limitation.

Leonardo strove for perfection, because without such a striving everything would blur—in his art by persistent verification and in his scientific investigation by the closest attention to detail. But only for a time. He could not, and had no desire to, accept limitations. He desired perfection in every particular, but was unwilling to lose himself in the process of attaining it. In a few great works he became a great artist, and in his scientific investigation he became a specialist. But he wanted everything to serve the one totality, which was always present to his mind and which made every shortcoming a hopeful shortcoming.

Wishing to build an edifice superhuman as a whole but preserving human proportions in every particular, Leonardo inevitably left behind him—apart from the few magnificent pictures, which anyone else would have regarded as perfect, and a few fully realized scientific experiments—a mass of painstakingly gathered but unused building materials.

In working out his ideas, in improving and correcting, in moving toward a purer truth, Leonardo was not able to preserve his sure, unique stamp (as Rembrandt did in every one of his drawings and engravings); he was unable to sustain his highest level in every one of his thoughts (as Pascal, Leibnitz, or Kant did in every note they jotted down).

But where he attained his best it is inimitable. In copies, in the work of his imitators, the essential is lost in favor of a beauty, an enchanting form perhaps, a deceptive perfection which, however, lack the uniqueness of vision, the reticence even in the smile, the indirectness of that which is made visible.

4. Leonardo has also been accused of other grave shortcomings. His life lacked roots. An illegitimate child, he was committed to neither family, home, nor country; he was a

cosmopolitan, who lived where he was paid to live, without allegiance or loyalty. It is pointed out that he did not marry and had no friends, but only patrons, pupils, and admirers; that he took no interest in human institutions, in law, politics, or history, and identified himself with no country.

Consequently, it is maintained, he had no sense of responsibility, he worked unceasingly at one thing or another, but never acted; his life was spent in irresponsible contemplation, bringing forth pictures of everything the world disclosed to him; he never attempted to change the world, never felt impelled to play a part.

It has also been said that the problems of ethics and religion interested him no more than those of politics; that his occasional ironies about the errors in the Holy Scriptures, the sterility of syllogistics, and about monks were the typical ramblings of a skeptic, with which he tried to justify his lack of faith and will, his inability to call evil by its name and combat it.

There is no unequivocal evidence to support these accusations. Leonardo's nomadic life, his exclusive concentration on his work, his indifference to politics are subject to varying interpretations.

He did not take a hand in the affairs of the world. He had no inclination to seek a position of power. Ambition, jealousy, desire for success seem to have been alien to him. He cared nothing for public life. What we know of his private life argues fairness, magnanimity, and simplicity.

Despite his many acquaintances and admirers, despite all those who cared for him and loved him, he was solitary all his life, but we have no indication that he suffered from his solitude. Leonardo relied on himself, without protection or desire to be protected. His self-reliance was unshakable.

His mind was too clear to be overrun by hidden, uncontrolled forces within him. For all his extraordinary qualities, he was without extravagance; for all his depth, we discern no eruption of hidden powers. Everything we know of him gives an impression of moderation and rationality. His existence was not grounded in any profound inner upheaval or consuming passion. What we see, rather, is patience, serenity, and an unwavering love of the glories of the world.

But his serenity was conferred by an enormous and unflagging activity. There is no trace of resigned, weak-willed sadness.

Leonardo's loving universality shone like the sun upon all things. But it had one limitation: it was a universality of active vision. His interests could be so universal, because he refused to be limited by identification with any historical action. He engaged in no ideological struggle, neither against the Church, nor against any political powers, nor any faith. He himself followed no system of philosophical ideas, but lived with an infinite openness to everything that can happen.

Leonardo was aware of the advantage of such contemplation of all things: "With the help of ideas we are universal and dwell simultaneously in all places; the will puts us in a single place and settles us there."

Nietzsche admired this universal impartiality. Leonardo, he wrote, "was supra-Christian in scope; he knew the Orient both inwardly and outwardly; there is in him a more-than-European quality, such as distinguishes every man who has seen too wide a range of good and evil things." Nietzsche counts him among the "magically unfathomable and inconceivable men, those enigmatic individuals who are predestined to victory and seduction." This strange characterization becomes valid only if reason itself, clarity itself, the pure love of the independent man, is regarded as enigmatic.

Leonardo's attitude toward Christianity was the unmilitant attitude of a man who does not know and is not touched. To him it was not a problem. He seldom spoke of it. He refuted the story of the flood, but on another occasion he wrote: "Do not lay hands on the crowned books [the Bible], for they are of supreme truth." He was said to have provided that the Church rites should be performed at his death, remembered the hospitals for the poor in his will, and left wax candles to various churches. Yet these reports are questionable, suggesting an ecclesiastical mind rather than Leonardo's. Leonardo lived with the transcendence of the spiritual; he speaks of God, but the God he speaks of is not the revealed God of the Bible. He does not tell us whether or not he prayed, and if so, under what circumstances. His painting of Christian subjects is no indication of Christianity. He lived in the perfect freedom conferred by the religious indifference that was possible before the Reformation.

Thus Leonardo was impervious to human desires and passions, and to the consolations of faith. But one thing remains. Though he was without ambition and uninterested in honors during his lifetime, he clearly expressed his desire for posthumous fame. It was a spur to unflagging activity. "One who spends his life without fame, leaves no more trace on earth than smoke in the air and foam on the water." "Oh, why do you not create such a work that after death you will be as one wholly alive, instead of sharing even in your lifetime the sleep of the pitiful dead." And he notes with certainty: "I will endure."

Here lie his greatest remoteness from Biblical religion and his kinship to antiquity and the Germanic world. The

absolute transience even of posthumous fame is forgotten.
For him, glory took the place of eternity, which can be
known only in radically different dimensions, making an
absolute of unceasing activity and leading him to forget
that for all its grandeur it is as nothing in the face of
transcendence. Here perhaps lies the hidden seed of a sublime inhumanity. And perhaps this accounts for the sudden
misgiving which sometimes tempers our enthusiasm for
Leonardo and which prevents us from being wholly at one
with him.

5. What impression did Leonardo make on those about
him? We hear of his physical strength, of his supremely
beautiful face, of his winning charm, his ease of manner.
We hear of the enormous impression made by his works,
which no sooner became known than they were declared
to usher in a new epoch in painting.

But in some accounts we sense that he may have struck
certain observers as personally forbidding, lacking in
warmth—and precisely because he was without passion or
anger or immoderation, vices which create a bond of common weakness and make us prize those who overcome them.

Even today the general impression made by Leonardo
has this sobering quality. This man—who needed no other,
who in his quest for knowledge relied wholly on himself,
who went through the world immured in solitude, without
communication of the kind which enables a man to come
to himself in relation to another self—commands our respect but does not draw us to him. His winning charm has
often been mentioned. But on many occasions he seems
to have made another impression, because perhaps he was
lacking in that truly human charm, the weakness of the
great man who for all his greatness stands in need of others.

Michelangelo and Raphael were idolized, whereas Leonardo, though welcomed by the King of France and various aristocrats, was not generally sought after.

When Leonardo and Michelangelo were both in Florence, the young men flocked to the much younger Michelangelo. When once Michelangelo in a group of painters shouted at Leonardo: "You who were never able to cast an equestrian statue, and the Milanese, those blockheads, had faith in you"—Leonardo said nothing and only blushed. He always maintained his distinguished bearing, while Michelangelo allowed his emotions to carry him away.

Michelangelo created figures which surpass Leonardo by the passion which informs them and the magnificence of their form. They reveal a world in upheaval, a despair that impelled to transcendence; Biblical faith became a new reality.

Leonardo and Michelangelo are two worlds between which there is little contact: Leonardo a cosmopolitan, Michelangelo a patriot; Leonardo serene and balanced, governed by moderating reason, Michelangelo beset by confused emotions from which he heroically rises; Leonardo controlling himself, calm amid passion, looking upon things and himself with detachment, Michelangelo given to shattering passions, unrestrained in his despair.

Leonardo produced unforgettable figures in the lucidity of reason; he reveals the mystery of reason itself, which seldom seizes upon things directly and is hard to understand in the depth of its lucidity. Michelangelo's creations, products of upheaval and eruption, carry infinite truth, and affect us in a different way; they are more torturing and more moving, more disturbing and more charged with memory.

Leonardo seems to live in an area of peace, unchanging amid happiness and grief; Michelangelo seems to reconquer himself in an area of continual crises, in gigantic oscillations between dejection and supreme exaltation.

Leonardo seems to contemplate the world of extreme human possibilities as a mere aggregate of natural phenomena; Michelangelo is part of it.

6. Those who meet with Leonardo are called upon to hear his appeal. Leonardo's mere fame is conventional. As long as we look on artists as a large group of men, all of whom have done good things in their way, we shall perhaps be dealing with art, but not with what speaks or fails to speak through it. Only if we feel the radical difference between mere art and art as an organon, shall we hear that appeal and be impelled to respond with our inner man from out of the Encompassing, whence words and images come to us only because we ourselves are in process of becoming. What do we hear through Leonardo?

The mute, unresponsive world demands to be known and loved. Leonardo's relentless activity pursued no other purpose than to see the world and to mirror it in the mind by means of the imagination.

There are few men who all through their lives are wanderers, seemingly detached from other men, wishing only to see the world and to communicate what they have seen. These men do for us what we can do only inadequately for ourselves. Constantly discovering and disclosing, they perceive with their whole being what we others learn to see through them. The fact that they do our work for us and allow us to look on to the best of our ability, gives them the privilege of standing aside while other men act and struggle and change the world of human affairs. Theirs is a different struggle, an intellectual struggle to perceive the eternal essences in the surface and appearance of the world.

And there is something more. We are fortunate in being able to meet in Leonardo an independent man, who, rising above society and history, neglecting both, lived in harmony with infinite nature through his vision of its revelations.

Our pleasure in accepting the gift of his manner of seeing and investigating, of his existence, does not imply that we ourselves should follow him in his way of life or mode of philosophizing.

Descartes

and Philosophy

Introduction

T HE fame of Descartes is uncontested; his influence has been enormous, and the study of his principal works is still indispensable to anyone who wishes to philosophize. Thus there is no need to demonstrate his *historical* greatness, especially as German philosophers, since Hegel and Schelling, have looked upon him as the beginning and source of modern philosophy.

We know Descartes's irreplaceable discoveries in mathematics. We know his extraordinary achievement in renewing the form of thought; anyone who comes to Descartes after reading the philosophers of the Renaissance feels that he has suddenly emerged into clearer air; the thought is pregnant, each sentence is undeviatingly in its right place; the superfluous and incidental are disregarded; the development is resolute and conscious of its aim; the reader feels that he has been taken in hand.

We see the great style of his disciplined life, his courage and nobility and practical wisdom; we note how he withdrew into solitude, and went to a foreign country for the peace and quiet he required for meditation; how he devoted his life entirely to the task in which he believed, the renewal of all knowledge.

Nevertheless, it is not an easy matter to go beyond such a general characterization of the man, his work, and his influence, to show more clearly and definitely wherein the *philosophical* greatness of Descartes resides. This greatness has been called into doubt. The literature on Descartes includes so-called exposures, purporting to unmask him as a hypocrite who did not say what he thought, as a coward whose fear and mistrust led him to hide his true colors; as a man who, for all his intolerable pride, was jealous of other men's achievements, who schemed and plotted to ensure his fame; as a revolutionary who wished to destroy the whole existing order. We hold with none of these judgments. But with all our admiration for his historical greatness, we are among those who doubt whether his philosophy, either in content or in method, constitutes an eternal embodiment of philosophical truth. For when it is asked: In what sense can we make this philosophy our own?—we come to see, behind the rational clarity of the surface, an extraordinarily complex philosophical operation, which seems to by-pass the truth whenever it tackles a crucial problem. If we go on to observe how Descartes's thinking developed in other minds, we are also led to wonder whether, by virtue of his greatness, he may not, in addition to kindling the philosophizing of all those who followed in his footsteps, have led it astray through his method as well as the content of his thinking. Because he dealt with matters essential to the modern era, he was able to influence the greatest minds; but since, by his way of approaching it, he missed or even perverted the meaning of what was true in his discovery, he became a danger to all those who fell under his spell. It seems quite possible that philosophy was corrupted by the tendencies whose fountainhead and foremost representative was Descartes, and that the depth of truth reached since Descartes has been achieved more in spite of Descartes than because of him.

Opposition to Descartes—which has been continuous from his lifetime until today—has sprung from very diverse and even mutually exclusive motives. Thus the mere fact of being against Descartes means nothing—it is the nature of the opposition that matters. The more opposition to Descartes is based on critical understanding, the more it gains in truth. Anyone who ventures to disclose the seeds of untruth in the source of truth, must at the same time keep in mind that original truth without which historical greatness would be incomprehensible.

Our analysis derives its sequence from the following consideration: Descartes is famous for having tried, through *method,* to raise philosophy to the rank of a science coinciding with science as a whole. His method is related to his equally famous *fundamental operation,* by which he sought to make certainty spring from universal doubt.

These two elements—the problem of method and the problem of the origin—merge into a whole in his philosophy, but this whole was formed from two originally different sources. In his search for method, Descartes seems to take the same path as what was then modern science. The fundamental operation which, while providing the foundation for certainty, develops the principles of all being, is, on the contrary, rooted in the age-old philosophical tradition. In this new form philosophy strove to create a foundation not only for modern science, but for man's life as a whole.

In the first part of this essay we shall analyze the "fundamental operation" and in the second the "method." On the basis of insights which, we believe, develop from these

analyses, we shall, in the third part, extend our inquiry to
the character of the philosophy as a whole and its position
in the history of philosophy.[1]

I
The fundamental operation

1. HOW IT WAS EFFECTED

Let us briefly recapitulate the steps taken by Descartes:

1. Dissatisfied—he said in substance—by the instability
of human opinions, by the doubt that has been cast upon
every philosophical assertion made until now, and by disputations which thus far have not yielded a single secure
result, I shall aim for real and enduring certainty.

In order to attain it, I shall first carry doubt to the
extreme. If with plausible reason I have doubted everything that I ever regarded as certain, and if I then find a
certainty that is secure against all modes of doubt, this
certainty must be the foundation of all further knowledge
that is accessible to us.

I can doubt the existence of the things outside me and
the existence of my body; I can go so far as to doubt mathematical truths, even if these are compelling as such; for
an evil genius might have created me and so organized me
that for all my subjective certainty I might still be deluded;
if that were so, I should be defenseless and might even fail
to recognize the most evident truth. Then I should be un-

---

1 This essay was written at the suggestion of the *Revue philosophique*
(Paris). It first appeared in French translation in the special Descartes
issue of that review (1937) on the occasion of the tercentenary of the
appearance of the *Discours de la méthode*.

able to know any truth; I might, to be sure, defend myself against the demon by resolutely refusing to accept any statement involving a doubt. Does this mean that I can no longer accept any statement?

2. In taking the decision to doubt and radically to withhold my judgment, I observe that even if all grounds for doubt are justified, one thing remains certain: as long as I think, even if I am mistaken in supposing my thought to be compelling, I am certain that I myself exist (*cogito ergo sum*): of this certainty I can no longer doubt. If an evil spirit, who was my creator, deceived me in everything else, he could not deceive me in regard to the fact that I, even while allowing myself to be deceived, nevertheless know that I am.

3. Once I have gained a basis in indubitable certainty, how shall I go on?

In the process of attaining this certainty, I also learn what is requisite for certainty in any matter, namely: to conceive clearly and distinctly. But I formerly believed that I conceived many things clearly and distinctly and yet fell into doubt, suspecting that even in clarity and distinctness a demon might be giving me an illusion of truth. Thus a universal rule, such as: everything must be true that I conceive as clearly and distinctly as the *cogito ergo sum*—will be valid only if I can convince myself beyond any doubt that I was not created by a demon of deception. The next step must lead to this certainty.

Now I see not only that I did not create myself, but also that consciousness of my existence is inseparably bound up in me with the idea of infinity, which is the standard by which I measure my finiteness. In other words: I find within myself the idea of an infinite and perfect being, that is, the idea of God. In order to understand this idea,

which was given me with my existence, I must clarify a
fundamental insight in terms of a rational idea, which I call
a proof of God's existence. I proceed as follows: I cannot
have produced the idea of God any more than I can have
brought forth my own existence. This I know on the
strength of an axiom which is given to me by natural insight, namely, that there must be as much reality in a cause
as in its effect. But since there is finiteness and imperfection
in me, which I am enabled to appraise by the standard of
my idea of the infinite and perfect, this idea of the infinite
cannot have its source in me, who am finite, but can only
come from God Himself. Therefore God *is,* and He is an
infinite and perfect being. In knowing that I am, I know
at the same time—even if everything else is illusion—that
I am not alone in the world. "We must of necessity conclude from the fact alone that I exist, or that the idea
of a Being supremely perfect—that is, of God—is in me,
that the proof of God's existence is grounded on the highest
evidence" (*Oeuvres complètes,* ed. Adam et Tannery—referred to in the following as A.T.—VII, 51).

But this being cannot be evil, for evil is imperfection.
He must be good in every way and therefore cannot deceive. Thus through what follows inevitably from the *cogito
ergo sum,* I can rely, also in every other realm of my knowledge, on the clarity and distinctness which in the *cogito
ergo sum* were able to withstand even a possible demon.

4. After clear and distinct knowledge has thus, on the
two foundations of the *cogito ergo sum* and the certainty
of God's existence, been proved to be reliable and beyond
doubt, most of the truths I had previously doubted are re-
stored at one stroke, in particular, the mathematical truths
and the existence of corporeal things outside me, in so far
as these are clearly and distinctly recognized, that is, in so

far as they have quantity, extension, form, position, and motion.

Descartes sums up this whole development in the statement of Eudoxus in the dialogue *Recherche de la vérité*: "For it is really from this universal doubt, which is like a fixed and unchangeable point, that I have resolved to derive the knowledge of God, of yourself, and of all that the world contains" (A.T. X, 515).

2. CRITIQUE OF THIS CERTAINTY

The most evident purpose of this operation is to provide an indubitable certainty, valid for every thinking being. In inquiring to what degree this certainty is achieved, we shall have to ask: *to what* does this certainty refer? what does *doubt* mean in this operation? and, is there *a way to further development* from the ground of certainty thus acquired?

1. *To what does the first certainty refer?* As Descartes himself expressly states, the *cogito ergo sum* is not an inference; for an inference would presuppose other truths from which the *sum* followed, whereas this thought itself is represented as the origin. We interpret Descartes: The *ergo* is employed only as an analogy to the syllogism, in order to bring out the fact that this is not an immediate, perceived certainty, but a fundamental reflexive certainty, a self-certainty. I become aware, in reference to myself, that I think, that I am. Here we have the unity of a unique act of thought, which in thought refers back to itself and becomes aware of this relation as something existing in itself. Any attempt to state this adequately raises insuperable difficulties. Since *cogito ergo sum* suggests an inference, but Descartes rejects the notion of an inference, we might attempt to change the wording. We might say: *cogito, sum*, but then we should merely have two unconnected words.

We might say: *cogitans sum* (if I think, I am); then, however, we should have a relation of consequence, the possession of being resulting from the fact of thinking, but
this relation would be almost empty and, moreover, it
would be stated in a definite form implying temporal existence; besides, the emphasis would be solely on the *sum*,
whereas the *cogito* is of equal importance; the origin of the
idea would not be appropriately rendered. Accordingly we
shall use Descartes's formula *cogito ergo sum* in the following, even though its syllogistic form lends itself to misunderstanding.

To recognize thought in myself as being is to attain
overwhelming certainty concerning the indispensable medium of all being that is being for me. But such certainty
does not know what it possesses, for it can have no definite
content.

Thus the *cogito ergo sum* as such cannot be doubted.
But both its power and its weakness reside in the fact that
its meaning remains utterly indeterminate and for that
reason cannot be clearly apprehended. I am supposed to be
certain of my existence as a thinking being. But in order
to attain clarity concerning this certainty, we must find out
what *thought* is, what the *I* is, and what the *being* of this *I*
is.

What is thought in Descartes? Let us consider, without
reference to explicit statements of Descartes's, what he may
have meant by thought: it is the unique action which in
acting knows itself, which consequently has immediate certainty of itself through its relation to itself. Because the
object of certainty is here at the same time its subject,
subject and object coincide; they are one and the same
thing, which is neither subject nor object and at the same
time both subject and object. This is what Descartes seems

to mean when he expresses his full confidence in the fundamental certainty of the *cogito ergo sum* as the foundation
of objective reality. But thought, which Descartes may
originally have conceived in this way, becomes something
more definite as soon as he begins to examine it more
closely. If he takes pure thought to be *self-sufficient,* it becomes an emptiness that can never be filled; if he *describes*
thought in greater detail, he is led to a psychological phenomenology. Both of the following extreme interpretations of thought are possible on the basis of his work:

Either: It has the character of divine thought (a conception that goes back to the ancients) which is and has
all Being in itself, because *in the process of thinking it
creates what is thought.* But human thought finds in itself
only the punctual emptiness of the "I think" without the
being that gives it content; for human thought requires
something other, the object that is given to it and con-
fronts it, without which it would vanish into the void of
self-thinking.

Or: The thinking that has immediate certainty of itself is not the identity of a self-certain one, but is split into
two things, namely, that within me which thinks, and that
which this thinking as thinking knows. But then the certainty is no longer immediate; it relates to something other,
which must, in order to be thought, have existed previously.
This seems to be what Descartes means when he calls that
which has absolute self-certainty in the *cogito ergo sum*
a "thinking thing, which doubts, understands, affirms, ne-
gates, wills and does not will, and which also has imagination and sensation" (A.T. VII, 28). This means that the
thought which is certain of itself has the same scope as
consciousness. But then everything that my consciousness
is is real in the same sense as the "I am." Then thought be-

comes consciousness and the being of thought is the *being of consciousness as a whole,* or the being of everything that is dealt with in a phenomenology of consciousness or in a psychology that analyzes and describes consciousness. If thought is conceived of as the totality of the acts and states of consciousness, my original certainty is replaced by an aggregate of highly uncertain insights.

Consequently—as we pursue our inquiry into the definite meaning of thought in Descartes—the certainty refers either to the punctual emptiness of self-thinking or to the reality of consciousness with all its innumerable vacillations. Whether we define thought in one or the other sense, the original certainty on which everything was supposed to rest vanishes.

What is the I in Descartes? Descartes, it is true, says that the statement *ego sum ego existo* is indivisible; but when he calls this *ego* a *res cogitans* as distinguished from a *res extensa,* he fails precisely to ask what distinguishes the *I* from the being of any other *res non extensa,* that is, from all mere consciousness, whatever form it may assume. The being of the *I* never became a philosophical question for him. In fact, because he reduced the self-certainty of the existence that thinks itself to an infinitesimal point that thinks itself, or denatured it by introducing psychological elements, the existence of the *I,* conceived of as an objectively existing thing like any other object of thought, remained outside the field of his investigations.

Because the *cogito ergo sum* expresses the I's discovery of its own reality, the philosophy of Descartes became in a later day the starting point for the philosophizing which, since Kant, Fichte, and Schelling, has investigated the riddle of the I. But before that, it led to subjectivist philosophies which soon took on a psychological character.

What is being in Descartes? Descartes's certainty relates to the being of the *cogito*. His propositions are not meant as formal truths; they are meant to express a thinking rational being's certainty of its own existence. But he does not question the meaning of being in his *cogito ergo sum*. He takes being for granted, and soon it becomes for him the mere presence of the *cogito*. In order to show what is lacking, let us compare Descartes's statement with ideas pointing in the same direction in Augustine, Kant, and Schelling:

In Augustine the *cogito ergo sum* is a function of my all-embracing need to gain certainty concerning the inner significance of Being, which is a mirror of the Trinity and speaks to me and through me in existence, life, knowledge, and love.[1] By reducing this thought to a general idea, useful as the starting point of a chain of reasoning, Descartes makes it into a certainty analogous, and in his opinion even superior, to mathematical certainties. But through the next step, the idea loses the depth of its content: a distinction is drawn between the substantiality of the *res extensa* and the substantiality of the *res cogitans,* and the being of the *res cogitans* becomes vitiated with an empty and by no means demonstrated durability. Descartes took a long leap from Augustine's self-certainty of the immortal soul to the purely rational idea of a substantial point, whose being consists solely in thought.

Kant elucidated the enigma of being by pointing out that the "I am" is an empirical statement (in so far as it affirms my existence as an object of psychology) and it is not an empirical statement (in so far as it designates the

[1] The numerous passages in Augustine, which should be considered in conjunction, may be found in Étienne Gilson, *Études sur le rôle de la pensée médiévale dans la formation du système cartésien*, Paris, 1930, pp. 191 ff.

indispensable condition of all thought). Then he realized that the "I am" does not tell me how I appear to myself or what I am as myself, but only *that* I am and this in an utterly indeterminate sense. Instead of considering these enigmas raised by the *cogito,* Descartes proceeded to identify the being of the *I* with the being of a *res cogitans* as a substance.

In an exposition of Descartes, Schelling criticized the meaning given to being in the *cogito ergo sum* (Schelling, *Werke,* X, 6 ff.). He recognized the justification of doubt as a means of arriving at being. But the doubt that is a doubt of being presupposes on the one hand that what is doubted exists in a certain sense, though not in the full sense of the word. As far as things are concerned, "one can only doubt that they *are* in an absolute sense; but that they are *in some sense* can be inferred in the same way as Cartesius infers his *sum.* It is just as correct to infer: I doubt the reality of things, therefore they are, or at least: they are not entirely without being. For I cannot even doubt what exists in no sense and not at all." On the other hand, I must also doubt *my own being.* For what is immediately certain, my own being, is incomprehensible to me. I must doubt my own being in the sense that my being, like everything that is doubted, is not a being grounded in itself, but a species of being, a being whose "reality is derived and therefore doubtful." Like all empirical existence, my own existence is a mode of being, situated between being and nonbeing; for thought, too, is only a state, a mode, of existence. Accordingly Schelling says: "The *sum* comprised in the *cogito* has not the significance of an absolute 'I am,' but only the significance of an: 'I am in a certain way, namely, as a thinking being.' "

Precisely because Descartes does not make the meaning of being into a question, because he neither looks into the abyss of the being of the I, nor conceives of absolute being as a standard, he slips from the certainty of his *cogito ergo sum* directly into a knowledge of the being of thought as *res cogitans* distinguished from a *res extensa*. Consequently the "I am" cannot for Descartes signify the absolute being of possible Existenz, which I know myself to be if I am relative only in reference to transcendence. Or at least it cannot preserve this significance in Descartes, who, on the contrary, takes it as a relative being, a certain mode of being as opposed to other being. And the *cogito ergo sum* becomes empty, in so far as it becomes a mere mode of being among other modes of being.

Schelling had no great esteem for the mode of being concerning which Descartes achieves certainty in the *cogito ergo sum*. He did not desire to follow Descartes, "who was not concerned with understanding things, but only with knowing that they are (the least one can know of things). . . ."

But if with the *cogito ergo sum* it is merely demonstrated that I exist in some way, the step I have taken away from universal doubt is by no means as weighty as it first seemed. I have not achieved a grounding in authentic being. Then, according to Schelling, "I doubt the being of the things outside me, therefore they are, is an inference no less valid" than that of Descartes: "I doubt, I think, therefore I am."

The consequence of Descartes's failure to inquire into the meaning of being in the *cogito ergo sum* is that every definition of this being annuls the philosophical force which was present, though unclearly, in the original idea.

2. *What is the meaning of doubt?* Descartes was accused of having sinned by his doubt: had he not gone so

far as to doubt the existence of God and to suggest the
hypothesis of a demon of deception? This gave Descartes
an opportunity to characterize his type of doubt (in a letter
replying to Buitendijck's question as to whether it was
permissible to doubt the existence of God). Descartes declared that a distinction must be made between the doubt
which concerns the reason and the doubt which concerns
the will. Intellectual doubt is not a matter of choice or
justification, for insight is a matter not of will but of capacity. Consequently, many must doubt the existence of God
in their reasoning, in so far as their reason is unable to
prove His existence, and still believe in His existence. For
faith is the affair of the will, and if I believe, I can nevertheless examine the question of God's existence with my
innate reason and so doubt it, without doubting in my
faith. Anyone who sets himself the goal of doubting in God
in order to persist in this doubt, is committing a grave sin.
But the conduct of one who undertakes to doubt as a means
of more clearly knowing the truth, is pious and beyond
reproach (A.T. IV, 62 ff.). In the *Responsiones* Descartes
repeats what he has already said in the *Discours* and the
Meditations, namely, that he had always excluded from
doubt "everything relating to piety and in general to customs" (A.T. VII, 476).

Thus as he speaks of it here, Descartes's doubt is a
methodological doubt in reason, not an existential doubt
in faith. It is a systematic, intellectual attempt to arrive at
rational certainty; it is not an existential experience. It is
an activity, of which Descartes remains master, not a fall
into the abyss of unbelief. His only standard is theoretical
evidence, not an awareness of the truth in the practical
course of life and action. Hence this doubt has not the
earnestness of an existential risk, but only the earnestness

of a conscientious effort at logical thinking. This doubt is merely a means of ascertaining the source of the theoretical certainty of reason by finding a clear and distinct concept that no one can doubt. It is not despair, it is not a crisis through which I can achieve certainty of a truth to live by. Thus Descartes's doubt presupposes that, even when I doubt, I continue to live by a source other than the truth with which this doubt is concerned.

Descartes's doubt also presupposes the acceptance of an absolute truth which is accessible to our human judgment. For a moment this absolute stands even higher than God; for if God were to deceive us as to this truth, He would be judged evil. The thinking man who doubts thinks on the basis of this truth, which, however, in the last analysis, is guaranteed only by God.

Now this truth is either a definite, particular truth— and then it is *indeed compelling* and universally valid; in this case it is scientific truth, but never the truth by which I live. Or else, it purports to state, in the *form* of compelling certainty, the certainty that is the ground of my Existenz; in that case, it must necessarily err, because we are unable to express such a certainty clearly and adequately in the form of a proposition. For this reason authentic philosophy, which follows this second path, cannot have as its aim the certainty that characterizes the *rationally compelling* sciences. An indirect indication of this is that every explicit philosophical position has had opponents, and that philosophy never achieves the scientific kind of knowledge which is valid for all men and capable of gaining universal acceptance. Descartes, who follows the philosophical tradition of Aristotle and St. Thomas in holding philosophical and scientific truth to be of the same kind, doubts, *because* all philosophical propositions put forward

up until his time have been contested. But the fact that
Descartes's own theses incurred the same fate was a source
of insight to later generations: the radical method by which
Descartes sought certainty confronted later philosophers
with the task of distinguishing scientific and philosophical
certainty.[1]

Because of this unquestioned assumption that the one
universally valid truth is the form of all truth and because
of this certainty, both of which are fundamental to Descartes's thinking, Kierkegaard—despite his esteem for Descartes—spoke ironically of his doubt and Nietzsche said that
he hoped to be a better doubter than Descartes. Both
understood that Descartes had taken the nature of truth
in general as something self-evident, which it is not.

3. *Descartes's certainty leads nowhere.* Despite the in-
definite and ambiguous content of the *cogito ergo sum,* it
nevertheless represents an incontestable advance from radical doubt. For all its indeterminateness, it is correct for a
mind that is looking only for a compelling argument. Before Descartes, the step had already been taken by Augustine. The difference between Augustine and Descartes is
that Descartes regarded the step as an essentially rational
argument and made it the principle of his whole philosophical system, whereas for Augustine it is on the one hand
an all-encompassing confirmation of the self, enriched with
the full content of one's self-awareness, while, on the other
hand, he employs it only incidentally as an argument
against skepticism.

Thus Descartes takes an unquestionable certainty as
his starting point. But his next step is intended to show
that clarity and distinctness are *universally* valid criteria

[1] Concerning "compelling" certainty and the relation between philosophy
and science, cf. my *Philosophie* (Berlin, 1932, Vol. I, pp. 89–94, 318–329).

of true knowledge. For this he requires the proof of the existence and essence of God (who must not be a demon of deception, capable of provoking false evidence). This proof required first of all a new assumption, namely, that the cause of an idea must be as perfect as its content; on the strength of this premise, the idea of God, which is present in our minds, cannot have been created by ourselves, but must have its ground in God Himself. This idea—having its sources in Descartes's religious belief—seems, indeed, to have the depth of a metaphysical elucidation of human existence; it possesses a force of conviction capable of appealing to a man without specific religious ties but fundamentally predisposed to faith; its meaning is inseparable from its undemonstrability. But once this idea is transformed from an inspiring appeal into a proof of the kind that gives us mathematical certainty, it collapses; it loses the truth that is peculiar to it and fails to achieve compelling validity.

Thus this first certainty is such that with it Descartes *runs aground.* From this certainty he can take no further step to a new certainty, having the same character of compelling evidence. He has struck ground, but his ground is a sandbank: he cannot go on, and he cannot even stay where he is.

This sterile certainty of the *cogito ergo sum* finds its expression in the peculiarly negative form of the reasoning that leads to it. The self-certainty of consciousness is achieved by the negation of all possible skeptical negations. Its outcome is doubt and not a source of its own. The primary "no" never gives rise to a creative "yes." Like all philosophical ideas that spring from a refutation and not from a positive source, Descartes's idea is striking in its simplicity, but at the price of leading nowhere. The same is true of another well-known idea, used to refute skepticism: The skeptic says there is no truth; in so saying, he maintains something that he regards as true; thus he contradicts himself, for in his statement he is doing something which his statement says to be impossible. Like Descartes's idea, this one is correct and useful as an answer to the negations of skepticism, but it too leads nowhere.

Self-certainty may be of two kinds. One is that of the absolute skeptic who can effect no judgment, because in thinking he is certain only that he thinks. The other opens the prospect of attaining to a deeper truth by seeking to confront all certainty with the certainty of the self—the actual presence of the truth—in other words, to raise all certainty to the level of self-certainty.

Descartes often gives the impression of choosing the second path, for a move in that direction is unquestionably present in the initial impulse of his thinking. Even in so abstract an expression of self-certainty as the *cogito ergo sum* there is something at work which speaks to the reader, which sets up a sympathetic vibration, and a more explicit indication of this impulse in Descartes is that he believes in God and needs Him as the indispensable source of all knowledge of the truth. But he does not incorporate God —taken as the fullness of Being, as the real source of real existence—into his philosophical movement. He makes use of Him as the mere idea of God, a God who, once His existence is proved, is no longer needed, because His sole function was to establish clarity and distinctness as criteria of knowledge, so rendering this knowledge absolutely independent. But a God who serves only to establish a criterion of truth is just as vague and empty as the *cogito ergo sum*. Where, on the contrary, the "I am" is bound up ex-

istentially with the idea of God, a reciprocal bond is present in the source: the "I am" becomes as rich as the idea
of God. Then the "I am" is actual Existenz oriented toward transcendence; it can no longer be adequately apprehended in any abstract logical idea and cannot be the
first link in a chain of reasoning tending to establish compelling certainty.

Because of this striving for compelling certainty, Descartes's first fundamental thought is without richness and
content. In every further step he attempts to recapture
richness and content, but he *never again attains certainty*.
He starts out with an empty certainty; but at the very next
step even this certainty is lost.

3. THE ENCOMPASSING

However, there is, in Descartes's fundamental operation,
something more than a striving for indubitable certainty.
In basing his confidence in clear and distinct knowledge
of the fact that God is the creator and cannot be a de-
ceiver, he gains awareness of the Encompassing which we
are and in which we are.[1] Though in Descartes's system
God is reduced to a mere function, and serves solely as the
guarantor of compelling certainty, nevertheless his thinking reveals an echo of profound philosophical reflections
relating to his own being as indissolubly bound up with
transcendence. Despite the precision with which Descartes's
propositions are formulated, the content is so indeterminate
as to make them meaningless. But for all this indeterminateness, they point to the Encompassing. We shall try to

[1] On the concept of the "Encompassing" see my lectures: *Vernunft und
Existenz* (Groningen, 1935), second and third lectures. English: *Reason
and Existenz*, 1955, The Noonday Press. Translated by William Earle.

show how in Descartes a philosophical meaning speaks through these pointers but also how, because of his method of philosophizing, it immediately falls silent.

We call *transcendence* the Encompassing in which we authentically are. We call *Existenz* the Encompassing that we ourselves are. The mode of our *Existenz* depends on the *meaning of truth for it,* and achieves reality through *inner action.* Consequently we shall examine successively, in Descartes's fundamental operation, the presence of transcendence, the starting point in my consciousness of my Existenz, the meaning of truth, and inner action. In conclusion we shall show how Descartes's thinking marks the beginning of a break in man, who saw the ground receding beneath his feet and then began consciously to look for new and reliable ground.

The presence of transcendence. Descartes's philosophy begins with the indissoluble bond between the thinking being's certainty of his existence and the idea of God. Even though this inseparability is taken at once as the basis for a rational proof of the existence of God, its source is no mere rational position but the Encompassing. This lends his subsequent steps a meaning which, however, gradually seems to lose itself in mere rationality.

We read, for example, at the end of the Fifth Meditation: "And so I very clearly recognize that the certainty and truth of all knowledge *depend* alone on the knowledge of the true God, in so much that, before I knew Him, I could have a perfect knowledge of no other thing" (A.T. VII, 71). Although the explicitly stated meaning of this passage is merely that knowledge of God's existence gives us confidence in clarity and distinctness as the criteria of knowledge, the original idea contains far more than this application which seems poor by contrast. In Descartes, however, *this* original idea is not developed.

We find in Descartes passages which not only bear witness to his piety, but show that he was aware of transcendence. At the end of the Third Meditation, he writes: "But before . . . I pass on to the consideration of other truths . . . it seems to me right to pause for a while in order to contemplate God Himself, to ponder at leisure His marvelous attributes, to consider and admire, and adore the beauty of this light so resplendent, at least as far as the strength of my mind, which is in some measure dazzled by the sight, will allow me to do so. For just as faith teaches us that the supreme felicity of the other life consists only in this contemplation of the Divine Majesty, so we continue to learn by experience that a similar meditation, though incomparably less perfect, causes us to enjoy the greatest satisfaction of which we are capable in this life" (A.T. VII, 52). In such passages it is as though Descartes had abandoned his role of sober rationality. The style here is not that of his demonstrations. In his innermost attitude Descartes preserved something of what he had taken over from scholasticism. His thinking—for brief moments at least—carries a transcendent mood, which does not express itself directly, but which is present and can be discerned by the perceptive reader despite the rationality which carries Descartes so far away from it.

The starting point: my consciousness of my existence. The self-certainty of the thinking being is more than one insight among others. It is for Descartes the starting point, and not only in the sense of a first statement in a series; it is being itself, one and incomparable, and only in relation to this being can anything else acquire being and truth for

us. Consequently Descartes holds that whatever is inseparably bound up with this self-certainty of the thinking
being—e.g., doubt, negation, affirmation, will, sensation, imagination—is just as real and true as the "I am." It is inseparable from my consciousness (*a mea cognitione*) and
my self (*a meo ipso*) (A.T. VII, 28–29). Consequently an
interpreter of Descartes can say quite rightly: ". . . and
everything which is as closely bound up with the idea of
your existence as existence itself exists for you and with
you with equal necessity, equal certainty!"[1] One is tempted
to think of Kant's words about the "starry heavens above
me" and the "moral law within me": "I do not merely con-
jecture them and seek them as though obscured in darkness
or in the transcendent region beyond my horizon; I see
them before me and I associate them directly with the consciousness of my own existence. The former begins at the
place I occupy in the external world of sense. . . . The
latter begins at my invisible self . . . and exhibits me in a
world . . . which is comprehensible only to the understanding—a world with which I recognize myself as existing in a universal and necessary . . . connection."[2] We
seem to find the same impulse at the source of Descartes's
fundamental idea.

But in Descartes this original impulse is not preserved.
What he designates as inseparable from consciousness (*cogi-
tatio*) is not only thought in the sense of judgment and not
only freedom to affirm or deny, but over and above these,
or rather far below them, the multiple contents of consciousness: "What then am I? . . . a thing which doubts,

[1] G. F. Hock, *Cartesius und seine Gegner*, Vienna, 1835.
[2] Kant, *Kritik der praktischen Vernunft*, pp. 288 f. English: *Critique of
Practical Reason*, Library of the Liberal Arts, New York, 1956, tr. L. W.
Beck, p. 166.

understands, affirms, denies, wills, refuses, which also imagines and feels. Certainly it is no small matter if all these
things pertain to my nature. . . ." (A.T. VII, 28). In re-
stricting the Encompassing to consciousness, Descartes reduces it to a field of psychological phenomena to be considered by the methods of psychology. This is no longer
the Encompassing but a kind of stage on which psychological phenomena are displayed. Both empirical existence as
the dark background of our reality, and possible Existenz,
as the absoluteness of a selfhood, that knows itself to be in
the presence of transcendence, are lost. Hence, in elucidating what is no longer the Encompassing Descartes loses himself in psychological (phenomenological and epistemologi-
cal) reflections. Thus he can no longer attain the language
of Existenz, often present in speculative thinking (and that
is why there is next to nothing of Anselm's "ontological
proof" in Descartes's second proof, which reduces it to a
mere logical operation); moreover, he attains neither the
reality of empirical existence nor the imperative that speaks
to us out of the possible Existenz of the self. And indeed the
connection between truth and my consciousness of my Existenz, or, in other words, this Encompassing which is authentic Being, is not brought out in Descartes. Only by
interpreting Descartes on the basis of what is known to us
from other sources, can we discover the seed of the idea that
moved Kant and Kierkegaard.

   The Encompassing and truth. Our conception of the
Encompassing is always correlative to a specific conception
of the nature of truth. Thus the idea of the equality of all
men is correlative to the mode of knowledge that is identical for all; and the idea that men differ from one another
in rank and essence is correlative to a conception of truth,

according to which the content of thought is by no means
the same for all men.

After starting from the self-certainty of his existence,
Descartes's thinking breaks away from its roots in the totality of the Encompassing; and this is reflected by the way
in which he regards all men as capable, and then again
incapable, of apprehending the truth.

On the one hand, the accent is on the idea that the
essential is always identical to itself and therefore accessible to all. All men become identical for him in an Encompassing which is nothing more than consciousness and
reason. For example: "I have observed, in examining the
natural aptitude of several men, that virtually none are so
crude or slow-witted as to be incapable, if properly directed,
of achieving the state of mind necessary for the acquisition
of the highest sciences" (to Picot, A.T. IX, Part 2, p. 12).
Another example: "Good sense is of all things in the world
the most equitably distributed, for everybody thinks himself so abundantly provided with it. . . . It is unlikely that
this is an error on their part; it seems rather to be evidence
in support of the view that the power of forming a good
judgment and of distinguishing the true from the false,
which is properly speaking called good sense or reason, is
by nature equal in all men. Hence too it will show that the
diversity of our opinions does not proceed from some men
being more rational than others, but solely from the fact
that our thoughts pass through diverse channels and that
the same objects are not considered by all" (A.T. VI, 1 ff.).

Nevertheless Descartes speaks of "weak minds," he
finds men's aptitudes very unevenly distributed, and expresses the belief that fewer men are fit for metaphysical
than for geometrical studies, and even goes so far as to say:
"The minds of all men are subject to certain limits which

they cannot surpass" (A.T. X, 215). But here we need not necessarily see a contradiction; for thanks to what is common to all men, they might all be guided into the right way. For Descartes, every individual as a human being has the possibility of participating in this reason which is common to all men: "There is no soul so lacking in nobility, so attached to the things of the senses, that it does not sometimes turn away from them to desire some greater good . . ." (to Picot, A.T. IX, Part 2, p. 4).

On the other hand, Descartes not only sees men varying in rank according to their aptitudes; he also seems to presuppose so radical a difference among men that he warns them against his own ideas, which were supposed to carry compelling, universally valid certainty and intended to provide sound methodological guidance for all. Considering the possibility that revolutionaries might make use of his ideas for their own purposes, he wrote: "My design has never extended beyond trying to reform my own opinion. . . . I do not do so because I wish to advise anybody to imitate it . . . the simple resolve to strip oneself of all opinions and beliefs formerly received is not to be regarded as an example that each man should follow . . ." (A.T. VI, 15).

The contradiction is astounding. Certain dangers incite him to warn others not to take the same path as himself, although his is the only methodical path to the truth. The only possible explanation for this is that Descartes senses the presence of certain powers of empirical existence and Existenz, which he had *not* gathered into his purely rational Encompassing—which is common to all men alike. Since Descartes unquestioningly posits only one interpretation of truth—that of compelling validity for all men—the meaning of truth in all its multiplicity is no problem for

him. Consequently, his Encompassing narrows down to consciousness and reason. It becomes an island cut off from the
actual world. When he speaks in this way, he has no inclination to concern himself with those who do not follow him
in his cautious conception of a truth far removed from action in the world; he expressly shuts himself off from them.

Inner action. The thinking of the Encompassing is
identical with a continuous inner action, in which I elucidate, produce, and transform myself. Descartes's doctrine
of liberty makes it clear that he philosophizes in the Encompassing, even though he immediately loses sight of it
in developing the content of his ideas.

In his fundamental operation, Descartes performs an
inner action which he examines more closely when he takes
freedom as a philosophical theme: in submitting to universal doubt, freedom of thought gains self-awareness. A man
need submit to no judgment, to no received truth; he can
suspend his own judgment until, having considered, pene-
trated, and surveyed all possible critical objections, he arrives at a certainty which he accepts as so indubitable that
he recognizes his own eternal essence in it forever.

In dealing with "freedom," Descartes reasons as follows: the world that we have learned to take for granted
in the course of our physical and historical development
does not disclose things to us as they intrinsically are. It
discloses them to us in a form corresponding to our physical
needs, ranging, according to the conditions of our existence,
from sensory needs to the practical requirements of human
society. The judgments which such experience has im-
printed upon us are prejudices, and they are well-nigh in-
surmountable. The traditional philosophy which Descartes
rejects is in his opinion nothing more than a kind of unconscious justification of these prejudices; in practice, he

holds, its system of the world merely reflects our needs and interests.

But once we have awakened to maturity, he believes, we can think independently of these needs and interests, that is, we can think not only in order to live, but also for the sake of thought itself. Then the aim of thought ceases to be our empirical existence alone, and becomes first and foremost truth as such. The power to engage in this thinking, which is a striving for pure knowledge of the truth, detached from the conditions of existence which formerly pressed in upon us, deceived us, and nourished our prejudices—that is the freedom possible for man. Descartes expresses the beauty of this freedom, of this philosophical upsurge which frees us from the old blind prejudices:

Freedom of judgment, that is, freedom to affirm or negate or to suspend judgment, is unlimited. I can restrict my affirmation or negation to what is absolutely clear and distinct to the eyes of my mind. In my freedom of decision I am secure against all error if I abstain from decision until the object of my judgment has attained the highest clarity and distinctness. Judgment is an act of the will; freedom of will enables me to confine myself to true judgments, and makes me responsible for every error, because in case of error I have judged without having previously attained full clarity and distinctness.

This freedom is complete only in thought, that is, in the realm of *theory*. In *action* we do not have time to achieve full certainty of judgment; but in action the indecision of theoretical judgment is not permissible; time presses and every situation demands a decision. In the realm of theory what counts is *compelling certainty*, which convinces by its evidence and is as such indestructible. In action, on the other hand, what counts is the *determination*

which leads me unflinchingly to carry out my decision once
made, even though its theoretical foundation may be inadequate.

In the realm of theory, freedom is unlimited. Here
alone can I venture—in action it would be disastrous—to
doubt everything with a view to attaining compelling certainty. To conceive this certainty with perfect clarity and
distinctness—that is freedom. As long as clarity and distinctness have not been attained in the course of my methodic progression, I can decline to affirm or deny, so preserving at least the freedom of indecision.

It is therefore my task, as a potentially free being, to
find myself in inner action, by thought and only by thought.
In order to arrive, through reason, at full certainty of the
truth and at the same time of my own Being, I must detach myself from everything else. In order to achieve such
detachment, I must, by means of universal doubt, free myself from prejudice—that is, from all opinions taken unquestioningly for granted—and I must free myself from
sense perception and imagination by practice in pure
thought, free from the sensory representations that cloud
our thinking and prevent it from becoming clear.

Descartes speaks with proud self-assurance of this possible freedom. Otherwise everything in human nature is
weak, finite, and limited over against God, in whose image
we are made: "It is free-will alone or liberty of choice
which I find to be so great in me that I can conceive no
other idea to be more great; it is indeed the case that
it is for the most part this will that causes me to know that
in some manner I bear the image and similitude of God."
This freedom consists "in our having the power of choosing to do a thing or choosing not to do it (that is, to affirm
or deny, to pursue or to shun it), or rather it consists alone

in the fact that in order to affirm or deny . . . we act so that we are unconscious that any outside force constrains us in doing so" (A.T. VII, 57).

With this grandiose conception of freedom of judgment, Descartes idealizes man's ability to disregard whatever he pleases, so that his thinking remains in a state of suspension. Such thinking can open up a vast area of freedom, but this freedom is empty. If it is to acquire content, the thinker must enter into his own historical substance and realize his relationship to transcendence. The weakness of Descartes's first operation is that, though he attains compelling certainty, its content remains questionable. This may be clarified as follows:

a) *Freedom of judgment* depends entirely on the clarity and distinctness of the content. Without a given substantial content, the clarity and distinctness are empty, and with them the judgment. The truth resides not only in clarity and distinctness as such, but also in the nature and origin and evidence of the content of my thinking. How I become aware of this content, how I perceive it and assimilate it—that is the decisive question. Indispensable as they are, clarity and distinctness are merely secondary conditions of truth. Moreover, suspension of judgment is in itself merely a renunciation, devoid of content.

b) *Pure thought*—detached from everything—is no longer the Encompassing as such; it is divorced from the total Existenz of man. In greater or lesser degree, it loses its ties with the reality of life and makes for an attitude of isolation, which has less and less content. The man himself in his Existenz, his all-encompassing possibility, is lost sight of.

c) Scientific inquiry and life itself can be fruitful only if we recognize the existence of contradictions, not in order to resign ourselves to them, but in order to surmount them. One who decides from the start to *sidestep all contradiction,* can only revolve in a barren circle, and his supposedly sound judgments can carry him no closer to eternal truth. It is worth remembering what great mistakes were made by Descartes, who hoped to exclude all error by confining himself to self-evident truths. Descartes is perhaps the greatest example of a thinker who erred precisely because of his striving for compelling certainty and who lost the truth by succumbing to the temptations of rationality.

As in the doctrine of freedom, inner action is discernible in Descartes's philosophizing wherever method ceased to be a mere technique and became a means of communicating with himself. Several of the Meditations end with an appeal for inner action; the First: ". . . a certain lassitude leads me into the course of my ordinary life. And just as a captive who in sleep enjoys an imaginary liberty, when he begins to suspect that his liberty is but a dream, fears to awaken and conspires with these agreeable illusions that the deception may be prolonged, so insensibly of my own accord I fall back into my former opinions, and I dread awakening" (A.T. VII, 23); the Second: "But because it is difficult to rid oneself so promptly of an opinion to which one was accustomed for so long, it will be that I should halt a little at this point, so that by the length of my meditation I may more deeply imprint on my memory this new knowledge" (A.T. VII, 34); the Fourth: "Nor have I only learned today what I should avoid in order that I may not err, but also how I should act in order to arrive at knowledge of the truth; for without doubt I shall arrive at this if I devote my attention sufficiently to those things which I perfectly understand; and if I separate them from these which I only understand confusedly and with obscurity (A.T. VII, 62).

To be sure, this inner action is not much more than a self-administered treatment of the intellect; it has to do with the purification of thinking, with intellectual exercise, and the discipline of clarity. Nevertheless it carries a vestige of the philosophical Encompassing that is at work in every method. For philosophy does not merely strive, like the sciences, to achieve methodical knowledge of something; it strives through knowledge to fulfill the encompassing essence of the philosopher.

Abyss and foundation. Although Descartes's doubt is presented merely as an attempt to prove that rational certainty is beyond doubt, it actually has deeper implications. The radical doubt which culminates in the hypothesis that my creator was an evil spirit of deception, opens up to me for a moment the possibility that my existence is without foundation. If the clarity and distinctness of compelling insight as such are no longer absolutely reliable, rational certainty ceases to be a foundation; reason is called into question. The only thing that prevents this shattering of all certainty is that Descartes does not think this thought in earnest, but only experiments with it. Anyone who is really convinced of this idea that Descartes puts forward experimentally—and here the idea of the creator-demon can be dropped as long as his illusory world with its innumerable ambiguities remains (as often in Nietzsche)[1] the sole reality—has not only lost confidence in reason but is faced with a bottomless abyss if there is no other ground than reason to sustain him.

Philosophically speaking, Descartes took an extraordinary step when, holding rational evidence in itself to be inadequate, he tried to confirm it from a deeper source. For a moment he was aware that rational evidence has its source in a prerational act. But taking the form of a purely

[1] Cf. my *Nietzsche*, Berlin, 1936, pp. 160 ff., 194 ff., 256 ff.

rational and compelling statement, this insight was instantly lost. Wishing to disclose the irrational source of rational evidence by rational arguments, he lost sight of it. In questioning reason, he did not depart from the solid ground of reason; no sooner was his question formulated than he was back at his starting point.

In order to make fully clear the relationship in Descartes between his fundamental operation and the evidence of rational insight in mathematics and the sciences, we should first have to realize the existence of two distinct types of certainty, and then derive one from the other in a new way which transcends all particular scientific intelligibility.

And it may be noted that Descartes actually tends to distinguish two kinds of certainty, when, on the basis of the proof of the existence of God, he writes that "the existence of God would pass with me as at least as certain as I have ever held the truth of mathematics" (A.T. VII, 65–66), and when, comparing the evidence of the existence of God with the evidence of geometrical insight, he writes: *"Whereas,* on reverting to the examination of the idea which I had of a Perfect Being, I found that in this case existence was implied in it in the same manner in which the equality of its three angles to two right angles is implied in the idea of a triangle . . . or even more evidently still" (A.T. VI, 36). But how can anything be more evident than the absolute evidence of mathematical insight? This passage might be explained by the existence of two different kinds of certainty. With his fundamental operation Descartes tries to gain a certainty on the basis of which mathematical certainty, already supreme among certainties, can be made absolute. From this we must infer that for Descartes mathematical certainty was lacking in the absolute necessity with which I must think God's being and my own existence. He seems to have in mind a certainty which is not rational, but is the ground of rational certainty, to believe that anterior to compelling certainty there is a still more compelling certainty. Stepping out of the purely rational cognition of mathematics and science, we must find a new approach to knowledge, the ground of another certainty.

It would be going too far to say that Descartes subordinated the compelling certainty of reason to the existential certainty without which rational certainty would sink into nothingness. Originally Descartes's ideas may have moved in this direction, but clothed in a rational, argumentative, demonstrative form, they soon lost whatever existential content they might have had. After having experimentally doubted rational certainty, Descartes found no other foundation for it than rational certainty itself, from which he had never seriously departed.

II
The method

The principles of Descartes's philosophy are disclosed in his fundamental operation. In so far as the goal is indubitable and compelling certainty, everything depends on deliberate method. Indeed, Descartes presents his philosophical effort as method even before conceiving his fundamental operation, and the fundamental operation itself provides the basis of his method. Thus the accent seems to be on method, on the cognitive process, and not on the contents of knowledge.

To have made method his central theme and as such the foundation of all philosophy—that was what Descartes's contemporaries and successors found so fascinatingly new in his thinking. He set the highest hopes in the results that might finally be attained by his method. Many of his successors have been so preoccupied by the idea of what *might* result from this method that they have overlooked or forgotten what actually *did* result. It is still pertinent to inquire what this method really was.

1. METHOD AS A THEME

Development of the notion of method. Descartes was weary of the diversity of men's thoughts and statements. It seemed to him that before his time men had been unable to distinguish the true from the false and had consequently failed to achieve compelling certainty, and that human knowledge, for all its riches, remained chaotic. For without method truth could be stumbled on only by chance and consequently, for lack of compelling verification, could not become our permanent possession. Accordingly, he held the first requirement for successful philosophizing to be the conscious application of a clear method. He believed that no such method had existed before him and that his particular task was to create one.

Descartes first applied his method in practice; then he became conscious of it; and finally, he made it the central theme of his investigations. That was the beginning of his philosophy.

Historically, Descartes[1] first experienced certainty in mathematics. Then he sought and tried to construct a

[1] The historical development of Descartes's ideas is not considered in the present study. See Henri Goulier, *La Pensée religieuse de Descartes*, Paris, 1924, and Gilson, *Études sur le rôle de la pensée médiévale dans la formation du système cartésien*, Paris, 1930, pp. 281 ff.

mathesis universalis, which would serve to unify and confer mastery of realms of knowledge that had hitherto been separate (all the mathematical sciences or all sciences in general). His attempt at doubt came only then, as a final step.

Once the methodic source of his knowledge was discovered, the order was inverted. From doubt issued the indubitable truths, the principles of Being, which for him constituted the area of knowledge. Self-evident principles and methodical progress are inseparable. The all-embracing universal method engenders universal mathematics, and from universal mathematics grow the specialized sciences. Thus from the principles recognized in the method Descartes went on to the knowledge of the world, of extended substance and thinking substance.

Philosophy and mathematics. Considering that in Descartes mathematics always seems to occupy the forefront and that mathematical certainty was his actual starting point, we must ask whether his philosophy reflects the influence of mathematics on philosophical speculation (that is, the transference of mathematical thinking to philosophical speculation) or whether, on the contrary, an authentic philosophical impulse exerted a creative effect on mathematics.

Apart from the biographical order of his intellectual development, there are other indications that mathematics held primacy with Descartes and that mathematics was the model on which he built his philosophical thinking. Time and time again, he compares his philosophical insights with mathematical insights; occasionally he even states his fundamental ideas in the form of Euclidean theorems (Answer to the second Objection to the Meditations: A.T. VII, 160 ff.). And often he stresses the value of mathematics: "Of the sciences already discovered, Arithmetic and Geom-

etry alone are left, to which the observance of this rule
reduces us" (A.T. X, 363).

However, the primacy of mathematics is by no means
absolute. Mathematics is a guide in this philosophical endeavor, but not its source.

The passages in which Descartes expresses the superiority of philosophy to mathematics and his contempt for the
mathematician who is nothing but a mathematician must
surely come as a surprise to anyone who supposes mathematics to be the source of Descartes's philosophy. "For,"
he writes, "really there is nothing more futile than to
busy one's self with bare numbers and imaginary figures
in such a way as to appear to rest content with trifles, and
so to resort to those superficial demonstrations, which are
discovered more frequently by chance than by skill . . .
that in a sense one ceases to make use of one's reason"
(A.T. X, 375). Moreover, in speaking of the rules for the
guidance of reason, he writes: "For I should not think
much of these rules if they had no ability save for the solution of the empty problems with which Logicians and
Geometers have been wont to beguile their leisure. . . ."
He speaks of "trifling," and declares that in taking "illustrations" from mathematics he had nothing less in mind "than
ordinary Mathematics . . ." (A.T. X, 373 ff.). This contempt, however, is never directed at the *method,* but only
at the *object* of mathematics, in so far as it is taken as an
end in itself. Descartes did not forget that his mathematical
thinking gave him the experience of method by means of
which he hoped to mold *all* cognition and raise it to certainty. But he wished to give mathematical knowledge a
logical and metaphysical foundation in something more
universal, from the standpoint of which the subject of
mathematics dwindles almost to insignificance.

In his period of philosophical maturity, Descartes distinguished explicitly between mathematical and philosophical knowledge: "The difference is that the basic concepts presupposed for the proof of geometrical theorems are accepted by all, because they accord with the evidence of the senses. Here, accordingly, the only problem is to draw the right inferences. . . . In these metaphysical matters on the contrary the utmost effort is required to apprehend the first concepts clearly and distinctly . . ." (A.T. VII, 157). But once this has been done, Descartes is convinced that his philosophical proofs "equal or perhaps even surpass geometrical demonstrations in certainty and evidence" (A.T. VII, 4).

But this difference between philosophical and mathematical thinking is not a radical one, as later in Kant, who drew a fundamental distinction between philosophical thinking based on concepts and mathematical thinking based on the intuitive construction of concepts (*Critique of Pure Reason*). For Descartes, on the contrary, a "synthetic" method, in the form of a Euclidean proof, is applicable also to philosophy, though it would not be convincing until the principles themselves had been made fully evident by "analysis." Once this has been done, the Euclidean proof, he believes, will be sound and compelling. Thus it is not correct to say that Descartes's successors, e.g. Spinoza, Wolff, etc., chose the Euclidean method because they had misunderstood Descartes, for he himself made use of it. Windelband is doing the followers of Descartes an injustice when he writes (*Geschichte der Philosophie,* 13th ed., p. 332): "The disciples confused the free creative thinking that Descartes had in mind with the system of rigorous demonstrations that they found in Euclid's Treatise on Geometry . . . ; a new method of investigation was turned back into an *ars demonstrandi.*" If it had any validity, this criticism would apply to Descartes himself. But Windelband's distinction is in itself false, because it sets up an opposition between elements which must go hand in hand: between investigation and form of presentation, between discovery and its theoretical foundations.

Description of the method. In the pursuit of his method, Descartes finds certainty by going back to the indubitable principles and then by developing with equal certainty the truths deriving from these principles. The first step leads to the *intuitive* certainty that we have of a principle for which we need seek no other foundation. The second step consists in *deduction* from these intuitively clear principles. In Descartes this method is characterized by three basic traits:

a) In order to gain clarity and distinctness of thought in intuition, we must rid ourselves of all sensory images. Sense perceptions and the representations based on them lead to the diversity and imprecision of endless particulars. Thought alone leads, by the evidence of intuition, to the realm of the One, which is authentic knowledge and in which all authentic knowledge is encompassed.

b) Since truth can be arrived at only analytically by way of simple principles or synthetically by the derivation of one theorem from another, the truth is never isolated or fortuitous; we can never gain certainty of a truth that stands by itself. A truth carries full evidence only in its place in the chain of analyses and deductions.

c) Knowledge has a single foundation—in the self-certainty of thought. But since there is only *one* knowledge, only *one* method, the task is to ground all knowledge in the methodic unity of one science, a *mathesis universalis.* This science must not be a classification of manifold data, which continue to escape an over-all view, but a means of mastering all possible knowledge, thanks to a method which can produce whatever knowledge is needed at any time. It is not merely a systematization and classification of existing things, but a rational technique, a method, which enables us to master by cognition everything that is within our reach. It is a key that enables us to open up every field that is accessible to us.

Indubitable certainty, unity established by a universal method, a technical mastery which opens up boundless possibilities of knowledge—these are the basic traits of Descartes's conception of method. Let us now examine the matter in detail.

1. *Intuition.* Ultimate, indubitable insight is based not on perception or imagination, but on clarity and distinctness as such. Descartes gives the name of intuition to the act by which we apprehend these qualities: "By intuition I understand not the shifting testimony of the senses . . . but a simple and distinct conception of the pure and attentive mind, of such a kind that no doubt remains concerning what we know, or, which amounts to the same thing, a conception . . . that springs solely from the light of reason" (A.T. X, 368). Examples of such intuition are "that each man can know intellectually that he exists, that he has consciousness, that a triangle is bounded only by three sides, and so on, and there are far more such propositions than most people realize" (A.T. X, 368).

Descartes insists over and over again that passing beyond sense perception and representation, we must apprehend the pure principles by intuition. We should not dwell on any particular object, on any isolated representation. Intuition is not achieved through the visualization of forms, actual things, or elementary phenomena, or through the study of known objects. Rather, it is by detachment from all definite sensory things that we arrive at the intuitive principles which enable us to master all reality. This procedure finds its most eminent confirmation in Descartes's invention of analytical geometry, which dispenses with the use of geometrical figures or arithmetical numbers for purposes of demonstration. While algebra frees us from the necessity of resorting to specific numbers, analytical geometry goes beyond all representations that make use of sensory elements, discovering the broader principle which is valid both for geometry and for arithmetic and enables us to master them both. By expressing lines, curves, planes, etc. in equations which refer to a system of co-ordinates, analytical geometry enables us to study the properties of geometric figures in algebraic terms, without the use of diagrams. This abstract principle, which has no recourse to sensory elements, can nevertheless be applied to various kinds of sensory reality. In it the two aspects of mathematical knowledge converge.

Descartes maintains that there is an essential identity between intuition on the one hand, clarity and distinctness on the other. If, to his mind, clarity and distinctness are the sole sources of intuition, it is apparently because he always has in mind the example of mathematical evidence. He was convinced that by combining geometry and algebra into analytical geometry, he had attained something that transcends all representation. Mathematicians are still discussing the problem of whether mathematical certainty requires a representational guide, and if so, what it should be. Descartes denied any such necessity. He believed that he was able to make decisive advances in knowledge precisely because he had transcended representation by means of pure clarity and distinctness. For him the source of knowledge was not clear and distinct representation but clarity and distinctness as such.

We must ask whether Descartes's concept of "intuition" means anything at all, and what happens if it is taken as a foundation.

The words "clear and distinct" are themselves clear only if they refer to the clarity and distinctness of something. Otherwise they are meaningless. Descartes does not distinguish between the clarity of an actual thought, bolstered up by images—an object, a principle, a symbol, etc. —and clarity as the rational validity of a relationship or form, which need contain no vestige of representation.

Descartes also overlooked the fact that there is a certainty which in no way implies clarity and distinctness. A magnificent example of this is the foundation of his own philosophy. His *cogito ergo sum* is a certainty, but its content is vague and both its principle and its object are utterly devoid of clarity and distinctness. Descartes confused the certainty of the representations that accompany the living experience of present possibilities unfolding ad infinitum, with the rational certainty implied by the empty form of propositions without defined content.

The consequences of this self-delusion about his own first certainty are extraordinary: In developing his system, Descartes confined his attention to the compelling validity of the statements which he derived from the *cogito ergo sum*. But he almost entirely lost sight of the profound meaning and rich possibilities contained in his first certainty. Concomitantly, he tended to regard the abstract concepts of reason (which he calls ideas) as self-sufficient truths, to suppose that with ideas he had the things themselves.

And yet in the original conception of "intuition," in spite of everything that he loses by transforming it into compelling rational certainty, there is a vestige of the Platonic striving to rise above the senses. Here, as almost everywhere, Descartes seems to begin at the philosophical source, which opens up an entirely different truth, but soon to run aground on the particularity of a compelling rational content.

2. *Deduction.* By deduction Descartes means "everything that can be derived with necessity from other things that are known with certainty"; "it is a continuous and nowhere interrupted movement of thought, which intuitively produces every single step" (A.T. X, 369). Consequently, the "fundamental secret" of method is to discover the "simplest element" and from it to deduce everything else. The simple elements are for him clear and evident; the rest, the other terms that are derived from them, form a chain of deductions in which there is likewise nothing unclear (A.T. IX, Part 2, p. 2).

The method differs essentially from a mere classification of things by categories (A.T. X, 381). It does not juxtapose data, but derives one datum from another: to know is to produce. The endless differentiation of concepts practiced in scholasticism was largely abandoned. Because in the progress from evidence to evidence, Descartes was not concerned with ordering an endless manifold, but in mastering it by rational operations, numerous previous distinctions were dropped; hence the frequent *"sive,"* with which he equates concepts that had formerly been distinct (examples in Eucken, *Geschichte der philosophischen Terminologie,* Leipzig, 1879, p. 88). Descartes despised the technique of solving problems by a *"distinguendum est"* and seldom made use of it.

There is something very ambiguous about Descartes's view of method. In a way his formulation characterizes the

"nova scientia," which Galileo had already perceived clearly
and applied with brilliant results, and which Kant later
summed up in the sentence: I know only what I can make.
The procedure is as follows: On the basis of a priori blue-
prints, I construct a hypothesis, the consequences of which
can be tested in experience by measurement. The method
is fruitful and leads to new knowledge if the investigator
stays close to reality and subjects every hypothesis to complete empirical verification. Consequently this method imposes limitations upon itself, admitting only of hypotheses
that are by nature subject to verification, confining itself
to quantitative mathematical constructions, because measurement is the only means of exact verification, and accepting no hypothesis before it has been checked against
experience.

Descartes showed his understanding of modern scientific method in his insistence on experiment. In that respect
he was clearer than Bacon but much less clear than Galileo.
Particular to him is that he did not follow the new method
—which started a new age in Western thinking—rigorously,
but applied it in the form of the old dogmatic systems.
This occurs wherever he formulates and employs it as a
hypothesis without verification, as a self-sufficient construction, as if dogmatic clarity and distinctness taken in themselves were a knowledge of reality. This side of Descartes—
as Maritain shrewdly remarked—confuses human knowledge
with the form of knowledge peculiar to the angels (as
conceived by Thomas Aquinas).[1] The knowledge of the
angels is intuitive, innate, and independent of things, and
on this model, Descartes wished to reform human knowledge, which however is not intuitive, but dependent on

[1] Maritain, *Trois Réformateurs, Luther, Descartes, Rousseau,* Paris, 1925.

logical inferences, not innate, but dependent on experience, and not independent, but dependent on objects. However, Maritain's characterization does not apply to the other aspect of the method, which is also present in Descartes's thinking, though in contradiction with it: Descartes knows not only intuition, but deduction as well, not only innate knowledge, but also experience, not only the independence of things in hypothetical constructions, but also verification by observation.

The consequences of Descartes's determination to divorce his method from the senses, from representation, and from experience, or at least of his failure to reunite them, are far-reaching:

a) After separating them so radically, Descartes is unable to recapture the connection between thought and perception, between thought and the corporeal world, although he always tries to maintain such a link.[1]

This is evident in the fact that he conceives the objects of mathematics and of the physical world in two different ways: in pure reason (*intellectio*) and in images (*imaginatio*). This last can be either the mental image (imagination) or the external representation of physical reality (perceptual images). Transcending them both, pure thought possesses the thing itself by virtue of the intellect (*intellectio*) alone: a straight line is not perceived by us through the senses, only the intellect can apprehend it; it is in essence an object of thought, not of perception; moreover, a physical object is what it really is "only in thought," as is illustrated by the example of wax, which

[1] On the following, see Goldbeck, *Descartes' mathematisches Wissenschaftsideal*, 1892 (reprinted in *Der Mensch und sein Weltbild*, Leipzig, 1925, pp. 296 ff.).

may be solid or liquid or gaseous: "We must then grant that I could not even understand through the imagination *(imaginari)* what this piece of wax is, and that it is my mind alone which perceives it" (A.T. VII, 31). Thus it is certain that "even bodies are not properly speaking known by the senses or by the faculty of imagination but by the understanding only . . ." (A.T. VII, 34).

But now the question arises: what role do the senses and the imagination play in understanding? Descartes speaks of the "application" of the mind to the body (quoted by Goldbeck, p. 298). The *imaginatio* has no independence, though it is an indispensable aid of the intellect (according to the interpretation of Gilson, *Commentaire,* p. 220); but in addition, it is everywhere a source of error, for those who depend on it cannot achieve understanding because their thinking is not free.

If mathematical objects are not only objects of thought, but also exist in reality, if they are forms of thought, yet at the same time modes of extended substance, because extended substance itself can only be known in the form of mind, we must ask how mind can enter into contact with the senses and how the senses can enter into contact with mind. The depth of philosophical thinking is disclosed by the way in which it mediates between the oppositions it sets up (without which there can be no movement of thought). An example is Kant, whose central theme is the problem of the link between intuition and understanding, between nature and freedom, etc. Descartes, however, draws a sharp distinction between *imaginatio* and *intellectio.* Though in the end he does not altogether deny a connection between what he has so strictly separated, this connection never becomes clear. Either he refers to it incidentally with a vague term such as "application," or he develops a purely arbitrary pseudosolution. Descartes's conception of method leads him to take dualism for granted.

b) As a second consequence, Descartes was so confident in mere clarity and distinctness, supposing that they conferred knowledge of things themselves, that he relied on them not only in mathematics, where verification on the basis of one construction or another can prevent thought from going astray, but also in metaphysics and natural science, where he lets his thoughts run riot and, on the sole strength of the intuitive certainty conferred by supposed clarity and distinctness, ventures to make the most astonishing assertions (in physics, or in psychology—theory of the passions, theory that the soul is localized in the pineal gland, etc.). Though his method was intended, among other things, as a foundation for the new natural science, he offered little resistance to the old scholastic habit of building up metaphysics and natural science out of pure thought. Though on a new foundation, he preserved the same confidence in the power of mere thinking to engender true knowledge. Descartes may have despised the syllogistic of the scholastics, but was far from despising their conception of pure thought which gains knowledge or reality by constructing itself.

c) Thirdly, his fundamental conception of method enabled Descartes to believe in the possibility of a universal method applicable to all knowledge. Starting from the well-founded and fruitful idea of a universal mathematics, he tried to develop a *mathesis universalis* and was led into a never-never land, where no results were obtainable.

3. *Mathesis universalis:* Descartes believed that by casting off sensory apprehension, which is always a source of limitation and unclearness, the mind apprehends, by pure

thought, what is *identical* in all knowledge. He consequently regarded mathematics as the best, in fact the only discipline which teaches the mind to discern the truth. "One who has accustomed his mind to mathematical reasoning will also have rendered it capable of finding other truths, for thought is everywhere one and the same" (*cum sit ratiocinatio ubique une et eadem,* A.T. V, 177, conversation with Burman). Descartes expresses the same idea when he says that "the sciences taken all together are identical with human wisdom, which always remains one and the same, however applied to different subjects . . ." (A.T. X, 360).

If all knowledge is the same, there can be only *one* method, which is universal, and one science, encompassing all knowledge. This is the *mathesis universalis.*

Descartes's enthusiasm for compelling certainty is increased by the insight that the method which produces certainty also teaches us to master all knowledge. Hence it is a "Method for the resolution of difficulties of every kind in the Sciences" (A.T. VII, 3), a procedure by which every science and every object are made accessible to knowledge. Such a method opens up infinite possibilities.

Descartes's primary concern is not with things but with method, not with any specific object of knowledge, but with the way in which the knowledge is obtained. Nevertheless the purpose of method is to produce objective knowledge. But as applied by Descartes, the method seems to become its own content, divorced from all objects. The question arises: can anything be known through such a method? Let us examine this question in the light of the grandiose program of the *mathesis universalis.*

Descartes had taken the step to analytical geometry, in which geometry and algebra are combined. He had discovered a single universal mathematics, embracing all the

special fields of mathematics: "But as I considered the matter carefully, it gradually came to light that all those matters only were referred to mathematics in which order and
measurement are investigated, and that it makes no difference whether it be in numbers, figures, stars, sounds, or any
other object that the question of measurement arises. I saw
consequently that there must be some general science to
explain that element as a whole which gives rise to problems about order and measurement, restricted as these are
to special subject matter" (A.T. X, 378). So far the idea
is convincing and justified by actual mathematical knowledge. But Descartes wants far more. What he has in mind
is not "ordinary mathematics," but "quite another science,
of which these illustrations [the branches of mathematics]
are rather the outer husk than constituents. Such a new
science should contain the primary rudiments of human
reason . . ." (A.T. X, 374). He is convinced that this science is the source of all the others and therefore superior
to all other knowledge transmitted only by human tradition.

Descartes inaugurated a discipline embracing all the
domains of mathematics and it has proved fruitful. But a
mathesis universalis going beyond universal mathematics to
embrace all human knowledge remains to this day an un-
solved problem, probably because there is no possible
solution. Considering that such a *mathesis* calls for pure
thought stripped of all specific sensory elements, and moving exclusively in the One, which is all knowledge, let us
ask a few questions:

Since universal thought calls for an all-embracing representation, must we not say that its freedom from representation is relative rather than absolute? Consequently,
must not, in the last analysis, this *mathesis universalis,* for

which Descartes was striving, finally require the guidance of sensory images, through which its knowledge takes on content, applicability, and reality? Is this *mathesis universalis* not ultimately an all-embracing mathematics, which reduces manifold sensory contents to a common denominator and is patterned on its own characteristic "intuitive" element, so that it can never really be a universal science of all being?

In casting off all representation and all ties with representation, would I not be entering into a field of knowledge that is empty and therefore devoid of interest—a knowledge which consists only in empty forms of communication, in propositions, formulas, and symbols which can signify everything or nothing, which express no content but merely exemplify possible forms of statement? If this method permits me to gain "exact" knowledge of any objects whatsoever, can the result be anything more than the empty precision of certain compelling formal operations, which either mean nothing or have a concrete mathematical character?

These questions apply to Descartes's attempts to establish a system of logistic based on his idea of a *mathesis universalis*. But there is more philosophy in his idea than is apparent in our questioning of its logical application. Unquestionably the demand for an all-embracing unity of knowledge has never ceased to fire those who concern themselves with philosophy. It is a necessary and central philosophical problem, and the response to it is a striving for totality and all-embracing unity. It inspired the "systematic" enthusiasm of the philosophers from Kant to Hegel and such systems as that of Thomas Aquinas. Descartes marks a specific aspect of this eternal philosophical striving. What we are questioning is not the striving, but the form that Descartes gave it in his program for a *mathesis universalis*.

The crux of the matter is: *how* is this unity sought? Is it expected to provide the principles from which "everything" is derived? In other words, is it held to be a universal method which is itself all science? Or is it regarded merely as a guiding idea, which we can never possess as an object or a plan, but which, by elucidating all the possibilities of thought, cognition, and will, leads us to an awareness of the Encompassing in which we gain knowledge? In the first case, the unity is present from the start as a content, and an image of the whole is derived from a small number of principles. In the second case, unity exists as transcendence, and with this transcendent unity in view, a never-to-be-completed system of categories and methods clarifies and critically defines the knowledge and experience that have been acquired. In the first case, perfection is the attainable goal, the whole truth is definitively grasped; in the second, we attempt to clarify the knowledge and the forms and possibilities of thought thus far attained within the Encompassing. In the first case, the universal method is the plan of the whole; in the second, there can be no universal method, but only particular methods. In the first case, unity is given; in the second, it is the quest for unity which serves forever as a goad to reason: it is the over-all relationship connecting all things accessible to knowledge, and as such a never-ending task. In the first case, the one true view of the world is a meaningful goal; in the second, totality exists only as an unfinished system of philosophical logic. In the first case, the one truth has been captured; in the second, our reflection on the meaning and scope of every method of apprehending the truth is eternally subject to critical limitations.

In *carrying out* his idea, Descartes follows the first alternative throughout, although the second possibility is discernible in the idea as originally conceived. Descartes is fully conscious of only one universal method. From this follow certain typical consequences:

a) Descartes has no understanding of the "inexact sciences" (e.g. history). He does not, like Aristotle, justify them by saying that there is an appropriate way of investigating every field of knowledge, but rejects them. He does not distinguish the fundamentally different ways of mastering or apprehending reality; for example, he does not distinguish the constructive certainty of mathematics from the certainty gained through the observation of nature, or the certainty that illuminates human Existenz. Hence he is also unable to distinguish the compelling methodic insight, which is identical for all consciousness and whose subjects are interchangeable, from the insight into existential possibilities out of the ground of a man's own being, an insight which, though it can be communicated, is not understood identically by all individuals.

The fascination of his idea of universal method further prevents Descartes from distinguishing scientific invention from a mechanized technique of demonstration; he seems to expect his method to serve both to *confirm* already acquired but not yet sufficiently grounded truths, and to *discover* new truth (consequently he expected his method, which he had made into an identically transferrable, almost mechanical apparatus, to carry on by its own momentum to new inventions ad infinitum. He had no understanding for the true creativeness of discovery and invention, for the incalculable process which leads to method but does not necessarily spring from method). Thus for him, the thinker's methodic development of his own faculties

is subordinated to a single aim: knowledge and understanding acquired through practice of a research method
become identical with insight resulting from the essential
self-education of man in inner action.

b) The universal method is directed toward everything that can be known; consequently, it must first free
itself from all content, and is afterward unable to recapture it. In its conscious striving, Cartesian thinking is limited to the quest for truth whose content is identical for
every thinking being, i.e. to truth that is existentially im-
material. And this knowledge is supposed to be achieved
by the intellect, which has nothing but itself to work on.

But the idea of a productive intellect can only be a
source of error, for the intellect can produce only by taking
in material that is not intellect. Truth varies according
to the origin of its content. A thinker who supposes that
the truth is already present in pure thought and who looks
upon pure thought in itself as a universal method by which
to investigate the truth, must inevitably incur certain consequences in his own being, since he is a living man with
existential potentialities. To discern them in a personality
as reticent as Descartes's is barely possible for us; if they
are not discernible, it is also because he is always more than
what is stated in his philosophy, and this is apparent in the
initial impulse of his thinking. But it would be in the logic
of the method, if it were seriously regarded as the whole
truth, to have the following consequences: To a thinker
adopting this way of thought everything "other," that is,
everything to which the method does not apply, would
appear irrational. Since it is neither apprehended nor elucidated, this "other" must either come to him in a confusion
of varying aspects, each presenting itself as an absolute,

and thus dominating life, or else he must consciously recognize it as a valid counterposition—but in this case his entire thinking is reduced to a mere game, a private experiment without relevance for others.

To the idea of a universal method and the related divorce of method from content is opposed the idea of a philosophical logic, which discloses the truth in the multidimensionality of its configurations and methods. In pursuing this path—at variance with that of Descartes—we find that the existence of rational man is invariably subject to the following conditions:

a) What is disclosed in true knowledge is directly related to the existential reality of the man to whom it is disclosed. There are hierarchies of possible knowledge corresponding to hierarchies of humanity. All knowledge can be perverted and diluted into a mere content of the intellect, an empty shell of what was once genuine knowledge, into supposedly clear thinking which is in reality nothing other than unclearness wrapped in concepts and definitions.

b) Methodological reflection concerning any knowledge raises the question: where is the *contact with reality*, for this is the basic requirement that knowledge must meet? Such contact can occur through the observation of nature, through measurement and enumeration, through the understanding of data of perception; it may occur in the spiritual activity by which I produce myself and am given to myself; or it may occur when I gain awareness of Being by reading the ciphers of transcendence and sensing its presence.

c) Method is never an end in itself, but must always be a *method of accomplishing something*. I employ it to gain an understanding of something, to experience reality, to fulfill myself, etc. The methodic operation has meaning only in so far as it helps me in such an undertaking; otherwise it is empty, endless, bottomless.

Although Cartesian thinking seems to lead far away from living knowledge, it discloses two impulses which retain their appeal for us, because, as first conceived, they embodied an aim that was subsequently lost:

1. *Method* can actually *coincide with reality* at one point, namely, where it is no longer concerned with the knowledge of something, but with the operations of thought in which possible Existenz transcends in the medium of reason toward metaphysical awareness of being. In this respect, the method contains within it something that has no object outside the method, and this is characteristic of authentic speculation. Descartes did not consciously look for speculative ideas and consequently he did not understand them when he found them. His speculation is hidden and almost lost, and yet it finds forceful expression in certain isolated sentences. This explains why the most authentic philosophers have admired Descartes, even though at the same time formulating their objections and criticisms.

2. The idea of the unity of all knowledge as the foundation of the unity of all the sciences is a truth which became manifest at the very beginning of philosophy. Even though a universal method and a *mathesis universalis* are not the appropriate means of achieving this unity, nevertheless, Descartes's reflections often show the influence of a passion for unity, which, because it is undefined, is not yet burdened by his specific solution.

Thus he opposes definitive particularization and specialization in the sciences. According to him, there is a radical difference between sciences and "arts": in the arts a man can achieve greatness only by practicing one at a time; if he attempts to practice several, they interfere with each other; different arts, e.g., farming and harp-playing, are not readily compatible in the same individual (A.T. X, 359–360). The sciences, on the other hand, further one another when practiced by the same individual. All the sciences are so interlinked that it is far easier to learn them all than to detach any one from the others. Thus if anyone wishes seriously to investigate the truth, he cannot restrict himself to any particular science (A.T. X, 361). Descartes finds the cause of this in the unity of human reason—a scientist cannot limit himself to a part of its domain without prejudice to the rest. Descartes's philosophical impulse drives him toward the *one* cosmos of knowledge. Without philosophical thought, a specialized scientist can make limited discoveries along lines of investigation that have already been laid down. But mere correctness takes on meaning only in relation to the One, the good understanding (the *bona mens*): "All other studies are to be esteemed not so much for their own value as because they contribute something to this."

2. THE APPLICATION OF THE METHOD

Only in application can a method show its worth. Let us then see what Descartes does with his method and what knowledge he gains by it. First we shall examine the *content* of the knowledge he obtained through the method; secondly, how the method is reflected in his scientific attitude; and thirdly, how his method contributes to the pursuit of the ultimate goal of philosophy, the Encompassing of all thought.

The method in natural science and in the development of our world view. Historically, Descartes's view of the world exerted an enormous influence. His sharp dis-

tinction between body and soul and his mechanical view
of nature were for centuries fundamental tenets. But we
must ask what these positions mean in Descartes and to
what degree scientific truth can be imputed to them.

In keeping with his method, Descartes constructs a
view of the world by first setting forth the *principles* of
reality and then deriving all reality from these principles.

The principles are already given in the first propositions in which universal doubt is overcome; the first certainty implies, for Descartes, a separation between soul and
body: "Thus considering that he who wishes to doubt
everything, cannot doubt that he exists while he is doubting, and considering that what thinks in this way and cannot doubt in itself . . . is not what we call our body, but
what we call our soul or mind, I took the being or existence of this mind as my first principle" (A.T. IX, Part 2,
p. 10). From the philosophical source of the *cogito ergo
sum,* Descartes derives his knowledge of the psychological
reality of consciousness.

Actually it is Descartes who for the first time revealed,
with all the consequences it implies, the enormous gulf
between consciousness and everything which, without itself
being consciousness, is an object of consciousness. From a
certain point of view this is a truth, indispensable to the
investigation of phenomena, and on this level it is irrefutable. But Descartes transformed it into a metaphysical assertion concerning *two original substances.*[1] Here he was
going too far, as though this separation disclosed the very

---

[1] Descartes introduces the concept of substance without justifying it. He
took it for granted because of his scholastic education. (In the scholastic
sense, he was not a nominalist but a realist, though in his case these terms
are no longer fully appropriate.) On the significance of the category of
substance in Descartes, cf. Gilson, *Commentaires,* pp. 302 ff.

roots of being. Moreover, such an assertion is false, because it implies *consequences* that contradict it.

1) Descartes tries to explain the fact that—even if mind and body are radically different—man is nevertheless mind *and* body, that we have no experience of a mind without body, and that the enormous influence of the body on the life of the mind is at the very least a condition without which there can be no life of the mind. How are body and mind connected? Descartes's answer to this question— that the contact between the two occurs in the pineal gland —is not based on investigation; it is purely arbitrary, a figment of the imagination. Such absurdities—the localization of a mind which has been characterized as aspatial, the influence of a punctual, incorporeal mind on corporeal processes—have made it apparent that this hypothesis, which is of central importance for Descartes's world view, is a very strange one, an impression intensified now that modern investigations of the anatomy and physiology of the pineal gland have shown it to be a minor organ which does not by any means determine the functioning of the brain.

2) Inevitably Descartes eliminated from his field of vision all those phenomena to which the distinction between mind and body brings no elucidation: for example, all phenomena of expression; the reality of man as man; even the living reality of animals which, with a consistency carried to the point of the absurd, he regarded as unconscious automata, because they are without thought.

These examples show that it is impossible to establish an intelligible connection between mind and body once they have been distinguished absolutely as two substances. What is correct phenomenologically, that is, for one aspect of reality—namely, the sharp distinction between consciousness as inwardness and spatial objectivity as outward extension—becomes a rigid metaphysical hypostasis, which on the one hand is sterile, and on the other hand raises insoluble and existentially meaningless questions. By taking a dualism that is justified within certain limits as an absolute, Descartes blocked off his horizon.

In his deduction, Descartes tried to investigate each of the two substances separately. He concerned himself chiefly with extended substance, that is, the existence of bodies in space. According to Descartes, bodies are what they are only in so far as they are clearly and distinctly known. But they are clear and distinct only in regard to magnitude, extension, form, etc. Hence such qualities as color, sound, and smell are subjective. In order to understand the world of nature in a purely mathematical sense as a purely quantitative process resulting from the pressures and collisions of bodies and forces, science must exclude these so-called secondary sensory qualities as objectively unreal: "In physics I neither accept nor look for any other principles than those of geometry or pure mathematics, for through them all natural phenomena can be explained and sure proofs concerning them provided" (A.T. VIII, 336 ad 78–79).

In the further course of this deduction of mechanistic physics, Descartes distinguishes the knowledge of nature *as a whole,* from the knowledge this makes possible of the endless variety of *particular* things. In the principles and in what is derived from them, he believed that he possessed knowledge as a whole. He rejected principles set up by the older philosophers; they "all presupposed as a principle something that they themselves did not fully know," such as gravity, the vacuum, the atoms, heat and cold, dryness and moisture, salt, sulphur, quicksilver, etc. (A.T. Part 2, p. 8). Descartes, on the other hand, puts forward principles which in his opinion are the only true principles, because they are clear and distinct. They provide a definitive insight into all nature, an explanation "of the first laws or Principles of Nature, of the way in which the Heavens, the Fixed Stars, the Planets, the Comets, and the whole universe in general are composed, and in particular [they disclose] the nature of this earth, of air, of fire, and of magnet, which are the elements that can be found most commonly everywhere on the surface of the earth, and of all the qualities that are noted in these elements, such as light, heat, weight, and so on" (A.T. IX, Part 2, p. 16).

Descartes thought he had explained all this by the principles. But "to explain in the same way the nature of each of the other more particular elements . . . namely, the minerals, plants, animals . . ."—that alone would provide "a complete system of philosophy" (A.T. IX, Part 2, p. 17). Descartes did not attempt to develop such a system in detail. For this he adduces a number of reasons: it would not be possible within the lifetime of one man; it would require many experiments, involving an expenditure which he, as a private individual, could not afford.

Let us now try to characterize Descartes's general world view. The belief was long prevalent that Descartes laid down the lines on which modern science built and exerted a determining influence on its development. In the course of his philosophizing, Descartes actually did take up the new mathematical science, which had been developed in and before his time by Galileo, Kepler, and Copernicus, presenting it as if it followed from his principles. But in so doing, he did not add to the certainty and evidence of this science; on the contrary, he lent it an absolute character that is alien to the scientific spirit.

Scientific inquiry is always directed toward particulars

and, vast as these particulars may be, its hypotheses are always limited. Consequently, science never embraces the totality, but oscillates between rational, hypothetical construction on the one hand, and on the other hand the measurement by which each hypothesis is verified, refuted, or corrected. Yet though our knowledge of particulars is far from complete, Descartes aims at a definitive knowledge of nature as a whole.

Whereas a science conscious of its concrete method pursues aspects of reality and investigates them in the appropriate way—and here reality is not considered as one, but is broken down according to particular perspectives—Descartes aspires to grasp the whole of reality, or at least its principles, in a single movement of thought. The result is not scientific investigation, but a purely rational derivation of reality, often reflected in groundless assertions contrary to experience and observation.

Descartes and modern science have this in common: both hold that only science based on mathematics is really science. But the ways in which they evaluate and apply mathematics are entirely different. For the scientist, the value of mathematics is that only mathematical theory permits of such exact constructions that the observation of nature can itself become exact enough to verify or refute a hypothesis. The older type of observation had served only to show that certain facts as described were vaguely and approximately in keeping with certain rational constructions. Now, thanks to the new empiricism grounded in mathematics, Kepler was able, for example, to deduce the true laws of planetary motion from an insignificant annual deviation of eight minutes (observed over a period of years). For Descartes, however, the importance of mathematics resided in its own evidence. It satisfied his dogmatic need for certainty and led him to mistake a construction for reality.

Thus Descartes's system of nature was constructed, not grounded in experience, and did not, like an exact hypothesis, promote investigation. His theory of vortices yielded a total world view comparable to those which philosophers had imagined time and time again; but it could not, through quantitative determination and verification, serve as a mathematical basis of investigation: it led to no new experience. The spirit which inspired it was not the spirit of science, for which the mechanistic view of the world was a fruitful means of research, but rather, the spirit of a mechanistic metaphysics. Descartes's successors often attacked the unbridled speculation of the past, but all they themselves produced was a new kind of speculation, restrained in form but not at all in content: the dogma of a world conceived as mechanism.

The consequences of this rationalistic system of nature in Descartes are obvious: developed apart from experience,[1]

---

[1] The word "experience" has several meanings. 1) Descartes was by no means lacking in the experience of the man of the world, who knows human situations, the dangers implicit in them, the exigencies of social life, and the consequences of action in this world. 2) He shows a kind of experience when, recollecting his travels and great events at which he was present (such as the siege of La Rochelle, the coronation of the Emperor at Frankfort, etc., or his days as a soldier), he writes: "After I had employed several years in thus studying the book of the world and trying to acquire some experience, I one day formed the resolution of also making myself an object of study . . ." (A.T. VI, 10). In all this he was probably more of a spectator than an earnest participant; even as a soldier, as far as we know, he was brave but without passion for any military or political cause. 3) Descartes made it his business to observe the works of man, ships, machines, fortifications, etc., and he occasionally witnessed dissections of animals and other biological experiments. But his biography provides no indication of a true contact with nature. He seems to have seen the visible world through a veil. 4) Descartes had wide knowledge of

it led Descartes still further away from the empirical world. The result was twofold: on the one hand his theoretical statements proved to be wholly false, and on the other hand, he put forward assertions so absurd that they could have been arrived at only by one blinded to reality and fascinated by an empty logic that had lost all contact with things themselves.

Hence it is understandable and characteristic that Descartes should have *failed to understand* the science of his time in the person of Galileo. "Everything that he (Galileo) says about the velocity of bodies falling in a vacuum, etc. is built up without a foundation; for he should first have determined what gravity is; if he had known the truth about that, he would know that it is non-existent in a vacuum" (A.T. II, 385; III, 9). But this is precisely the scholastic attitude which we find also in Bacon, whereas the new science, which was to prove so fruitful, set aside the question of essences as unanswerable and concentrated on investigating empirical laws. Unlike all previous systems of the world, the new science made no attempt to establish the fundamental principles of things, and contented itself with constructing methodical, always particular hypotheses suggested by a fortunate inspiration, and with projecting and conducting exact observations, that is, ex-

---

the scientific investigations of his time. But his attitude toward them was predominantly intellectual, he refuted and constructed theoretically, as though an idea could have meaning apart from its bearing on reality. Certain of his ideas, to be sure, "anticipate" future discoveries, but this has been the case with all builders of philosophical systems of the world from antiquity to our own day. Such ideas become significant only when the discoverer comes who—usually without knowledge of his purely speculative precursors—connects them with experience by showing what kind of measurement can make them accessible to experimental verification.

actly verified answers to the questions submitted to nature. The new science was interested in real knowledge. Descartes reproached Galileo for having neglected what it was *not* interested in: "Without having considered the first causes of nature, he merely looked for the causes of certain particular effects. Thus he built without a foundation" (A.T. II, 380). And characteristically, Descartes also found this supposed scientific deficiency in Galileo's style of thinking: "I find, in general, that he is a much better philosopher than most, because to the best of his ability he relinquishes the scholastic errors and tries to examine physical facts by mathematical reasoning. In this I am entirely in agreement with him and I hold that there is no other way of finding the truth. But it seems to me that he is very much at fault for continually making digressions and not stopping to explain a subject fully; which shows that he has not examined it methodically" (A.T. II, 380). Descartes fails to understand the free and thorough approach of the scientist who undertakes only to examine particulars. Galileo's use of mathematics gave Descartes a feeling of kinship with him, but he did not understand the core of the new scientific method. Galileo and Kepler really understood one another, but there was a gulf between Galileo and Descartes.

In view of all this, it is not surprising that scientists should have repeatedly rejected Descartes's scientific thinking. Speaking of Descartes's vortex theory, which for a time (thanks no doubt to the high prestige of Descartes the *philosopher*) was able to compete seriously with Newton's theory of gravitation, Newcomb wrote: "Had Descartes been able to show that the parts of his vortex must move in ellipses having the sun in one focus, that they must describe equal areas in equal time, and that the velocity must diminish as we receded from the sun, according to Kepler's third law, his theory would so far have been satisfactory. Failing in this, it cannot be regarded as an advance in science, but rather as a step backward" (*Popular Astronomy*, 2nd ed., London, 1883, p. 73). In his *Histoire de l'astronomie moderne* (Paris, 1821, Vol. II, p. 235), Delambre wrote: "Descartes renewed the method of the ancient Greeks, who speculated endlessly, without ever calculating; but error for error, fantasy for fantasy, I prefer Aristotle's solid spheres to Descartes's vortices. With the spheres men were able at least to make planetaria which roughly reproduced the movements of the heavens; . . . they were able to find approximate rules for calculation; *no one has ever been able to derive any benefit from the vortices,* either for calculation or for machines."

Here a distinction must be made: Descartes's valuable discoveries assure him a permanent place in the history of mathematics; on the other hand, his influence on the history of science has been nonexistent or negative.

But thanks to its unity and the elegance with which it was presented, its purely logical consistency, its grounding in an all-embracing philosophy, and the promise which the method seemed to hold out, Descartes's world view, based not on observation but on pure construction, has carried an enormous appeal. Over the centuries, Descartes's total view has exerted a paralyzing fascination, for which neither the new science nor philosophy was to blame. A historically unique combination of motives in Descartes led him to his strange edifice: scholastic and dogmatic in its origin, in its substance modern and scientific, and in form rational and compelling (though compelling only in appearance).

The method and Descartes's scientific attitude. In order to understand the strange combination of motives at work in Descartes's scientific attitude, we must consider the impulses that characterize modern science. These are: 1) the desire for compelling and indubitable certainty; 2) the conviction that no idea is valid unless it is confirmed by experiment; 3) interest in the knowable particular rather than in the unknowable whole and the hope of contributing, by investigation, to an endless and unlimited progress of science; 4) the striving for technical achievement; 5) the passion for novelty. These five features of the scientific attitude characterize modern science, which, first making its appearance in isolated precursors, expanded in Descartes's time into a broad stream that has not been interrupted since. They are all present in Descartes, but he takes none of them in the sense specific to the new science and develops each one of them in a way that is incompatible with this science.

a) The desire for compelling certainty: Descartes wished to "compel the mind" (*intellectum convincere*), to attain "a certitude equal to that of the demonstrations of Arithmetic and Geometry" (A.T. X, 366). Thus he rejected "all merely probable knowledge" (A.T. X, 362).

From this he drew conclusions that were perfectly in keeping with modern science. Conscious of the limits of our cognitive faculty, he wished to limit himself to objects "to which our mental powers seem adequate" (A.T. X, 362). In order really to attain the knowledge that is possible, we must make it our rule not to waste our time, "as many do, who neglect all easy quests and take up their time only with difficult matters; for they, though certainly making all sorts of subtle conjectures and elaborating most plausible arguments with great ingenuity, frequently find too late that after all their labors they have only increased the multitude of their doubts, without acquiring any knowledge whatsoever" (A.T. X, 364). Accordingly Descartes warns that "it is much easier to have some vague notion about any subject, no matter what, than to arrive at the real truth about a single question, however simple that may be" (A.T. X, 366).

Here Descartes expresses the truth of a new scientific tendency. But he himself loses this truth, first by neglecting all modes of certainty other than that which he regards as absolutely compelling, and secondly, by taking this certainty as an absolute, indubitable, and definitive insight. Of course he is right in insisting on reliable knowledge and in criticizing those who waste their energies in putting forward complicated and fruitless conjectures or in imagining possibilities without end. But he fails to consider the legitimacy of mere probability or to realize that exact investigation can be conducted on the basis of probabilities; and he failed to recognize the rights of the nonexact sciences, the subject matter of which by its very nature does not admit of cogent knowledge, or the fact that any reasoned method of apprehending existentially meaningful truth has its justification. Because he saw all truth on the one plane of compelling certainty, Descartes missed the truth itself. And the most striking example of this is that in the field of natural science most of the ideas which he took for certainties have proved to be false.

b) Thought and experience (experiment): Descartes once remarked that the things of experience can often be derived from his principles in a variety of ways. To find the right derivation there is no other "plan but again to try to find experiments of such a nature that their result is not the same if it has to be explained by one of the methods, as it would be if explained by the other" (A.T. VI, 65).

This sounds as if Descartes had understood the meth-

odological principle of modern science: the interdepend-
ence of constructive hypothetical thought and experience,
or in other words, the necessity of confirming, correcting,
or refuting an idea by experiment. But Descartes was not
clearly conscious of this idea and was therefore unable to
retain it. When he speaks of the innumerable experiments
that remain to be carried out, he is as vague as Bacon. And
indeed his manner of seeking knowledge is governed by
an attitude which is contrary to constructive experimental
science.

Descartes did not employ Galileo's method of exactly
deriving, by mathematical construction, hypotheses accessible to empirical verification by measurement and thus
opening the way to exact, methodical inquiry. "Experience"
remained for him a vague, general concept, namely, the
experience which, on the basis of his intellectual constructions, he regarded as possible. He contented himself with
the experiments and observations that chanced to come his
way, or explained nature on the strength of his memories:
"Passing over in my mind all the objects which have ever
been presented to my senses, I can truly venture to say that
I have not there observed anything which I could not easily
explain by the principles which I had discovered" (A.T.
VI, 64).

Descartes sacrificed true scientific method in favor of
a logical form, which he believed to be universally applicable, but which actually led to nothing but an empty construction, remote from all reality.

Even when Descartes spoke of the many experiments
that remained to be performed, he did not mean that they
would serve to verify his physical view of the world. For
he had already discovered the principles of nature. He
meant only that such experiments would amplify and com-

plement our knowledge of particulars, and he was convinced that he already possessed an all-encompassing vision
of what these experiments would be. "Moreover, I have
now reached a position in which I discern, it seems to me,
sufficiently clearly what course must be adopted to make
the majority of the experiments which may conduce to
carry out this end. But I also perceive that they are of such
a nature and of so great a number, that neither my hands
nor my income . . . could suffice for the whole" (A.T. VI,
65).

c) *The whole and the particular; the progress of science:* In respect of the whole, a scientist can only form
theories, and his relatively certain knowledge applies to
particulars; his conceptions of totalities (which are never
the whole of natural reality) are subject to perpetual,
though methodic, change, so that they comprise at all times
both truth and the need for correction by future experience.
Consequently, the proponents of the science that was then
new strove for certainty in particulars and were conscious
of working for posterity, for an indeterminate future, on
the way to which they merely took a few steps, without ever
knowing the whole.

There are passages in Descartes which give him the
appearance of a modern scientist in this respect, as for
example when he says that the truth "reveals itself little
by little" and that "the knowledge of some small amount
of truth" is preferable "to the vanity of seeming to be ignorant of nothing" (A.T. VI, 71). In reading such words, one
has the impression that Descartes is expressing the same
idea as Galileo when he writes: "I esteem more highly the
discovery of a single truth, even insignificant, than discus-
sions of the most essential problems when not a single
truth results from them." Yet if they remain isolated, these

particular truths, even when they are as vast as Newton's insights, signify little in relation to the whole truth. Newton himself said that he felt like a little boy playing on the seashore, who is delighted if occasionally he finds a smooth pebble or a beautiful shell, while the vast ocean of truth lies before him unexplored.

But this is not true of Descartes, since he believed himself to be in possession of principles that were absolutely true and eternal. Progress, for him, consists merely in the development of the principles through the particulars. At times he approached the attitude of the experimental natural sciences, as it were unconsciously, only to betray it again and swing back to its opposite attitude, a quest for the whole, for perfection, for a systemized knowledge of all nature.

The principles, he believed, gave him an essential knowledge of the whole, and this fundamental attitude changes the meaning of those of his utterances that sound supremely scientific. He sees himself as working for the future; all knowledge should be made public "in order that the last should commence where the preceding had left off . . ." (A.T. VI, 63). He justifies occupations which are without utility to our contemporaries and provide them with no immediate advantages, but "which will bring much more advantage to our descendants" (A.T. VI, 66). Considering future possibilities, he admits that the little he has thus far learned is as nothing compared to what he does not know (A.T. VI, 66). But at the same time, thanks to the definitive character of his principles, he believed that he held the future of science in his hands, since other scientists would proceed simply by deduction, without adding anything to the principles: "I am also well aware that several centuries may pass before all the truths have been derived from these principles, that can be derived from them . . ." (to Picot, A.T. IX, Part 2, p. 20).

d) *The striving for technical achievement:* The enthusiasm for technical devices that was to usher in the modern development of technology made its appearance in the seventeenth century. The tendency to rationalize machinery gave rise to a "feverish hunt for inventions" (Max Weber, *Wirtschaftsgeschichte,* Munich, 1923, pp. 268 ff., English translation, *General Economic History*). This movement which now achieved self-awareness had begun centuries before in the art workshops and mines. The first rational patent law was promulgated in England in 1623. At that time science was far more the consequence than the cause of technological development. Not until much later did exact science inspire new technical inventions.

Descartes participated in this movement. He read Bacon. To him it was self-evident that technical utility was one criterion for the value of science. Very much like Bacon, he attached great importance to the practical utilization of his methodic science, especially for the improvement of human health (medicine) and for the facilitation of human labor (mechanics). He took a keen interest in all the crafts, in navigation, in the building of fortifications, in the technical aspects of medicine and of music (the construction of instruments, acoustics, etc.). His principles showed him "that it is possible to attain knowledge which is very useful in life, and that, instead of that speculative philosophy which is taught in the Schools, we may find a practical philosophy, by means of which, knowing the force and the action of fire, water, air, the stars . . . as distinctly as we know the different crafts of our artisans, we can in the same way employ them in all those uses to which they are adapted, and thus render ourselves the masters and possessors of nature" (A.T. VI, 62).

In accordance with the spirit of his age, Descartes had technological visions of the future. He expected technical results from his thinking, though he never took any concrete step in this direction. But by extending technological conceptions to the whole of science—that is, in his case, to philosophy—he cast a darkening shadow over it. He was capable, for example, of putting the simplification of labor, medical science, and ethics on the same level. Thus the universal welfare of man becomes the ultimate aim of philosophy, and everything else is subordinated to the problem of technical production.

e) The passion for novelty: Their enormous self-assurance had impelled the philosophers of the Renaissance to stress the novelty of their thinking. The emergence of the individual personality had made a distinction of novelty. But it was in connection with modern science that an objective value came to be attached to the word "new." Thinkers began to claim "priority" for their ideas or discoveries and were often prepared to fight for their claims. Such an attitude is quite in keeping with the spirit of modern science. For in the days when philosophy was metaphysics, a thinker lived in an enduring whole. Content with the *philosophia perennis* in which he believed, he did not distinguish between the old and the new in his thoughts, for all of them were rooted in the whole. He judged ideas not by their novelty, but by their authenticity. The sole value of thought was the satisfaction conferred by awareness of the truth and of being. In modern science, however, every discovery is only a rung in an endless ladder. Satisfaction resides not in knowledge possessed, but in progress, not in the

sense of security provided by the whole, but in search along
paths whose end is not in sight. The essential value of the
individual resides in his distinct and recognizable contribution to progress. Apart from his enthusiasm over the
endless quest, the scientist now achieved satisfaction in the
thought that his contribution, however negligible from the
standpoint of the whole, would be identified with his name.
That is why all scientists since Galileo have attached great
importance to their priority and in many cases taken steps
to safeguard it.

An attitude that is appropriate to modern science will
also be valid for a philosophy that regards itself as identical
with scientific investigation. Consequently the scientific attitude expressed by Descartes in his philosophy is identical
with that of the scientist. He lays stress on novelty, for example, on the difference "between my principles and those
of others" (to Picot, IX, Part 2, p. 20). And even in his
strictly philosophical ideas, he stresses novelty. When for
example Arnauld and others showed him that the *cogito
ergo sum* already occurred in Augustine, his answer shows
that he was aware (and, it might be added, not without
objective foundation) of what was essentially new in his
cogito: "But even if all these truths which I number among
my principles have at all times been known to everyone,
no one up until now, as far as I know, has recognized them
as the principles of philosophy, that is to say, principles from
which the knowledge of all other things that exist in the
world can be derived" (to Picot, IX, Part 2, pp. 10–11).

The new discovery—his new philosophy—seems to have
struck Descartes as so exclusively valid, so self-sufficient,
that he preferred not to know the old; those, he declares,
"who have learned least about everything that has hitherto

been termed philosophy are the best suited to learning the true philosophy" (to Picot, A.T. IX, Part 2, p. 9).

This emphasis on the value and significance of novelty has its rightful and necessary place in modern science; Descartes transferred it to philosophy, where it does not belong.

In Descartes the five basic traits of the modern scientific attitude have this in common: according to the context, they ring true in some of his statements, while in others they strike a false note or become untrue. He seems to pervert their meaning without knowing it, so that they shift into their opposites. Thus compelling certainty is lost in Descartes's purely constructive manner of investigating nature. Although he stresses experience and experiment, they actually play no more part in his work than they had done before, nor does he give them new meaning. Although he insists on the value of reliable particular knowledge, his dominant concern is with knowledge of the whole. His striving for technical achievement is limited to fantastic visions of the future and leads to no concrete action; in addition, it takes on the character of an absolute and is extended to fields where it is out of place. Apart from his mathematical discoveries, where his claim to priority is justified both in theory and in practice, his insistence on having done something new applies to a realm—philosophy —that does not have the absolute validity of science. Moreover, the novelty of his philosophy is by no means demonstrated, nor is its value enhanced by such claims.

All these perversions [1] have the same cause, namely, that

---

[1] By the "perversion" of an idea I mean an imperceptible and unintentional displacement of its meaning. The form remains the same, but something alien or opposed to its original content is taken into it. Per-

artes willed philosophy, but in the spirit of modern
ce. As a result, his philosophy becomes perverted and
science escapes him. His thinking springs from two impulses
which he misleadingly identifies and never distinguishes:
1) modern scientific method, which yields cogent particular
insights as links in a chain of endless progress, and which in
itself is unable to create a view of life and the world except
in the sense that the method of investigation is itself an
element of such a view; 2) man's eternal philosophical
impulse to gain awareness of his existence as a whole, of
the roots of his life in the world, of transcendence. The
source of perversion in Descartes was the interweaving of
these two impulses. He conceived the aim of philosophy
in terms of a scientific attitude which he took as an absolute
and misunderstood.

Thus Descartes falsified the attitude of the philosopher
by representing scientific conceptions as philosophy and in
general failing to distinguish between philosophy and science. At the same time he falsified the scientific attitude
by setting up a purely rational construction, to which he
imputed certainty, and disregarding all the methodological principles of true scientific investigation. That is why
Descartes, with a sense of perfect certainty, could turn out
scientific absurdities and mistake them for philosophy.

---

version is not merely a reversal, it is also an amalgamation of essentially
different elements. This is a source of error, for the rational form of an
original truth now embraces contents that negate this truth. It is not
sophistry, for it does not spring from purpose or interest, but from an
unconscious concourse of motives. It is not patent insincerity, for such an
intermingling of motives seems to be inherent in the nature of things. Perversion springs from an untruth which quite possibly slips into our human
knowledge at the very origin of its development, but which is not insuperable. Because of this connection with the origin, perversion, unlike
mere errors, has philosophical relevance.

The method in the final purpose of philosophy. Descartes defines philosophy according to its etymology as the "study of *wisdom*." By wisdom he means "not only prudence in daily affairs, but a perfect knowledge of everything a man can know, pertaining to the conduct of his life, the preservation of his health, and invention in all the arts" (to Picot, A.T. X, Part 2, p. 2).

Taken as the methodic knowledge that leads to compelling certainty, philosophy, he held, should form the foundation of man's whole life. Considered in this light, knowledge becomes everything. Descartes aspired to distinguish the true from the false "in order to see clearly in my actions and to walk with confidence in this life" (A.T. VI, 10). Through knowledge he believed himself to be assured of acquiring "all the best things which could ever come within my power . . . it is sufficient to judge wisely in order to act wisely" and to acquire "all the virtues and all the other good things that it is possible to obtain" (A.T. VI, 28).

Descartes conceived the highest hopes of a philosophy based on his principles; it would, he claims, extend to every field of life. We shall see "to what degree of wisdom, to what perfection of life, and to what happiness it can lead" (A.T. IX, Part 2, p. 20). All this Descartes sums up in an image: "All philosophy is like a tree, whose roots are metaphysics, whose trunk is physics, and whose branches, issuing from this trunk, are all the other sciences, which are reduced to three principles, namely mechanics, medicine, and ethics; by this last I mean the highest and most perfect ethics which presupposes a complete knowledge of the other sciences and is the highest degree of wisdom" (A.T. IX, Part 2, p. 14).

But this tree has not yet grown. Descartes wishes to

plant it. It is only in a distant future, he believes, that a true morality will one day be born of the totality of the knowledge thus gained through the method. But meanwhile man had to live and likewise Descartes, who at his own risk had embarked on the endeavor whose ultimate aim it was "to regulate our morals" (A.T. IX, Part 2, p. 3). Since he could not wait for the ethic that would ultimately see the light, he required an ethic for the present. This he formulated in the *Discours* as the "provisional ethic" of the three rules of life (A.T. VI, 22 ff.).

When we inquire into the relationship between this provisional ethic and the ultimate ethic, we find no clear answer; what we do find in Descartes is an ethical ideal which for practical purposes has nothing to do with either.

a) The provisional ethic seems to be required only until the definitive ethic has been attained, that is, until life itself can be based on knowledge. But here there is an ambiguity. It is not made clear whether the provisional ethic will really, some time in the future, be replaced or confirmed by the ethic born of rational wisdom, or whether this "provisional" ethic is not really provisional at all, but valid for all man's temporal existence. The latter idea is expressed, for example, in a letter to Princess Elisabeth (A.T. VI, 264–267). Here he says that this ethic in itself will lead to the highest good, to beatitude, to peace of mind and inner contentment. This is a significant departure from the provisional rules as stated in the *Discours,* according to which "resoluteness" impels us only to carry out a decision once made even if it is insufficiently grounded in reason and based only on a probability or on a choice between two equal probabilities. For in the letter Descartes speaks of carrying out the counsels of reason itself.

Moreover, even the provisional ethic, to be observed while we are on our way to perfect knowledge, involves attitudes that are not at all provisional. The lasting satisfaction we feel when we discover truths—the "pleasure which is found in the contemplation of the truth [is] practically the only joy in life that is complete and untroubled with any pain" (A.T. X, 361)—seems to be a fruit of the philosophy which in itself constitutes the meaning of life. Another definitive benefit obtained along the way is the habit of methodic knowledge, which makes us better able to judge the objects we encounter. And most significant of all are the consequences we can expect from the perfect certainty of the principles, for, quite unlike the scholastic controversies which only make people pettier and more quarrelsome, it "will eliminate all grounds for dispute and thus dispose men's minds to gentleness and harmony" (A.T. IX, Part 2, p. 18).

b) Independently of the growth of knowledge and of method, Descartes's philosophy expresses an ethic which is neither his provisional ethic nor that which derives from the methodic progress of philosophy. In so far as Descartes lives in this ethos, he draws on an Encompassing which is not a part of his consciously deduced philosophy. This is shown by the following examples:

In the letter to Princess Elisabeth, Descartes expresses a state of mind based on knowledge of God's existence, the immortality of the soul, and the greatness of the universe. Such an attitude is only seemingly derived from his philosophy. The existence of God, he writes, teaches us to accept with equanimity whatever befalls us. Knowledge of the nature of our *soul* prevents us from fearing death: we learn to withdraw our desires from the things of this world and to consider with contempt everything that is in the

hands of fate. Insight into the greatness of the universe
frees us from presumptuous prejudices, from the ambition,
for example, to participate, as God's counselors, in the
government of the world, an ambition which would fill us
with vain and incessant unrest (A.T. IV, 291–292).

After these remarks in the famous letter to Princess
Elisabeth, Descartes goes on to develop an active ethos: Although we are all separate one from the other and each
of us has his special interests, we must always remind ourselves that we cannot live alone in the world. We must prefer the interests of the whole, in which we are a part, to our
private interests. If we related everything to our own interest, we should have neither true friendship nor any loyalty, nor any virtue at all. Such reflection is the source and
origin of all heroic actions. Assuredly, men who risk death
out of vanity or stupidity are more to be pitied than praised.
But when a man risks death because he believes it to be his
duty, because he believes it to benefit others, he always
does so on the basis of this reflection which—if only unclearly—is present in his thoughts. The consequence is a
satisfaction of mind and a contentment which incomparably exceed the petty and ephemeral pleasures of the senses
(A.T. IV, 293–294).

The philosophical attitude that Descartes expresses in
such passages is not derived from the principles of his philosophy. It is not the fruit of the definitive morality which
grows on the tree of all science, but an ethos characteristic
of Descartes's personality.

Let us sum up: In his ethical thinking Descartes takes
two paths that have no explicit relation to one another.
One leads, by way of the provisional ethic, from the principles of his philosophy to the idea of a future ethic attainable through methodical knowledge; if this ultimate purpose of philosophy is identified with a methodical planning,

which purports to produce morality side by side with technology and medicine, it seems to me that philosophy ceases to be philosophy. The other path discloses a philosophy which is no longer methodic and informs an active ethical attitude of a grandeur that reveals traits of the classical and humanist tradition.[1]

III
The character of the Cartesian philosophy as a whole

Our analysis has shown that Descartes's thinking loses sight, time and time again, of its authentic beginning. An impulse sprung from the depths of philosophy seems, through perversion, to forget its source. In studying his works, we gain the impression that in this admirable personality philosophy fell into a radical error, which cannot be seen clearly in any particular position or proposition, but is more in the nature of an attitude which pervades the spirit of the whole, a hidden rot which undermines what seemed at first to be so clear and solid an edifice.

We shall now attempt to clarify our critical analyses of Descartes's astonishingly intricate creation by summing them up under a few heads.

1. REASON AND AUTHORITY

Descartes's philosophy seems to be entirely a philosophy of reason; he is regarded as *the* representative of self-sufficient

---

1 Cf. the excellent analysis of the virtue of *générosité* in Descartes, compared with the μεγαλοψυχία of Aristotle and the *magnanimitas* of Cicero and Thomas, in Gerhard Krüger, "Die Herkunft des philosophischen Selbstbewusstseins," *Logos*, XXII, 225 ff., 1933 (see pp. 251–271).

reason. And yet he recognized the existence of something other than reason, which he did not incorporate into his philosophy but on which he touched repeatedly in his thinking. One wonders whether, because of this, his conception of reason may not have been vitiated at the root; whether the fundamental attitude of this philosophy may not have been affected by the security which the thinker actually found in revealed faith; and whether the way in which he conceived reason and faith may not have prevented both from coming into their rights, so that his reason could not be the whole of reason and his faith could not be authentic faith. In fact, Descartes seems to live both in reason and in faith, but in neither of them entirely. An examination of his thinking in regard to what is other than reason may serve to reveal a hidden flaw in this philosophy.

The limits of knowledge. Descartes did not claim that reason is all-powerful. He knew the limits of human knowledge.

First of all, he held that the human mind as such is incapable of understanding everything. "In truth only God is perfectly wise, that is, endowed with full knowledge of the truth of all things" (A.T., Part 2, p. 2). It would be absurd for man to direct his search for knowledge toward realms other than those where it can attain its goal. Let us seize with all our powers that which we can know, but not concern ourselves with what cannot be known. For Descartes, "no more useful inquiry can be proposed than that which seeks to determine the nature and the scope of human knowledge"; we are able "to define the limits of that understanding of which we are directly aware as being within us" (A.T. X, 397 ff.). If we do so, we see how futile it is, for example, to quarrel about the secrets of nature, the influence of the heavenly bodies on this world, the prediction of the future, and so on. Similarly, the final cause, that is, God's will and providence, is beyond our understanding, whereas we *can* investigate causalities in the world. Once we have recognized the limits of our knowledge, we make it our rule either to master completely the object to which we direct our knowledge, or to demonstrate that the object in question is beyond all human understanding (A.T. X, 400).

But such caution and renunciation are inadequate in practical life. A *second* limit to our knowledge results from the fact that our temporal life calls for action in concrete situations, even if we do not possess all the knowledge that would give us complete certainty concerning the right way to act. When the moment presses, we cannot wait until all the conditions for compelling, indubitable evidence have been assembled. In our action, we must consequently draw on sources which lie beyond our always limited insight. We must make up our minds and act on the opinions that seem to us most probable (to Princess Elisabeth, A.T. IV, 295). Descartes saw that this implied a human weakness, but also the possibility of a strength which does not spring from the mere knowledge of truth. "It cannot be denied that human life is often subject to error in particulars, and the weakness of our nature must be recognized" (A.T. VII, 99). But because we must live our lives in spite of this weakness, we require a kind of strength, which Descartes calls "resoluteness." What does this mean?

The double truth. As we have seen, Descartes takes a twofold attitude toward the knowledge of the truth: reason strives for compelling truth; but though such truth is not yet available, we must, in our active lives, make decisions as if we possessed it. A distinction must be made between *contemplatio veritatis* and *usus vitae,* between theory and practice. In rational knowledge, to be sure, we can accept only what we see clearly and distinctly. But "in practical life I am so far from supposing that we must assent only to what we know clearly, that on the contrary I believe we should not even await the probable in every case, but are sometimes obliged to choose one among many things that are totally unknown" (A.T. VII, 149).

Nevertheless decision in practical matters (*usus vitae*) is not without foundation. Although its source is inaccessible to our understanding, it is not utterly fortuitous. *What* is the source of this decision?

In regard to our *physical needs,* we are guided by our senses and by an instinctive certainty that is related to the senses. Our instincts, which we share with the animals, impel us to preserve our body and to satisfy our bodily desires (though we are not always obliged to follow them— A.T. II, 599). They play no part in Descartes's philosophy except in connection with his explanation of life as the bond between body and mind and his analysis of certain errors (A.T. VIII, 35 ff.; see Gilson, *Commentaire,* pp. 165 ff.).

In questions of *action* I am guided by the state and the customs of the country, by the example of the best among my fellow men, and by resoluteness.

In questions of *faith* I am guided by revelation, by the supernatural light, and by the decision of ecclesiastical authority.

These realms, which cannot be replaced by reason, are subject, according to Descartes, to rules which guide the *will* as opposed to the rules which guide the sure progress of science:

1) He took it as a maxim to be firm and resolute in action and, once he had decided in their favor, to follow even the most questionable opinions no less resolutely than if they were completely proven (A.T. VI, 24).

2) Descartes did not intend to attack the state, the form of government, the customs of the country. He did not wish to provoke reforms, much less revolutions. Just as it is not good to tear cities down in order to build better ones, it is not good to rebuild the state from the bottom up, and he advised others against attempting to do so: "In the case of great bodies it is too difficult a task to raise them again when they are once thrown down, or even to keep them in their place when they are thoroughly shaken. . . . And finally the imperfections are almost always more supportable than would be the process of removing them" (A.T. VI, 14).

3) As for revealed truth, Descartes professes his belief that "matters that have been divinely revealed" are "more certain than our surest knowledge, since belief in these things, as all faith in obscure matters, is an action not of our intelligence, but of our will" (A.T. X, 370).

But Descartes's theoretical attitude is opposed to this practical attitude. For himself alone—not as an example to others, whom he warns not to follow him—he resolved, in the realm of knowledge, to take a course which he rejected in connection with the state, customs, society, etc. "As regards all the opinions, which up to this time I had embraced, I thought I could not do better than endeavor once for all to sweep them completely away, so that they might later on be replaced, either by others which were better, or by the same, when I had made them conform to the uniformity of a rational scheme" (A.T. VI, 13).

There is an extreme contradiction in Descartes's think-ing: on the one hand, absolute recognition of faith and authority; on the other hand, their rejection in favor of reason. An understanding of what faith and authority meant to Descartes should make possible a deeper insight into the philosophy by which he actually lived than is con-veyed by an analysis of his reason.

Ambiguity. It is impossible to indicate with precision how Descartes conceived the relations between authori-tarian ethics and philosophical ethics, between theology and philosophy. His statements are contradictory.

We have seen that the relationship is not made clear between the provisional ethic outlined by Descartes and the definitive ethic of the future. But he also fails to state clearly whether the definitive ethic to be brought forth by philosophy is the whole of ethic. If philosophy is destined to reform all life on the strength of rational knowledge, the authority of state, Church, and custom will one day be superfluous. Philosophy will confirm or reject it on the basis of fully unfolded reason. Descartes also insisted on the ethic which is prescribed by the authorities and inviolable; the consequence is that his provisional ethic seems to con-sist largely of rules for a line of conduct at which the au-thorities will not take umbrage. He states expressly that he has no wish to write about ethical matters, because to regulate the morals of others is the concern of sovereigns, or of authorized persons (to Chanut, A.T. V, 86 ff.; cf. Gil-son, *Commentaire*, p. 234). Though he had attempted to regulate his own conduct by reason, he had no desire to write on the subject. "For where morality is concerned, everyone has so many ideas on the subject that there might be as many reformers as heads if others than those whom God had established as sovereigns over peoples, or whom

He has endowed with sufficient grace or zeal to make them prophets, were permitted to undertake the slightest change in it" (A.T. XI, 71).

Nevertheless, as we have indicated in our remarks about the ultimate intention of Descartes's philosophy, he developed an ethic which serves as a foundation for life and permeates it. There is a contradiction, real though unperceived by him, between these ethical maxims which activated him and which he enunciated, and his Christian, ecclesiastical faith. As Adam convincingly shows in his biography of Descartes (pp. 57 ff.), these maxims are not Christian. If for Descartes philosophical acceptance of the world order is more essential than harkening to the will of God, if his self-reliance is so unshakable that he rejects the pangs of conscience as useless, if there is in him no hope in God's grace, because he requires no such hope, then Seneca, Montaigne, and Charron are the source of his ethics, and not the Gospel.

Descartes's ideas about the role of reason in the relationship between philosophy and theology are no freer from ambiguity than his ethics.

The question arises: does the relationship between reason and what is other than reason imply for Descartes that we are led *by* reason to carry out decisions which are not *grounded in* reason? Does reason, for example, impel us to follow a faith that we have not understood? The answer to such a question can only be contradictory. It would seem that we must answer in the affirmative in so far as reason is the Encompassing and hence the source of faith itself, and in the negative in so far as reason is *at odds with* such "positive" and dominant contents as revealed faith, grace, the customs of the country, the authority of a prince.

Descartes does not discuss the sources of the conviction carried by authority and custom. But in accordance with the Christian tradition, he examines the positive source of the clarity characteristic of faith: "The clarity or perspicuity, by which our will can be moved to assent, is twofold in nature: one stems from the natural light, the other from divine grace" (A.T. VII, 147–148). Divine grace creates a supernatural light in the believer: "Although we say that faith relates to obscure things, the power by which we are moved to embrace it is not obscure, but clearer than all natural light" (A.T. VII, 147). The effect of this supernatural light coming to us from God is that we believe "that what is proposed to our belief comes from God Himself" (A.T. VII, 148).

This sharp distinction between reason and faith, i.e. between natural and supernatural light, and consequently between philosophy and theology, is a scholastic tradition, as is the way in which Descartes reconciles them or the way in which the two spheres, which are never clearly separated, infringe upon one another. If they were absolutely distinct, there would be no resort but the doctrine of the double truth.

We have evidence of such an infringement or of a movable and hence imprecise dividing line between the two spheres of philosophy and theology, when Descartes apprehends *by reason* what by its content is the concern of faith, when, for example, he tries to demonstrate outside the sphere of faith, what is most essential to faith: the existence of God and the immateriality of the soul (considered as a substantial entity independent of the body). In the dedication of the *Meditations,* addressed to the Sorbonne, he insists, for example, "that nothing more useful can be accomplished in philosophy than once for all to seek with care for the best [proofs of the existence of God and of the substantial being of the soul] and to set them forth in so clear and exact a manner that it will henceforth be evident to everybody that they are veritable demonstrations" (A.T. VII, 3).

Then again Descartes invokes revelation in essential matters, such as the immortality of the soul (A.T. VII, 154); there is reason to hope for it in view of the proof that it is different in nature from the body, so that the destruction of the body does not bring with it that of the spirit; but certainty in this respect is obtained only through God's will, which He has imparted to us by His revelation. Thus the dividing line between what can be demonstrated by reason and what is certain only by virtue of faith in revelation, is no clearer in Descartes than in scholastic philosophy.

This ambiguity in defining the limits of reason has its counterpart in Descartes's contradictory view of theology:

He assigns to theology its special field: It is the truth that aims at the salvation of our soul; its content is supernatural revelation. Everything that does not relate to the salvation of the soul is irrelevant to this domain. And what is necessary to the salvation of the soul is just as accessible to the ignorant and unlearned as it is to the learned. In this realm, speculation is a superfluous complication (A.T. VI, 8). These truths are so far above our understanding that Descartes says: "I would not have dared to submit them to the weakness of my reasonings" (A.T. VI, 8).

But here again Descartes is inconsistent. He does not always refrain from reasoning about theology. Gilson goes so far as to say (*Commentaire* on the *Discours,* p. 133) that Descartes envisaged the possibility of a Cartesian reform of scholastic theology, and cites passages in support of this contention. Since Descartes's philosophy is the only true one, it is also, in Descartes's opinion, the only one which can, without contradiction, coexist with faith.

All the contradictions and ambiguities we have been

discussing are related to the question of the meaning of authority. We shall first consider Descartes's attitude toward authority and then take up the problem itself.

Descartes's attitude toward authority. In reality Descartes, in carrying on his philosophical activity, was aware that the ecclesiastical authorities, who were at the same time the sovereign power in his world, had to be handled with care. He knew the dangers that arise when the servants of this authority interpret a published philosophy (like his own) and reject it (he was well acquainted with this power through the Jesuits and the Dutch Protestants). For that reason he attempted—for example, by dedicating his *Meditations* to the Sorbonne—to obtain the support of persons in authority, "since the truth is held in low esteem when it is alone" (to Mersenne, A.T. III, 184).

But Descartes did not rebel against this pressure. He inwardly recognized the rights of authority, for he remained true to the faith. He was more than circumspect; in his letters, when there was no need for it, he attested his zeal for the Catholic faith, his veneration for its dignitaries, and his unshaken faith in the infallibility of the Church to which he belonged (A.T. VI, 60).

Thus Descartes did not fundamentally reject authority, as many of the philosophers of the Enlightenment were to do. Although he dismissed the authority of Aristotle and all others in connection with the judgments of reason, which are based on clarity and distinctness (e.g., A.T. X, 366), he recognized authority in regard to action, life itself, and public statements. As far as he was concerned, authority remained the foundation of life, and pursuit of reason, outside of all authority, was a purely personal undertaking, for the present far removed from life itself, and hedged round with precautions and warnings. Thus authority anchored in encompassing faith seems in practice to have occupied the higher rank in his thinking.

The problem of authority. If Descartes had sharply distinguished two realms, on the one hand the world of faith and customs, Church and state, authority and obedience, and on the other hand the world of cognition which leads, through the autonomous power of reason, to compelling insight, we should have had a clear though disastrous separation. Then, life would be the realm to which knowledge does not apply, and the pursuit of knowledge, except for its technical aspects, would be irrelevant to life.

But this is not at all the case in Descartes. For all the precautions and limitations that hedge it in, his thinking actually aspires to be far more than a private experiment on the part of a reason submissive to authority. It is also a search for the insight by which men live. Nevertheless, he adhered to the authoritarian revealed faith. He did not adopt a philosophical faith that renounces revealed religion. He did not take this step, but in his philosophizing he touched on origins and followed paths which should have meant that he did. The consequence was that his faith lost some of its vitality, and that on the other hand philosophy had not yet become active in him as a nourishing matrix. This accounts for the ambiguities and contradictions that characterize his whole system. But this lack of clarity is an expression of the profound problem of authority, which is bound to confront all philosophizing that approaches maturity.

It may be that because of the limits of human knowledge, the source of our faith and the actual foundation of our lives must always remain authoritarian (and that the essence and dignity of human life are ultimately based on the form and content of the prevailing authority); it may be that in social and political life blind obedience to authority is ultimately necessary to self-preservation, because it alone lends a community the power to assert itself, and that we are free only to choose what this authority should be (actually the individual does not even have this choice); it may be that there are two authorities which in essence are mutually exclusive, that an authority imposed from without cannot become the inner authority; and it may be that an inwardly accepted authority, as that of God, is beyond the grasp of reason: to philosophize, however, is not merely to register objective facts; especially with regard to authority, a philosopher must strive for awareness of the senses and the conscience; it is not enough for him to know authority sociologically and psychologically as an established fact, he must also elucidate it philosophically. There seems to be a simple solution: to reject all authority and the prejudices of faith, and proceed to live by pure reason, in the naïve conviction that everything will come out all right. But that is impossible. Actually philosophy faces an enormous task: instead of exercising reason in a vacuum, it must strive, through reason, to apprehend the positive sources of authority.

Descartes developed no philosophy of authority (to this day, as far as I can see, no one has really succeeded in doing so). Although he recognized the importance of authority, it did not become for him an object of penetrating philosophical interpretation. In philosophy he strove for reason, whereas he accepted authority without trying to understand it. In so doing, he showed indirectly that reason alone is not enough. It was not merely his circumspection that led him to recognize authority; he felt that reason, in fact, cannot sustain itself. But he evaded the abyss by leaving authority unquestioned in all its rigidity and inflexibility. He accepted ecclesiastical faith and the state of society, making no attempt to understand them or even to question them. His attitude seems almost to reflect Hobbes' recommendation to the effect that it is better to swallow pills unchewed than to make them bitter and unpalatable by reflecting on their composition.

If his decision to let doubt range unchecked, until all objects of doubt came to an ultimate point in the immediate certainty of the *cogito ergo sum* and thus were rehabilitated, were carried out radically, in all its possible depth, the consequence would be either rejection of authority or else the reconciliation of authority with this immediate certainty. Then it would be possible to fathom the innermost meaning of authority. But in so far as Descartes effects a total separation between reason and authority, one would expect a complete cleavage in his own life: in the theoretical realm of contemplative knowledge all authority is rejected on the basis of all-encompassing reason; in the practical realm of public speech and action, obedience to authority (which is identical with the effective power in the world) is grounded in all-encompassing faith.

Thus Descartes's "certain knowledge" becomes a veil, concealing the two equally disastrous possibilities of this thinking: if it looks upon itself as absolute truth, it can no longer recognize authority and for lack of an absolute existential consciousness[1] must fall into the bottomless abyss of empty reason; if, on the other hand, it is aware of its relativity (for compelling knowledge can only be relative), it is reduced to unreason in the face of an authority which is not encompassed in a profound faith, a power that is neither elucidated nor susceptible of elucidation. Only

[1] Concerning "absolute consciousness," see my *Philosophie* (Berlin, 1932), Vol. II, pp. 255–291.

by envisaging both possibilities might Descartes have developed an authentic philosophical faith. Instead, he vacillates between a thinking without foundation and obedience
without understanding.

The following situation results: In Descartes's ideas
concerning the necessity of the exercise of the will under
the dictates of time, concerning unconditional faith and the
authority of churches and princes, we find a personal interpretation of the Encompassing in which he actually lived
and in which alone it is possible to philosophize. Though
frequent in Descartes, such ideas are incidental: they do
not, strictly speaking, form part of his philosophy. But in
so far as his philosophy raised the higher claim to provide
a foundation for the encompassing realities, its formulations were bound to be contradictory, for it oscillated between two mutually exclusive poles. In so far as his thinking turns its back on the world and delves into itself to see
how far it can go with compelling evidence, it neglects to
elucidate authority, faith, the state—they remain foreign
bodies which escape understanding and are without interest
to philosophy. But in so far as authority is recognized as
absolute, this rational thinking loses its absolute validity
as a foundation of life. Under such conditions neither authority nor reason can preserve its vitality. They merely
exclude one another.

Thus Descartes's philosophy does not become a complete philosophy. By splitting into two irreconcilable modes
of the Encompassing, it seems, time and time again, to
cease being philosophy. As long as Descartes is truly philosophizing, there remains a vital tension between his philosophical elucidation of the Encompassing and his cogent
reasoning, based on evident principles, which is the expression of this elucidation. Where only the latter form of

reasoning remains, confronted by something other, by an authority that is not subjected to the process of understanding, he ceases to be a true philosopher.

2. THE LOSS OF BEING

We have tried to show that in almost every connection Descartes's thinking leads from an initial truth to a perversion. Far from being a reliable methodical progression, his procedure is misleading and seems to culminate in a vacuum. His philosophy has the startling effect that after experiencing its initial attraction one ends by feeling let down by it. This philosophy, as it were, loses sight of being, the very thing it set out so vigorously to grasp. The loss becomes obvious not in its origins but in its end results.

Freedom for emptiness. Descartes drew not only the body, but also the soul in its dependence on the body, into his mechanistic view of the world. His doctrine of freedom was conceived as a counterweight to this crushing conception. But from the outset this freedom—originally rooted in the exalting belief that man's mind is fully independent and can achieve knowledge by its own efforts—proves to be astonishingly devoid of substance.

According to Descartes's fundamental dualistic conception, man is a combination of two substances, mind and body. The mind can liberate itself from the influences of the body, for it is self-sufficient: I am in so far as I think; actually I myself am only thought; I am connected, but not one, with the other, the body (which fetters me to sense perception, desires, and passions). As a thinking being, I am complete without a body.

This freedom of my thinking is total, since I am capable in my judgment of assenting only to what I recognize methodically, clearly, and distinctly as irrefutably certain.

But it is in the nature of this freedom to oscillate between indecision in the form of suspended judgment and the experience of logically compelling certainty. Such freedom remains empty, because its action is negative when it suspends judgment and passive when it submits to compelling certainty. It is dependent on the content of this certainty, and utterly empty when this certainty has no content.

Descartes *isolates* an essential and indispensable human possibility—the possibility of pure thought, detached from everything. But in so doing he discloses only the indeterminate, unoccupied space of an empty freedom. Such freedom acquires content only if it moves me to enter into the historical substance of my own existence.

Because of his unyielding insistence on independence and freedom, Descartes's freedom is without content; it merely denotes the abstract possibility of choice. In empty freedom, he passes being by.

Pure thought. Freedom in detachment from everything is pure thought. But in casting off sense perception, this pure thought loses all contact with experience. It becomes estranged from nature. The mechanistic thinking required by clarity and distinctness does not gain knowledge by investigating nature; rather, it transforms the world into a machine and living beings into automata.[1] The empirical investigation of things is replaced by unreal,

[1] The total conception of life and soul, originating with Aristotle, which classifies phenomena according to a hierarchy in which all things, from inanimate objects to thought, are harmoniously interrelated, was shattered by Descartes as well as by modern science. But to substitute convenient total conceptions of this kind for Descartes's imaginary construction is merely to revive a traditional metaphysical image, equally hostile to true scientific investigation and to the philosophical penetration of Existenz. This applies also to Schelling (10, 23–28), whose partly illuminating critique of Descartes leads to an equally distorted view of reality.

purely cogitated construction. All that remains is a supposedly correct judgment based on compelling certainty.

But mere insistence on correctness proves to be empty, and when method was taken as an absolute, when Descartes achieved the certainty that method is absolute truth, the striving for correctness became a prejudice. In attaining this certainty, Descartes did not press his questioning far enough. To achieve certainty of truth, we must keep in mind that in our striving for truth the important thing is to discover an original ground which is itself substantial and which can be elucidated by questioning. Then the origin which, in its unclear stage, has not yet achieved truth, is on its way to truth, not through pure thought, but in the development and growing awareness of thinking Existenz.

Reason that isolates itself and detaches itself from all content becomes alien to being and empty of being, unreal and imaginary, a barren understanding in a medium of seeming clarity. If one were tempted to ask in the spirit of Cartesianism whether Descartes invented reason, the answer might be: He assuredly did not invent it, but perhaps he transformed it into a bloodless phantom.

Descartes had the urge to empirical investigation, a will to technical mastery of nature, a philosophical attitude rooted in existential ethics; he was able to state the principles of real experience with convincing simplicity (e.g., when he said: man acquires experience only when he really incurs the consequences of his acts). All this, however, does not spring from the characteristic method of pure thought; it belonged to Descartes as an inherited capital which little by little and without showing results was consumed by the method. Descartes did not devote himself to the investigation of things themselves. His discoveries were limited to the realm of thought. And this pure thought had little bearing on the reality of life, on experience and being.

When others adopted this manner of thinking with its claim to absolutely correct judgment, it served to mask a certain hypocrisy, characteristic of those who represent themselves as champions of absolute truth. The illusion of clarity can become a means of shutting oneself off from oneself, from others, and from transcendence.

Loss of history. Thus Descartes seems to renounce the experience of nature, and to look upon God as a demonstrated God; his consciousness of Existenz shrinks to the minimal point of his *cogito ergo sum.* Along the same lines, his philosophy claims to be detached from all historical reality: aiming at timeless truth in a world without tradition, it loses sight of history in order to become the existential void of this abstraction, the thinking individual as such. By way of demonstrating the evidence of his philosophical principles, Descartes insists "that they have been known at all times and even accepted as true and irrefutable by all men" (A.T. IX, Part 2, p. 10).

But at the same time Descartes claimed that this truth, which he believed to be identical at all times and therefore timeless, was an absolutely new departure. For timeless truth can be understood without recourse to history (A.T. IX, Part 2, p. 9).

Descartes takes a similar attitude toward the traditional humane sciences. He classes them with travel (A.T. VI, 6) and entertainment. As for philosophy, it "teaches us to speak with an appearance of truth on all things and causes us to be admired by the less learned" (A.T. VI, 6). He regards the ancient languages as superfluous; our native language—regardless of what it may be—suffices for the attainment of the supreme science: "Those who have the strongest power of reasoning and who most skillfully arrange their thoughts in order to render them clear and intelligible, have the best power of persuasion, even if they can but speak the language of lower Brittany (A.T. VI, p. 7). Maritain (*Les Trois réformateurs,* p. 93) finds in Descartes a trait of inhumanity, characteristic of modern science. But such a trait is by no means inherent in modern science; it originated with positivist philosophy. Descartes anticipated this antihumanism in formulations which followed from his rationalistic logic, but which he himself did not live up to. It was an attitude quite out of keeping with his age, which Maritain was perfectly right in calling an age of historical erudition (Mabillon, Du Cange, etc.).

Descartes's rejection of history was based on a confusion. All authentic philosophy is original and not a repetition: but this does not mean that it starts from scratch, that it arises out of nothing. For a primordial ground cannot be elucidated in a vacuum—as though I derived my being entirely from myself and had accidentally dropped into some part of the world—but only through the historicity of my human substance.

Of course this primordial ground cannot, like an object of knowledge, be perceived again, as it were, from outside; it cannot be understood as part of a known totality, nor as a natural phenomenon, nor through combination of facts and situations encountered elsewhere, nor on the basis of a universally valid historical revelation. All philosophy springs from a primordial ground which, because it is a primordial ground, can never be adequately apprehended as an object. Original thought is perpetually starting all over again, but in the medium of a tradition which it elucidates and appropriates even when calling it into question (thus Descartes and all his thinking were rooted in the scholastic tradition, though he was quite unaware of the fact). Without tradition no authentic original philosophy would be possible. Philosophy would be blind or would artificially blind itself. Philosophy cannot go back to the beginning of history; rather, an essential feature of philosophy is its manner of understanding and so transforming this beginning. History is a transcending through appropriation, not a break and a fresh beginning, as though nothing had ever been. If Descartes's indifference to history became generalized, it would mean that the next generation—unlike Descartes himself—would acquire no meaningful knowledge. The breaking off of memory would inevitably give rise to a barbarism in which, because the beginning had vanished, there would also be no authenticity.

The loss of being in the cogito ergo sum. Descartes's conception of being and his identical conception of indubitably certain truth, provided the original impulse which enabled him to emerge from radical doubt. But from the outset he conceived being in a way that could not lead him onward into the depths of being. In his eagerness to master reality as a whole, he lost sight of the realities that constitute it. He hoped to find solid ground in indubitable compelling certainty by exercising his freedom to disregard the contents of reality, but in this he did not succeed. What he found was a dead center, indubitable but barren. In the *cogito ergo sum,* awareness of empirical existence and possible Existenz appear at one moment to be everything, but a moment later they are nothing, reduced to the mere concept of clarity and distinctness, which is meaningless unless there is something to be made clear and distinct. In thus starting from nothing, Descartes could not arrive at authentic being.

Thus Descartes himself could not take his fundamental

idea as the truth by which he lived. It is true that when in developing his idea he sought to elucidate the Encompassing, the proof of the existence of God gave him certainty of the being through which and for which I am; but a moment later his idea ceases to be anything more than an objective operation which, taking radical doubt as its starting point, seems to aim at theoretical knowledge of something, which is then held to be "known." In so far as a sense of being is present in his fundamental operation, although this operation bogs down in logic, we may say that if Descartes did not *live by* the truth of his first principle, he at least kept it constantly in mind. This is the source of the power which in spite of everything gives his thinking its great philosophical stature. And yet as a result of his insistence on a compelling formulation of something which loses its being in the process, being slips away from him at every step in his thinking.

3. THE NEW DOGMATISM

With all his detachment, Descartes did not achieve the ultimate detachment. In order to gain certainty, he doubted everything he could. But he did not doubt this mode of certainty. One might say that to doubt this certainty would be pointless; for then we should move in a circle and contradict ourselves. This is an oversimplification. It fails to take into account a human possibility, awareness of which can lead to extraordinary consequences. Descartes never knew the philosophical vertigo of a radical doubt, such as was experienced by Kierkegaard and Nietzsche. For all his radical power of abstraction, it never entered his head to abstract from his conception of certainty, to which, for better or worse, he entrusts and subjects himself and his readers. Because he could not abstract from this certainty, but was as it were imprisoned in it because he took it for granted, Descartes developed a new dogmatism. In its existential ground his clarity was still inherently unclear. For all his freedom from prejudice, he was caught in the toils of an absolutized reason. The clarity of his fundamental operation seems to have served only to imprison us in a lifeless mechanism.

The dogmatization of the fundamental operation. Let us briefly recapitulate how Descartes's original philosophical idea, once communicated, is hypostasized and is so rationalized as to become a dogma and cease to be truly philosophical:

Existential self-certainty as the source of my awareness of being is transformed into a philosophy of consciousness and then into a psychology; or else it becomes a doctrine of logico-mathematical principles and then a formal, logical construction alien to reality. The new possibility of an authentic human Existenz is perverted into subjectivity or into the empty abstraction of a reason which is nothing other than a logical function.

The inner action essential to true philosophy degenerates into a mere thinking about something, and this object thinking without existential commitment is held to be evident to the mere understanding and therefore universal.

The Encompassing, which we glimpse at times, is transformed into a particular object. Having thus safeguarded itself against a shallow conception of the Encompassing (the customs of the country, the state, the authority of the Church), this manner of thinking, characterized by compelling certainty, ceases to be anything more than a logical experiment without bearing on the world.

A dogmatic view of the world. We have seen that Descartes misunderstood the spirit of the new science. In his thinking, investigation was replaced by the dogma of a universal method, to which corresponded an equally dogmatic view of the world:

Descartes failed to discern the *particular* and *relative* character of the methods employed by the sciences and vitiated their meaning by subordinating them to a single, supposedly *absolute* and *universal* method.

Galileo's method of *empirical investigation,* in which nature discloses itself ad infinitum, through the continuous interaction of hypothesis and experimental verification, he transformed into a purely *deductive* method, according to which the principles and the totality of nature are known *once and for all.* An experimental hypothesis became a metaphysical absolute. The world had frozen; the ocean of being had been transformed into clockwork.

Accordingly, Descartes reduces the idea of scientific progress to an unfolding, down through the centuries, of his own already definitive principles. He loses sight of possibility, that is, of the idea so stimulating to scientific development, that all our knowledge and its principles as well are subject to endless growth. Because of this tendency to dogmatism, he did not proceed in a spirit of open-minded empirical inquiry, but derived and contrived purely rational constructions.

Because in Descartes the new science degenerated into a universal view of the world, he ignored the experimental method in favor of scholastic argumentation.

Dogmatic certainty and the tendency to special pleading. The dominant factor in Descartes's philosophy is his way of striving for certainty. Ever since the beginning of philosophy men have striven for certainty. But the character of this certainty has varied according to its source. The new science found certainty in the experience of nature. It was

able to do so and later (not until the nineteenth century on
a large scale) to exert mastery of nature because, renouncing
the hope of knowing the totality of nature or the essence
of things, it remained resolutely particular and—conscious
of its limits and of the uncertainty of all knowledge—open
to correction. This kind of certainty characterized the thinking of Copernicus, Galileo, Kepler, and Newton, but not
of Bruno and only in part of Bacon. Descartes espoused it
only in appearance, for he misunderstood it and transformed it into absolute certainty. By attempting to make
this absolute certainty the form of philosophical certainty,
he lost the specific certainty of science and at the same time
corrupted the certainty that is attainable in philosophy.
For fundamentally his certainty was *a new form of dogmatism*. In the cloak of pure rationality, his thinking was a
dogmatic striving for absolute, total knowledge.

Thus the new scientific attitude was perverted by a
dogmatic approach that was anything but new. The consequence was that armed with supposedly absolute certainty
Descartes continually made statements which were by no
means certain, and many of which were absurd, incorrect,
and contradictory to reality. Reason isolated from reality
can prove anything. Authentic truth springs from contact
with reality, under conditions of rationality.

Once a certain number of propositions are adopted as
certain, this purely rational, dogmatic certainty takes on an
argumentative tone, which might be called forensic. Its
chief characteristics are as follows: without regard for the
whole of reality and without sufficient account of any concrete, present object, Descartes puts forward abstract statements, which are necessarily subject to varying interpretations, and operates with them as with an exactly defined
conceptual currency. Investigation is replaced by special

pleading with the unconscious aim of justifying a precon-
ceived opinion against all attacks, of defending it and sav-
ing it at all costs, of dogmatically preserving a construction
or some obscure tendency of the will. Objections bring forth
answers and the argument goes on indefinitely. The truth
is simple; it is arrived at by a decision which may be empirical or philosophical; by a sure methodical progression,
in the awareness that every result achieved is only provisional; or in the simple presence of an object or Existenz,
which does not lend itself to polemics and merely asks to
be understood. In forensic thinking, however, the truth is
taken as something which is already known but must nevertheless be proved; this "truth" is repeated over and over
again in circular arguments, and no amount of proofs and
guarantees carry it one step forward.

It seems to me that this manner of thinking appears
in Descartes's thought processes, especially in his way of
treating objections. It is a polemical attitude inseparable
from dogmatism; according to his state of mind, a reader
may find it interesting and stimulating or merely boring.

Obscurity at the ground of dogmatism. If certainty
embraces the whole of Being, that is, if it takes the form
of philosophical certainty, the question arises: how is it related to other certainty? As absolute truth, it seems to
admit of no other absolute truth beside it or above it in the
same individual. This, however, is not the position of truth
in Descartes, for he recognizes the superordinate, revealed
truth of authority.

In the sciences, on the other hand, all certainty is taken
to be *relative* and *limited,* cogent only within a particular
method of investigation and in a particular context. Such
a view can still admit of the possibility that the whole in
which we live may be true in a very different way, pro-

vided that the truth of this whole is such as not to negate
the validity of the method in scientific investigations. But
this relationship between truth as compelling certainty and
an Encompassing does not obtain in Descartes, because for
him science was not a relative and particular certainty but
a philosophy, and philosophy was a self-contained whole.

In view of Descartes's failure to decide between these
two clear and unequivocal possibilities, the question arises:
did he, in the last analysis, know what he wanted? For all
the certainty of his compelling evidence, for all the clarity
of his theses, the ultimate ground of his truth, the basis
of his conviction, is not clear. Through perversion a grave
untruth can enter into the existence of one who seeks truth
only as certainty or as an authority which he makes no attempt to understand. The Encompassing which originally
embraced faith and reason vanishes, giving way to a rigid
dogmatism in which knowledge and authority form two
separate spheres. Thus objectified, thought undergoes a
gradual perversion, and indeed, on close study, Descartes's
rational, dogmatic thinking may well produce the impression of a splendid game. There is magic in the form, but
this form is not so much a form of knowledge as a style of
thought, which derives its devices and ornaments from
mathematics, science, and scholastic speculation. The scholastic notions lose their meaning and are used as pawns in
an ingenious game of sophistic argumentation.

This game, however, is not presented as a game, but
as dogmatic certainty, and this has another consequence:
precisely because a purely rational dogmatism is inevitably
the emptiest of all dogmatisms, its absolute character in
Descartes's formulations is correlative to the absolute character of something radically different, namely, of faith
grounded on mere authority. Descartes's attempts to show

that there is no contradiction between these two absolutes are purely artificial. The conflict between them never ceases, and a clear conscience is impossible on both sides. The consequence is a paralysis of the human soul and a pervading *dogmatic atmosphere*. This interpretation enables us at least to understand why certain *consequences* of Descartes's system become a general feature of other systems. It is no accident that orthodox believers, as well as freethinkers who fanatically rejected all authority and believed themselves to be building exclusively on reason, have been drawn to Descartes the philosopher. The former were able to invoke Descartes as a devout son of the Church, while the latter could maintain that the pressure of the times compelled Descartes to be circumspect. The former were able to regard him as fundamentally a scholastic, while the latter looked upon him as a modern philosopher of reason, who was obliged to wear a mask.

4. DESCARTES'S PERSONALITY

At first sight Descartes's work is distinguished by a clarity and openness which exert a powerful attraction quite independent of interest in the subject matter.

There is a strange tension in his writings, which are meant to impart the purest science and which are at the same time masterpieces of form. There is more to this literary form than rigorous thinking. Descartes shows a great deal of taste in deciding what to treat in detail and what succinctly. In general the pace is rapid, and the author never seems to lose sight of the whole. His good taste leads him to avoid the Euclidean form of demonstration, although the subject matter would seem to permit of it (the only exception is a part of *Responsiones II,* in which he attempts it on request). He was guided by a distinctly literary and

aesthetic instinct and tried to make his work as readable
as possible; his prose is carefully polished. Not only are his
ideas, but his expression as well is luminously clear.

Descartes had still another means of making his otherwise sober thoughts, which might have proved tiresome on
prolonged reading, not only interesting but passionately
absorbing. In the *Discours,* he relates the development of
his thinking as though telling the story of his life; the
most impersonal ideas take on a personal form. Despite
the universal character of the content, which is represented
as valid for all men on the basis of pure insight, the reader
finds himself challenged by a confrontation with the unique
personality of Descartes. Descartes does not present results,
but thought itself in the process of searching. The fascination of the work lies more in this movement than in the
results.

But although Descartes is a classicist in form and although he sets forth his thoughts with the clarity of personal experience, his personality itself is anything but transparent. The very nature of his work in which he seems
to speak so freely, and which he wrote in French rather
than in Latin, because he wished to speak to all men, stands
in strange contrast to his aristocratic aloofness; he did not
demand to be imitated and spoke only to an enlightened
elite.

Actually, Descartes seems to be the *soul of mystery.*
And it was not only his caution that made him inscrutable.
This mystery is disturbing, because it is not possible to
discover and interpret what lies behind it. Because Descartes does not lay bare his soul, we are tempted to look
for it. But we do not find it. Everything he says carries
more than one possible meaning, and in the end we en-

counter an ambiguity which is not meant to conceal, but seems to be inherent in his very nature.

It is not possible to penetrate this enigma. All one can do is to come near it with some hints, though confessing at once that merely by formulating them they acquire a definiteness which rather describes what Descartes *might* have been than what he perhaps really was.

Because of their perversion, even his scientific statements present a riddle in their contrasts: He aims at compelling certainty, but produces a total construction in which little is compellingly certain and much is absurd; he aims at method, but loses sight of scientific method; he starts with true philosophical speculation but then reduces it to a mere knowledge of something and virtually drops it. In every case he involves himself in a contradiction which may be expressed in the following dialectical form: At the beginning of his philosophizing, Descartes knows more than he actually expresses in his operations; thus he seems in a way to be wiser than he is. When he pursues his concrete ideas, which are sometimes so absurd, he seems to be forsaken by common sense; then he appears to be less wise than he is; paradoxically enough, this man of lordly intelligence seems to reveal astonishing depths of stupidity.[1]

[1] Admirers of Descartes have not infrequently expressed their astonishment at certain of his ideas: in connection with the doctrine of matter and of the corpuscles, for example, Schelling writes: "Every trace of science is lost, and it is hard to believe that this is the same Descartes who wrote the first *Meditations*" (*Werke*, XI, 271). And in regard to Descartes's hypothesis that mind and body meet in the pineal gland, Spinoza wrote: "I cannot get over my surprise that a philosopher, who had undertaken to derive nothing except from self-evident principles . . . and who had so often criticized the scholastics for attempting to explain obscure facts by occult qualities, should have propounded a hypothesis that is more occult than any occult quality" (*Ethics*, Book V, Preface).

The *extremism* of Descartes's thoughts and actions is disturbing. With its radical shifts and breaks, his life presents a picture not of harmonious human development, but of violent contrasts; in his thinking he was attracted by the startling, and absurd inferences did not frighten him. In his life he was no coward and displayed bravery in times of danger. But he side-stepped the true destiny of man, which calls for participation in the real world and an unconditional bond with our fellow men. Thus the absurdities of his thinking lack the force of the absurd; in their absurdity, they preserve a semiplausibility which reduces them to utter emptiness. Here again the riddle resides in an apparent link between disparate qualities, in a juxtaposition of platitude and depth.

It is disturbing to note the *passion* that sustains this seeming emptiness. In his passion for a compelling certainty, valid for all men at all times, an unparalleled *will to power* is discernible. Such a will to power cannot, like the genuine scientific attitude, born of a love for things themselves, content itself with the particular, with an infinitesimal but imperishable discovery. It demands totality, in the form of definitive principles. Descartes felt himself to be the dividing line between two epochs, the end of error and the beginning of truth. His will to power was not concerned with immediate effect, but with lasting influence, for the sake of which he was willing to suffer solitude and obscurity. A monstrous self-assurance and a boundless confidence in rational knowledge are clearly discernible throughout his work. There seems to be no room for life and spontaneity in this rigid and entombing system. It is this inhumanity in Descartes which occasionally overwhelms the student of his works with something akin to horror.

This impression is enhanced by the fact that Descartes was not a simple rationalist, but that the foundations of his philosophy disclose a *mystical impulse,* which is attested in his biography. Since Descartes rejected all the superstitious tendencies of his day including astrology, there is little reason to attribute this mysticism to the times. The two absolutes which were otherwise distinct in his thinking—his rational insight and the authority of the faith he professed—seem to converge in those days of November, 1619, when Descartes, in a period of enthusiasm over a new discovery (the unity of all knowledge in the *mathesis universalis*), had dreams which, he felt, could only come "from above." They summoned him to his vocation, which was to establish single-handed the unity of the sciences. In gratitude he vowed to make a pilgrimage to Loretto and later did so. Though Descartes makes no further mention of this experience, he also never disclaimed it (Gilson, *Commentaire,* p. 125). It is essential to an understanding of Descartes's personality.[1]

Then there are the portraits of Descartes, which show a face of extraordinary and impressive aloofness. Enormous power, but without love, without inner beauty, without the gaze of the dreamer who believes that he can read the ciphers of transcendence.

With the memory of these portraits in mind, we can, as it were, yield to the physiognomic impression of his philosophical work and, on the basis of his thoughts, form a picture of Descartes the thinker.

We seem to see a dark goblin enveloped in luminous reason. This thinking with its ahistorical striving for universal validity may well give the impression of a subter-

[1] Cf. Adam, *Vie et oeuvres,* pp. 48–56. *Olympica,* A.T. X, 179–188. *Cogitationes privatae,* X, 216 ff.

ranean force, passionately searching for human dignity, but
mistakenly expecting to find it in the thinking of empty
reason. This reason itself seems comparable to an elemental
force, comparable to the obscure life of nature, which under the eyes of the biologist always behaves so surprisingly
and, observed under inappropriate conditions, now ab-
surdly and awkwardly, now meaningfully and inventively.
This "prehuman" life of man, present throughout the
world, attractive and repellent in its infinite manifestations,
is discernible in Descartes's thinking, in the amazing
pseudo-clarity of something which is inherently unclear.

Descartes is not the "exception," now struggling to
emerge from the darkness of natural being to greater consciousness, now sacrificing consciousness for the obscurity of
transcendence. He is satisfied with his universal thought,
grounded in perfect self-discipline, and his confidence that
he is laying the foundations of definitive truth makes him
the exact opposite of an exception. Descartes may well strike
us as a man who failed to find himself, though he did not
know it. But this man stands before us as a consummate
aristocrat, dominating men by the force of his thinking and
the indefinable spell of his personality.

5. THE HISTORICAL INFLUENCE OF DESCARTES
If in a schematic simplification we consider the periods in
the intellectual development of man as clear, self-contained
units; if we set up a sharp dividing line between medieval
scholasticism and modern thought, Descartes seems to fit in
nowhere. He cannot be regarded as a mere phenomenon
of transition between scholasticism and modern science. He
presents the enigma of a unique philosophy, which can
appear to be decidedly scholastic or decidedly modern,

while it is neither of the two, and yet forms a self-contained whole, the essence of which is ambiguity.

Descartes *despised scholasticism* and thought it a waste of time to concern oneself with its fruitless disputations. But he knew these disputations to the extent that he made use of their conceptual tools without being aware of their origin.[1]

Descartes was a man of the Renaissance, a modern man of the world; his tastes, attitudes, and skepticism were molded by the ancient philosophers and Montaigne, and he had cast off habit and prejudice. But living in this modern world, he strove for the very opposite of skepticism, for certainty, method, *mathesis universalis*. In his thinking he disavowed the humanistic foundation on which he stood.

It is characteristic of his ambiguity that in a later day some have regarded him as a devout Catholic, others as the first Protestant philosopher, and still others as a revolutionary of reason. Such availability for the use of every conceivable faith even of quite different origin is characteristic of mere rationalism. Cartesian rationality became an appropriate medium for many faiths, widely varying in content, but all dogmatic and tending to fanaticism. I do not believe that a devout Catholic or a devout Protestant or a truly rational man can recognize himself in Descartes. His thinking satisfies those who neither live, nor wish to live, by and toward the One, whose being is essentially characterized by a definitive dualism and pluralism. His trou-

---

[1] Étienne Gilson, in *Index scolastico-cartésien*, Paris, 1913, has shown to what extent scholastic ideas are present in Descartes. See also, É. Gilson, *Études sur le rôle de la pensée médiévale dans la formation du système cartésien*, Paris, 1930; and v. Hertling, *Descartes' Beziehungen zur Scholastik*, 1897–99, reprinted in Hertling, *Historische Beiträge zur Philosophie*, Munich, 1914, pp. 181–242.

bling ambiguity made possible in others something that was
alien to Descartes: a secretly relativist manner of thinking,
a new scholastic rigidity of form, a style of rationalistic
thinking without passion for the truth, and finally, a deep-
rooted nihilism in the guise of this or that dogmatism.

Perhaps no philosopher has ever had true inner communication with Descartes. But many have been attracted,
indeed captivated, by his thinking. What is the source of
this attraction? Perhaps it is a tendency, cloaked in rational
universality, to isolate ourselves from the world and our
own potentialities; perhaps it is our desire to acquire the
false independence of empty reason after losing our existential independence; perhaps it is a polemical attitude
born of hidden resentment. But of course there are also very
different motivations: an objective examination of the pros-
pects which Descartes gave to knowledge, in his idea of a
mathesis universalis, for example; and above all a philosophical enthusiasm over the positive sources of Descartes's
philosophy.

When we speak of the influence of Descartes's philosophy, we do not mean that Descartes was its sole cause. The
deviations and perversions rooted in human nature take on
a character of triviality only when the common herd of
intellectuals takes possession of a great thinker and waters
down his very mistakes. By his greatness and authority
Descartes was suited to confirm such deviations and appease
the conscience of those who succumbed to them. Those who
indulged in these deviations could invoke him as a guarantor.

We shall now try to characterize his influence. Several
different factors may be distinguished.

His influence. Descartes is a great example of the influence of a *one-sided* view which imposes itself by its seem-

ingly compelling logic. He has been a spur to *radicalism.* His thinking has neither its object nor its origin in a vision of wholeness, in man or the world seen as a whole. His thinking is like a drill, which penetrates cautiously, but without concern for the damage it may by doing. This is a radicalism that is easy to imitate, for those who wish to think in this way have no need to commit their own substance.

Descartes has also exerted an influence by setting an example of *independent* thinking. His seemingly radical doubt is immediately transformed into an absolute reliance on reason. Because the audacity of his doubt culminated in the idea of mastering all things through philosophy, it was able to call forth a euphoria of confidence in the autonomous power of thinking—for in this philosophizing the other, the sensible world, history, and authority, played no part, but stood on the fringe, ignored by thought. This possibility of disregarding everything other made for a sense of freedom, and this freedom was thought to reflect the Godlike nature of man. There is a magic even in unlimited possibility, when such possibility, though devoid of substance, is mistaken for freedom. Similarly, the thinker mistakes his purely subjective abstract certainty for definitive possession of the truth.

The influence of Descartes's distortion of the meaning of modern science. I believe that Descartes exerted a profound influence with his misinterpretation of modern science. Such misinterpretation springs from a tendency inherent in the human mind, but Descartes provided the first conspicuous example of it.

His principles were *not methodic hypotheses.* Newton's *"hypotheses non fingo"* was directed against Descartes, who reasoned but did not investigate. For the new science,

the principles applied to each particular case are mere instruments of research; for Descartes they in themselves
represent compelling knowledge of reality. Consequently
Descartes, in indefatigably elaborating the details of his
mechanistic view of the world, extending from the astro-
nomical to the physical and biological phenomena on our
earth, proceeded by pure thought, contenting himself with
general observations and invoking no new experience. But
in thus giving the impression, which has fascinated so many,
of setting forth a new cosmos with his closed mechanical
explanation of the world, he excluded himself from the
process of scientific development. His constructions did not
become a factor in the growth of science, which had, on
the contrary, to rid itself of Descartes's mistakes.

The treatment of scientific subjects occupies a great
deal of space in Descartes's work. There are long passages
in which we have the impression that what we are reading
is not philosophy but unsound and inadequate scientific
disquisitions, relevant only to our historical and biographical understanding of Descartes. The philosophical element
in these passages is the unified conception of the world, a
conception which no one before him had ever developed
with such thoroughness and consistency. There is a distinct
analogy to the Aristotelian view of the world. Through
substantial forms, through the characteristic system of co-
ordinates provided by his categories based on form, development, hierarchy, etc., Aristotle explained the qualitative
richness of reality, which could be "visualized"; in fact he
was the first to give us a vivid picture of the cosmos. By
his mechanistic categories on the basis of quantity, corpuscles, pressure, thrust, vortices, etc., Descartes explained a
world which, seen through these categories, loses its rich
qualitative character and is no longer a vivid picture, but

a set of mathematical formulas. In both cases, the total conception is a finished product, not a spur to inquiry. Those who accepted such conceptions lost their power of free investigation.

Thus, while Descartes concurred with the new science in his conscious opposition to scholasticism, he actually went counter to its spirit by fashioning a new form of scholasticism from its content.

His essential perversion of the spirit of the new science was able to exert a great historical influence for the following reasons:

Descartes's conception of the world fell in with *the common penchant for easy solutions;* we would like to know with certainty, once and for all, the whole of nature and all its possibilities; we would also like to possess, in the form of compelling science, precisely what is not accessible to knowledge; we are dogmatists by nature, attracted to simple, striking schemata of the world, into which everything that occurs can be drawn: we conclude that apart from this process that can be understood in mechanical terms, there is nothing.

A second factor was that the contents of modern science, as it actually developed, seemed to concur with Descartes's conception of the world. Descartes's philosophy gained enormously in prestige, as though it had actually been *confirmed* by practical *findings.*

Actually the opposite was the case. Science developed in a direction contrary to that of Descartes; but time and time again its findings, interpreted from the Cartesian point of view, were associated with absolute conceptions that were not at all appropriate to them. This fundamental perversion in Descartes's thinking is of the utmost interest, because it *typifies* a powerful current which arose at that time and has flowed persistently through the cultural history of the West, detracting from a true scientific attitude and obscuring the meaning of the researcher's findings. This current, which extends down to positivism, has sustained a pseudo-science consisting of empty words and of schemata devoid of experience. Mechanistic mythologies have impeded the investigation of the qualitative and above all of life, and because of them even fruitful mechanistic investigations have suffered the consequences of a mechanistic world view, purporting to provide knowledge of reality as a whole. Because of its absolute character, Descartes's thinking is, to a great extent, of the type which obstructs investigation and drives man into the blind alley of illusory knowledge. This type of thinking is the source of the repeated deviations of the modern mind, which time and again have nullified true accomplishment and have sometimes falsified the whole scientific perspective. This perversion contains the seeds of disastrous mistakes on the part of reason and science, both of which are led to misunderstand their own nature. In so far as Descartes is its representative, we may regard him as anything but modern, as an obstacle to progress, to the fruitful exploitation of the new possibilities.

From this type of thought developed a consequence which Descartes did not suspect. In the main he himself followed reason considered as an absolute. He did not abolish faith, but set it aside, beyond the scope of autonomous reason. Thus his successors were able *to eradicate the whole world of faith* and with pure reason—which in Descartes was without positive existential content of its own —create a desert of faithlessness such as had never before existed in all history. In the Cartesian system God still retained a formal function, though in Descartes's actual thinking this function dwindled almost to nothingness. Once He was wholly eliminated in favor of self-sufficient reason—for essentially God was superfluous from the very first to reason taken as an absolute—what was left for posterity was a desert: a world swallowed up by mechanism, no world, no God, only an intellectual machine, the mechanization of everything, life as a struggle among mere machines.

All this was certainly not the consequence of modern science as such, nor of autonomous reason as such; it resulted from the intellectualism that treated science and reason as absolutes and from the philosophical interpretation of nature, inaugurated by Descartes.

The effect of this false interpretation and of the attitudes and beliefs it engendered was to cast discredit on science and technology themselves. They were blamed for consequences which are not inherent in them but result from a misunderstanding.

Influence of the idea of the "mathesis universalis." The idea of a *mathesis universalis* led to various philosophical efforts, differing from one another but all oriented toward the unity of the cognitive process, of human reason, and hence of the knowable world.

Leibnitz' ideas are closely related to those of Descartes: he strove to promote the *mathesis universalis* by a universal theory of signs. He was not successful. The signs he invented proved fruitful only in mathematics.

In his *Wissenschaftslehre,* Fichte tried to derive the unity of knowledge from a source which, despite its analogy to the *cogito ergo sum,* was very different. Nevertheless, he too sought to derive the whole of knowledge from a single principle. His system, as unnatural as it is ingenious, was a purely personal achievement, without general significance.

Symbolic logic is perhaps the undertaking that came closest to Descartes. No one denies that the logisticians have made correct statements. The question is: what do these correct statements mean in relation to the whole of human experience; that is, are they important, or are they merely correct, but without consequences? In the latter case, they would be empty, serving only as a game to be played by people who happen to like it and are prepared to accept its rules.

Influence springing from the possibility of reinterpreting "I," "method," and "science." Precisely because of the vagueness which attended Descartes's "clarity," the great themes of his philosophy have been open to continual reinterpretation. From these seeds grew plants as divergent as Spinoza's metaphysics, Kant's critique of the transcendental presuppositions of consciousness, Fichte's philosophy of the *I*, etc. From Descartes all these philosophers received an impetus which subsequently impelled them to turn radically against him. This, in particular, has been the influence of the ideas of the *"I"* (in the *cogito ergo sum*), of "method," and of "science."

a) Down to Kant, Kierkegaard, and the present, the *cogito ergo sum* has been regarded as a cardinal point of philosophy. Schelling believed, not without justification, that Descartes had struck the keynote of modern philosophy, although he added that this *cogito ergo sum* had "had the effect of a magic spell, imprisoning philosophy in the sphere of subjectivity and of the purely subjective consciousness" (Schelling, *Werke* X, 8).

b) The *method* exerted an influence because Descartes had taken it as his principal theme. It was something new at the time to come out in public with a program: and this method by which all our knowledge could attain its goal with certainty was a challenging and extremely promising program. In philosophy, the essence of which is the constantly present truth, the truth by which a thinking man lives, the accent now shifted to the future. Philosophy was presented as an unfinished process, which invited the participation of every man. Ostensibly it did not supply men with a finished body of knowledge, but showed each man how he too could become one of those who made new discoveries. Since then a number of scientific movements, fruitful or not, have arisen in philosophy, all based on methods by which supposedly every man can accomplish something. In such movements even those who know nothing of the underlying ideas can contribute outwardly. Since the method is supposedly technical, universal, and sure, everyone can take a hand and, by mechanically applying the rules, produce a semblance of scientific investigation. The result was a leveling of science. Descartes's program gave rise not to the communication among a few friends which kindles intellectual achievement, but to the school for the many, each of whom jealously guards his intellectual property and looks askance at the others.

The method exerted still another sort of influence. It became a point of departure for a new elucidation of the Encompassing, for true speculation. But such philosophy could escape deformation only where Descartes was quickly abandoned. Most of those who had learned clear reasoning from Descartes contented themselves with mere logical form, which appeared to be mathematical and exact, but on the one hand was not truly speculative (like the music of the great purely formal thinkers) and on the other was devoid of empirical content. Whether trivial or enormously

complex, their thinking, supposedly based on exact observance of the rules, was an essentially meaningless mouthing
of the jargons of the various schools.

c) Philosophy had always been *science* in the sense
of clear expression and truth rationally stated. Enthusiasm
for the new science ushered in a deep-seated philosophical
trend, whose adherents stressed the importance of universally compelling science for philosophy and ceased in principle to distinguish between philosophy and the sciences,
but conceived of philosophy as the *one* science in which
every other science occupies its appropriate place. This is
why Descartes stressed the novelty of his philosophy as
opposed to everything that had gone before. This idea—the
idea that he had founded a new and for the first time
scientific philosophy—has also been frequently repeated
throughout the centuries down to our own time. This attitude—in Descartes and in all others who have taken it
—implied the expectation that the new scientific philosophy
would soon gain acceptance as the universally valid truth,
and each of these philosophers consequently prided himself on being the cornerstone and founder of the true
scientific philosophy.

Actually none of these philosophies has ever gained
general acceptance. Nor were they, like superseded views
in the development of the sciences, preserved as links in the
chain of progress. They were forgotten; or if they were remembered, it was because, despite their fundamental fallacy, they possessed some other substance.

Here was also the starting point for the rationalistic
intolerance that is so widespread in the modern world:
the dogmatic presumptuousness of reason made for an attitude of self-assurance. Actually this omnipotent rationality
produced nothing but a blindness to Existenz and a means

of concealing very different impulses and purposes beneath the cloak of absolute reason. This scientific attitude in philosophy engendered arbitrary irrationality masked as rationality.

It cannot be doubted that Descartes has exerted an extraordinary influence down to our own time. That is all the more reason for asking whether we should count him among the creators of the modern spirit and whether we should regard him as the source of modern philosophy.

Because of the many motifs interwoven in his thinking and the perversion to which his philosophical impulses succumbed, we regard him—by comparison with the great philosophers before him, in his time, and after him—as a point of convergence of intellectual currents, each one of which, taken by itself, becomes ambivalent; everything that he thought seems to stand in a half-darkness.

If by modern spirit we mean an error that ought to be rejected and if, in surveying the thought of the last centuries, we concentrate on certain aspects that we regard as disastrous, we may be inclined to reject Descartes as well, because of his part in initiating the modern spirit. But if on the contrary we find in these modern times a magnificent positive content veiled by folly and misunderstanding—a content which it is still our task to develop—then Descartes becomes one of those dangerous figures who have kindled a spark in men, but at the same time led them astray.

The significance of the error. We do not regard the perversions we have attempted to point out in Descartes's thinking as accidental error. This error is significant, because it seems to be necessary, an error that human nature could not have avoided under the conditions in which modern thought developed, a false move that had to run its course before it could be fully overcome. But to surmount this error in all its many forms is a task that will have to be undertaken over and over again. It is probably impossible to guard against such perversions of thought except by trying them out and so coming to see through them.

Consequently we cannot overcome this error by a general refutation, but only by testing the specific articulations and contents of Cartesian thinking, by a critical examination which opens up this whole philosophy to us. It is only through error made transparent that philosophy attains full clarity.

But even though true philosophy cannot be achieved without the conquest of fundamental error, even though those who have not consciously overcome it keep falling back into it, Descartes's work will endure forever even if thoroughly understood. Anyone who philosophizes must know Descartes if he is to be safeguarded against these seductive illusions, to which he will succumb if left to his own resources. He must think through the mistakes that Descartes made with so much logical consistency, if he is to avoid repeating them and if he is to safeguard his thinking against them. Thus the study of Descartes remains indispensable. In Descartes we see, in its origin and beginning, what later became the enduring enemy of philosophy, and this applies even when we believe ourselves to be in agreement with Descartes's truth. Descartes is a historical crossroads in the sense that everyone who philosophizes must inevitably appropriate Cartesian thinking and by the manner of his appropriation come to a decision concerning himself.

Descartes is also significant because the *character of our opposition* to him is a test. Opposition to Descartes is almost general; but the agreement between his opponents is purely negative. The bases of opposition are so heterogeneous that inevitably one opponent combats another when he combats Descartes. We can attain clarity concerning philosophy by analyzing the erroneous ways in which he is combated:

Those, for example, who reject Descartes's distinction between two substances, body and mind, often also drop the true phenomenological distinction between consciousness and the spatial reality of things, and yet the distinction between the two, whatever problems it may involve, functions as a goad as long as we remain sincere with ourselves. In sacrificing this distinction, they succumb to the vitalism which maintains that there is one total substance, which oscillates between nature and spirit and is now one and now the other—an empty assertion which provides no fruitful path to knowledge.

Those who attack the logic of Descartes's proofs of the existence of God, also make the mistake of rejecting the philosophical speculation that elucidates Existenz and transcendence, in favor of a trivial positivism and empiricism, or of logicism.

And finally, those who condemn the modern world, science, and technology, rationalism and the mechanization of life, and put the blame as it were on Descartes, usually fall into the error of condemning not Descartes's perversion, but science itself, the possibility of clarifying reality with the help of reason, and hence true philosophy. They are falsely rejecting something which Descartes himself failed to see clearly, are confusing those deviations of Descartes's thinking (mechanical view of the world, reason taken as an absolute) which actually have their counterparts in the modern world (the mechanization of consciousness instead of human mastery over all possible mechanisms; vitalism instead of a life oriented by transcendence), with the genuinely creative modern spirit which, amid enormous perils, has made it possible for man to rise to unprecedented heights.

It is our task to create a philosophy which has passed through the fundamental errors of Descartes, which, developing with his help and that of the standard he provided, opposes him by presenting a whole: our human, historical substance as the source by which we really can and do live.

We must create a philosophy whose rationality is grounded in a deeper source, whose reason does not shut itself in but is all-encompassing;

which is open to all reality and thought, and free to speculate, to transcend with sober passion, to perceive the ciphers of the hidden transcendence;

which takes cognizance of every reality without loss of the Encompassing;

which recognizes compelling certainty but also understands that it is relative;

which leaves the road open for modern science and its consequences, but preserves the sciences from taking their findings as absolutes;

which resolutely accepts the possibilities offered by science but is aware of their limitations;

which is open to every conception of the world based on genuine proof, but dispenses with any one and absolute conception of the world;

for which all knowledge is only a means, which it appropriates as such, never regarding it as a final goal;

which is historically grounded in the Existenz from which it grows, but keeps its eyes and ears open to every other Existenz, always approaching it as such and not as a content of knowledge to be classified;

which is able to enter into contact with the substantial in any form, because it is itself the product of a potential substance;

which aims at boundless communication, without knowing where it will lead and what the totality is;

which neither degenerates into dogmatism nor evaporates into skepticism or nihilism;

which elucidates the unconditional (which is historical and hence not universally valid) and is at the same time receptive to the universally valid (which, because it is universally valid is not unconditional but relative);

which does not anticipate transcendence as something known and does not claim transcendence for itself alone— and which therefore breathes historical and existential life even into unconditional unity, but does not set it up as *the* absolute unity embracing all things and all men.

Max Weber

as Politician,

Scientist,

Philosopher

Preface

MAX WEBER (1864–1920) was the greatest German of our age. I know that in making such a statement I am anticipating the judgment of future generations. And still I make it, for I have lived with this conviction for almost half a century.

This essay on Max Weber, which can give only the barest hint of what he was, was first published in 1932. Amid the rising tide of National Socialism, it was intended as a reminder of the true voice of Germany. At that time Germany was confronted by a perverted image of her spirit, and it seemed to me that my own attitude might be most effectively expressed by an evocation of the great man.

Max Weber is here considered as a politician, a scientist, and a philosopher. Politics was an important aspect of his life. He took a passionate interest in it, and it often appeared as if he were on the verge of active participation, but in fact he confined himself to political thinking. Illness prohibited political activity.

Max Weber's life coincides with an age of unparalleled peace and security in Europe, which from a global point of view is known as the age of imperialism. He was intuitively aware of the historical moment: portentous, unpredictable events were in the offing. If Germany did not want to rest on her achievements, lulled in a false security, she had to summon

her energies and become a politically conscious and active nation. Max Weber did not demand colonies for Germany, but
he did demand a voice in the council of nations in the matter
of future global decisions. He was concerned with securing for
Germany unhampered participation in international trade, as
being indispensable for the economic existence of the German
worker. He despised German self-satisfaction and self-delusion.
He postulated a training ground for German statesmen in
which they could develop their capacities, something that was
impossible within the imperial "system," as he called it.

The subject matter of his political thinking, in so far as
it concerns active politics, is of purely historical interest today.
He was the last German nationalist. His point of departure
was a powerful German Empire, whose defeat in the First World
War he barely lived to see. Today, the conditions of political
life have changed radically and have nothing in common with
the perspectives of Max Weber's time. As we read him, we are
reminded of a past that is irrevocably destroyed. But his political thinking is of imperishable significance. It is the substance
and goal of national policies that determine a nation's dignity.
Max Weber sensed the hard pressures of reality, the greatness
of responsibility which grew out of Germany's historical position. When a prominent Swiss visitor said to him: "We must
love the state," he replied: "What! On top of everything, you
want us to love the monster?"

In considering Max Weber, one has to go back to a past as
dead as if centuries separated it from today. In order to understand the greatness of Max Weber's political thinking, though
in the Germany of his time it met with failure and fell on deaf
ears, one has to be willing to set aside all prejudice caused by
the evil of Hitlerism and the crimes committed by Germans in
the name of Germany. One must not allow our present knowledge of the presuppositions to totalitarianism and of analogies
of meaning to cast its shadow backwards on all that preceded
the totalitarian state in Germany.

Max Weber's political thinking cannot be subsumed under any of the historically known categories of thinking at the turn of the century. This essay speaks of a form of nationalist thought which as such was still possible before and during the First World War, but which was uniquely Max Weber's own. The reader has to be warned against misconceptions that might be aroused by certain passages in this study. In a time like ours, when the gravest threat to political liberty emanates from nationalism, with its insistence on national sovereignty, a certain effort may be required to see what is really essential in Max Weber's political thinking, namely, his sense of political freedom, of human dignity in politics—considerations which transcend all passing political situations.

Max Weber the sociologist and historian will always be remembered. His scientific achievement is stored up in great works. With him as with Galileo discovery went hand in hand with the most lucid methodological awareness. His contribution to our understanding of social phenomena is comparable to Galileo's contribution to physics. It is difficult to follow his thinking; his work with its precise and widely ramified concepts has impressed many as a great granite boulder which they are afraid to climb. It has only begun to exert an influence, especially in America, but also in England, France, and Germany. He found sociology sunk in conversational generalities, cheap banalities, and insane speculations—"Most of what goes by the name of sociology," he once said, "is a fraud"—and transformed it into an empirical science.

All this diversified scientific endeavor, so amazingly rich in experience and knowledge and method, is integrated by the personality of Max Weber. He himself always spoke of his subject and only reluctantly of himself. He was a man of integrity, hence a true scientist. His scientific effort was sustained by an immense passion, not easily held in check. He was given to excesses, which he was able to correct. His great heart was everywhere. His ethical intransigence remained free from fanaticism. His personality can be fully felt only by those who knew him. In his work it is discernible through the philosophy which, though seldom stated explicitly, encompasses the whole.

His life was an encouragement for all who enter the future without illusions, active as long as they can be, hoping as long as everything is not lost. He was the modern man, who veils nothing from himself, who in this integrity finds the motive force of his life, and allows himself no escape into despair. He suffered long periods of illness, and he was dismayed at the onrushing current of history, but like reason itself he prevailed in the end and realized the best that was in him.

KARL JASPERS
Basel, 1958 and 1964

Introduction

GREAT historical figures show us what men can be; they open up to us the realm of the possible in which we live. But each individual historical figure is remote from us, because we have not met him; these men did not live in our world. It is through our contemporaries, men who belong to our own world and share in its fate, men with whom we are in personal contact and who are real to us, that we gain the standards and the faith which enable us to approach those who are far from us and strange to us.

In Germany, in the years before and during the First World War, Max Weber was for many the man who embodied human greatness, whom they believed, by whom they oriented themselves, and above all whom they loved with the love that elevates us and causes what is authentic in us to grow.

Max Weber was born in 1864; he studied law; he was active as a professor of economics from 1894 to 1897 at Freiburg University and from 1897 to 1899 at the University of Heidelberg. After 1899, in consequence of a nervous disorder, he lived in retirement in Heidelberg, gradually recovering his health. As a captain in the reserves, he vol-

unteered for war service and administered the Heidelberg
military hospitals in the first years of the war. In 1919 he
took over Brentano's chair at the University of Munich.
Noted among his colleagues, esteemed by many individuals
as the man who had awakened them, he was scarcely known
to the general public when he died unexpectedly in June,
1920, of pneumonia, at the age of fifty-six.

What he really was is not so self-evident. His academic title and the volumes of his works show that he was a
scientist. But he was not exclusively or ultimately a scientist; he spoke disparagingly of his activity as a lecturer,
although he exerted great power over his audience; despite
all the vigor and productivity of his scientific endeavor, he
seemed in some way not to find it important.

All his life he followed political events with passion,
took political positions, and spoke his mind; for brief
periods, toward the end of the war and afterward, during
the revolution that marked the collapse of Germany, he
spoke in public, and what he said was always strikingly to
the point. But if this should lead us to suppose that he was
really a statesman, prevented by fate and circumstances
from coming into his own, we should have to think of him
as of a Raphael without arms, a potential great man.

Neither his political activity nor his scientific achievements—impressive as they are—explain why he occupies so
unique a position in the hearts of many Germans: Max
Weber stood supremely for the meaning of failure in our
time. He assimilated the whole range of German culture
and lived in a German state at a time when both were
already disintegrating; this he did, not in passive acceptance, but in lucid awareness of what was happening. And
his awareness was not that of a skeptic, who observes the
course of events with unruffled equanimity; in spite of all
he knew, he confronted the present, particular reality with

faith, and fought for his faith even in hopeless situations. He was a man who actively fulfilled himself in a time of decline. Because, with exemplary clarity in word and action, he accepted this role—which he had not chosen—as his destiny, he was a *philosopher*. To be a philosopher is not at all times the same thing, but something original and new for every period. But all philosophers have one thing in common: they are what they know; every philosopher is the lucidity of an unconditional being. The being of other men, confused and unable to understand itself, can come to itself through him. This concrete philosophy is fully developed in Max Weber's work and only in his work; its medium is political judgment and scientific investigation. Similarly his life may be characterized as a philosophical response to the concrete situations that confronted him.

If Max Weber was a politician, a scientist, and a philosopher, he was not the one *and* the other; rather, he was a whole man, who derived a vast vision of the world from the depth of his own being, which, indivisibly one, represents what a man as a man can be: a seeker after truth. Both in his political thinking and in his scientific investigation he was above all a philosopher.

The Politician

Max Weber did not become a ruling statesman; he remained a political writer. But although he did not act, he lived in constant readiness. His thinking was the reality of a man who was political in every fiber of his being; it reflected his will to influence current political developments.

But there is a profound gulf between political truth

and political action. Often in history, insight has been
powerless in its time and taken up as a legacy only by later
generations. A glance at Max Weber's attitude toward the
situations and events of his lifetime suggests the questions:
why had he no influence? what might have happened if
he had been allowed political leadership? what is the enduring import of his political thinking?

THE STRUGGLE AGAINST THE SYSTEM
Even in his youth, during the dazzling Bismarck period,
the events of which became known to Max Weber through
contact with the National-Liberal and Liberal politicians
who frequented the home of his parents in Berlin, he was
vaguely uneasy about the situation. He admired Bismarck
but saw with dismay "the terrible destruction of independent opinion that Bismarck has brought about in our country." He deplored "the treacherous gift of Bismarckian
Caesarism, universal suffrage," which, as he saw, does not
mean equal rights for all in the true sense of the words.
He condemned what was then current in every section of
society, "the worship of ruthlessness militaristic and otherwise, the culture of so-called realism, and a philistine contempt for all those who hope to attain their ends without
appeal to the evil qualities of men, in particular, brutal-
ity." He disapproved both of the *Kulturkampf* and the
way in which it was called off. To his mind the inglorious
peace was an admission of injustice. To say that Bismarck
carried on the *Kulturkampf* on purely political grounds,
not as a matter of conscience but only of expedience, is to
admit that violence was done to the conscience of the
Catholic people; it could not be considered as a struggle
of conscience against conscience. "In that case we acted
without conscience and we are morally the losers, and that

is the bitterest part of the defeat." The rise of ethical
indifference and hypocrisy in the age of Bismarck led the
young man to take a dark view of the future.

When he came of age, Max Weber voted Conservative
and joined the Pan-German League (*Alldeutscher Ver-
band*): to his mind, everything hinged on the life and
power of the German nation. When he saw that the League
put the big landowners' interest in cheap Polish labor before the national interest in a stable German peasantry,
he resigned. When after the dismissal of Bismarck the
Kaiser reduced Germany to impotence in world affairs by
his political dilettantism and catastrophe threatened, but
the Conservative Party, to safeguard the power of the
classes represented in its membership, defended the system,
which alone made the Kaiser's dangerous activities possible, Max Weber became the bitter enemy of the party,
which in his opinion was imperiling the future of the nation.

At an early date Max Weber became aware that German policies were leading to disaster. His alarm took on
definite form: "The politics of Europe is no longer made
in Berlin." "It is only by a miracle that we are not yet
confronted by a really serious diplomatic situation" (1892).
From then to the outbreak of the First World War, Max
Weber's political thought and activity revolve around this
one point. From time to time in a concrete situation (in
1906 and 1908, for example) he tried—if only in personal
letters—to open the eyes of political figures with whom he
was personally acquainted. All informed persons seemed to
be of one mind concerning the person of the Kaiser, and
even the top-ranking military leaders knew that wherever
he interfered, disaster ensued. Many were also aware that,
as Max Weber said, the person of the monarch was not the

determining factor. Every hereditary monarch is a political dilettante unless he happens to have the political genius of Frederick the Great. The determining factor is the system. It was widely known that the German form of government was a pseudo-constitutionalism. But Max Weber attacked this mode of government not on the basis of natural right or on doctrinaire grounds of political freedom as such, but on grounds of national interest and national honor. For he regarded the system as responsible for the lack of ability in the leading political figures. True, the great Bismarck, who had perfected the system as an instrument of his power, was himself a product of it. Bismarck himself, however, tolerated no men of character, but only flunkies about him—and the system offered no resistance to this tendency of his. Over a period of decades, he had managed affairs in such a way that after his dismissal there was no one to take his place. In Max Weber's opinion, the only remedy was an authentic constitutional monarchy, in which true statesmen could take the helm; only then, he was convinced, could the nation safely engage in global politics and evade catastrophe.

But if the system were modified, would this in itself produce statesmen from among the people? This became a crucial question for Max Weber.

As early as 1895, in his inaugural lecture, he treated the question of *where* political leaders might be expected to come from. He inquired into the political maturity of the different *classes*, that is, their ability to set the enduring economic and political interests of the nation above all other considerations. It was first and foremost by this political criterion that he judged the classes. But nowhere did he find such maturity:

The Junkers, who have led Germany up until now,

Weber reasoned, can no longer be expected to carry out the country's mission in world affairs. It is dangerous and in the long run incompatible with the interests of the nation that an economically declining class should preserve political leadership. True, the strong political instincts of the Junkers were formerly one of the greatest assets of the state and its power politics, but today they are engaged in an economic death struggle and no economic policy on the part of the state can restore them to their former social function. Moreover, the problems of the twentieth century are not of the kind that they might solve. For a quarter of a century the last and greatest of the Junkers headed the German state, and it was precisely under his government that the work of his hands, the nation to which he gave unity, underwent an irresistible change in economic structure. In the last analysis, this is what brought about the partial failure of Bismarck's life work: it should have led not only to the outward, but also to the inner unification of Germany, and in this he failed.

As for the other classes, to whom the shift in economic power brought political domination, Max Weber found them, at that time, still less politically mature. He spoke with exasperation of the apolitical spirit that Bismarck's creation had engendered in the German bourgeoisie, a class drunk with success and thirsting for peace. He lamented the silent abdication of the politically-minded upper bourgeoisie of the mid-nineteenth century, which, because few of its leading figures had taken an open political stand, had remained without influence. Now the bourgeoisie had changed in character: This glutted class believed that after many centuries of achievement German history was at an end and imagined that, in view of the triumphs registered by the German nation, sheer modesty

forbade world history from returning to its normal order
of the day. Max Weber fluctuated between indignation
over the cowardice of the bourgeoisie, which either yearned
for a new Caesar or relapsed into philistinism, and his
fury at Bismarck, who was partly to blame for this development. "One is almost inclined to think that the overpowering sun which occupied the zenith in Germany,
causing the German name to shine upon the most remote
corners of the earth, was too strong for us and so consumed
the slowly developing political judgment of the bourgeoisie."

After noting the inadequacy of the Junkers and the
bourgeoisie, Weber went on to ask whether the *working
class* was capable of producing leaders. But at that time
(1895) the German workers struck Weber as flabby and
immature. He found "no spark of the Catilinarian vigor"
that had animated the men of the French Revolution.
They were lacking in the great instincts of power.

In view of this situation Weber wrote: "We must realize that the unification of Germany was a youthful prank
which the nation performed in its old age and in view of
its costliness had better left undone, if it was to be the
conclusion and not the starting point of a German policy
of world power." Consequently, the purpose of social-
political endeavor was not material well-being, but, in prep-
aration for the harsh struggles of the future, the *social
unification* of the nation, which had been shattered by the
economic development of modern times. If it were possible
to create a labor aristocracy that would represent a political
idea, "then alone might the spear, for which the arm of the
bourgeoisie does not yet seem to be strong enough, be en-
trusted to those broader shoulders." The essential task was
to develop a sense of national policy in the leaders of the

working class; for to Max Weber's mind, the "illusion of independent social-political ideals" had been dispelled by the great questions of world power politics.

In this doubly deplorable situation—the absence of classes capable of providing the state with leaders, and the failure of a system which had proved incapable of raising to leadership those statesmen who might have made their appearance among the people—Max Weber was obsessed by the danger that Germany would fall a victim to its foreign policy. During the period of national good fortune, few men seem to have seen the impending evil as clearly as he did. Hoping to avert this danger at the last moment, he decided in favor of a *parliamentarianism* which, beginning in 1917, he envisaged as the only possible *means of selecting* political leaders. From then on, he urged immediate domestic reforms. It was imperative, he held, to take the right action at once, in domestic as well as foreign affairs. Max Weber advocated a democracy, in which the people would choose a leader whom they would trust and support. Such a leader would rule with authority but would be personally responsible to the people, prepared to pay for his mistakes with his life if need be. For Max Weber the form of government was purely a technical, not an ideological, question: he was concerned solely with the effective power of the nation, which could be secured only by the superior intelligence of its statesmen. He had no doubt that only a government supported by the people could raise the powers of the nation to their highest pitch. The primary concern of his political thinking was how to create an active harmony between democracy—which was inevitable in any case—and the authoritative leadership of truly able and responsible statesmen. During the war and the ensuing collapse he wrote the great political essays in which he

developed his ideas in detail. Although they were intended
for the moment, these essays embody a doctrine that will
remain permanently valid.

More than twenty years elapsed between Max Weber's
first intuitions and the Great War, which broke out at a
time when Germany was isolated by her own political
blunders and put an end for the present to her position as a
world power. Throughout these years, situations arose in
domestic politics, which impelled Max Weber, despite his
illness and his academic position, to speak out; he kept
thinking that a change might still be possible. In 1906, for
example, when the Reichstag was dissolved because the
Catholic Center Party and the Social Democrats had rejected
the Kaiser's colonial budget, he attempted to make it clear
to the Liberals that their campaign platform must not be
a vote of confidence for the Kaiser; it must be directed,
rather, against the Center Party, not merely because it had
rejected the Emperor's budget, but because this party
stood, not for the real power of the parliament against the
government, but only for patronage. He stressed the need
for a strong parliament, that would bring real leaders to
the fore and put an end to the extravagances of a politically
incompetent monarch. "The measure of contempt which is
shown us as a nation—and rightly so, that is what counts—
by foreign countries, because we put up with the regime of
this man, has today become for us a power factor of primary world importance. . . . We are becoming isolated."

MAX WEBER AND THE GERMAN COLLAPSE

For two decades Max Weber's political thinking pursued
one and the same course. His ideas were extremely simple,
but extremely difficult to carry out. He saw the fundamental cause of Germany's decline, but was powerless to

change it. No government called on him, nor would the masses have followed him if he had become a political leader.

When the war broke out in 1914, Max Weber was passionately involved. What he had been predicting for twenty years had now come to pass. But he had always thought it possible to avert the catastrophe, and continued to do so. The military victories in a situation which all non-Germans regarded as hopeless for Germany reinforced his hope, but did not cloud his vision. Even in the moment of Germany's greatest military superiority, he still believed in the possibility of a peace without European annexations. In this situation mere insistence on Germany's legitimate rights would amount to the greatest of victories and vastly increase German prestige throughout the world. He condemned the policy of greed, in favor of practically possible, attainable demands; he condemned the "policy of aplomb," in favor of a reasonable diplomacy carried on in an effective tenor; he condemned the demagogical agitation for intensified submarine warfare, saying that such decisions were entirely up to the country's military and political leaders; he condemned the fulsome promises of the war bulletins and demanded cool, honest reports on the situation. In every case his battle was directed against the political stupidity that caused us to lose what might have been attained.

Weber's pessimism never reflected a lack of courage— only those who are afraid demand spurious enthusiasm of themselves and others—but a sincere effort to consider everything that might favorably influence the course of events. His overpowering faith in Germany becomes fully apparent only with the collapse, though his ideas at the time were not clearly defined.

As soon as unrestricted submarine warfare was proclaimed and America's entry into the war became a certainty, Max Weber saw the turning point: "I suffer less now than throughout the twenty-five years during which I saw the hysterical vanity of this monarch ruining everything I held dear and sacred. Now the consequences of human stupidity have become a reality. And realities can be dealt with."

When years of hypocritically trumped up enthusiasm were followed by the collapse and large sections of the people merely flung themselves from one illusion into another; when, "by a swing of the pendulum, this revolution followed Ludendorff's insane gamble," he knew that a new order resulting from this terrible defeat and disgrace would not readily take root. He spoke of the revolution as of a kind of narcotic and expressed his horror "of all these empty phrases, vague hopes, and amateurish schemes for a happier future"; he assailed the political masochism of a pacifism without dignity, wallowing voluptuously in sentiments of guilt, "as though *success* in war were a divine judgment, as though it intrinsically proved anything, and as though the Lord of hosts were not with the larger battalions (not *always*, as *we* have shown)." In 1919 it seemed to him that everything that had constituted the greatness of the nation had crumbled; it was his cruel fate, he thought, to witness the moral abjectness of this people: the nation had bowed to the Kaiser, a dilettante without dignity; now it mistook the bloody carnival of the collapse for a revolution and was proud of it to boot. And now these men were scurrying to Versailles, eager to be present, whereas every German should do his best to keep away from these negotiations and disgraceful scenes. The simple dignity that had been ours seemed lost; and even among those who had been respon-

sible for the political and military blunders, the consequences of which the people had endured with unparalleled courage for four years, there were some who had the
audacity to accuse this crushed people of having made
victory impossible by their cowardice or treacherous stab
in the back. This was Max Weber's reaction on his return
from Versailles, where the government had sent him first
to draft an opinion as to whether or not the Allies' terms
should be accepted, and later to collaborate on a note
about the question of war guilt. Though at times he had
abandoned all hope either in the upper or the lower classes
of the nation, he realized that the starvation and deceptions
to which the German people had been subjected for four
years were beyond human endurance, and that under such
circumstances it was inhuman to accuse.

From the standpoint of those who believed in a social-
ist future, Max Weber was without faith; he saw the future
of Germany in the *German people*: Since the onset of the
war his love for his people had grown as he saw the simple,
unassuming bravery of those going off to battle, and the
decency which those returning preserved in spite of the
terrible experience they had been through, and again as
he witnessed the simple directness of the trade unionists
and soldiers whom he met in the Heidelberg Workers'
and Soldiers' Council. The Germans, he was convinced,
were a disciplined people; their weaknesses were known,
but also their competence and their sensitiveness to the
beauty of everyday life, in contrast to other peoples, who
looked for beauty in emotional transports or gestures. One
hundred and ten years ago, Germans showed the world
that they—and they alone—were able, in spite of foreign
rule, to become a great civilized nation. Let us do it again
now. "I believe," he wrote, "that this Germany is inde-

structible, and I have never felt the fact of being a German to be a gift of fortune so much as in these dark hours of Germany's shame." Looking back over the years, he said: Germany is the only nation to which history twice, after the total collapse of 1648 and 1806, granted a renewal. It will have a third renewal after the icy night through which it is now condemned to pass.

Max Weber's nationalism, however, never was a blind acceptance of the German people as it is, but an appeal, directed as much at himself as at the people, to become all that it potentially was. In its integrity and soberness it stood in sharp contrast to the then current German nationalism, with its pompousness, its willful blindness to truth, its false security and stupid arrogance, its wallowing in emotions, its readiness to risk death when military obedience demanded it, coupled with an utter lack of individual moral courage. The "German ideas of 1914" he regarded as a "product of the literati."

In his judgment of the Germans, Max Weber's nationalist feelings could reach the height of exasperation. He speaks of the type of glutted German who cannot bear not to be on the side of the winning cause, who boasts and brags of his realistic politics. Max Weber abhorred the crude philistines of realistic politics. During the war he happened to watch a body of soldiers in a railway station, and he comments: "They amount to something only in uniform, then they look less nondescript and are in their element." And earlier: "The Hohenzollern dynasty knows only the sergeant's concepts of power: Command, obey, stand at attention, boast and brag" (1908). In 1906 he wrote to Harnack: "Much as Luther towers above all others . . . Lutherism, in its historical manifestations, is for me, I can't deny it, the horror of horrors." And, "That

our nation was never in any form schooled by rigorous asceticism is the root cause of all that I find despicable in it
(as well as in myself)."

But against generalized criticism of all things German,
against the wholesale harsh and irresponsible rejection of
the entire nation, Weber raised at all times his "and yet."

The war was lost, and the Germans consequently
found themselves in an utterly new political situation. Max
Weber's way of political thinking demanded that politics
should be informed by an absolute supreme principle.
Without such a principle, no spirit of sacrifice, no exalted
passion, no enlightened action is possible. This supreme
principle is not a matter of dogma but one of substance.
Up to the defeat, it had been provided by the absolute
sovereignty of the nation. Could this still be the case? In
speaking, shortly before his death in 1920, of the irrevoca-
ble loss of Germany's status as a great power and of America
as a rising global power, with Russia as sole competitor, he
gave at least a hint of his thinking.

Today the main principle of political life is no longer
the sovereign nation, but the unity and solidarity of the
free Western nations as repositories of a common Occiden-
tal tradition. From 1919 on, the only meaningful policy
for Germany, the only policy conducive to national sur-
vival, would have been to collaborate unconditionally in
the struggle to preserve Western political freedom. In
insanely forsaking this path, the Germans brought catastrophe upon themselves and the world.

SOUND POLITICAL JUDGMENT IN CONCRETE SITUATIONS
The first prerequisite for political action is a clear vision
of what is to be done in the present moment. If we look at
actuality from a distance and are not really in it, we reflect

endlessly on the reasons for this and that and lose ourselves amid the innumerable possibilities; the simple essential is submerged by secondary considerations. Like the
sure touch required in a physical situation, thinking in a
political situation is the power to grasp the simple thing
that can and must be done. A simple solution is indeed a
result of complex thinking; but this result is something that
everyone can understand and take as a basis for action,
because, when it is put before the people, it seems to answer
their expectations. It was Max Weber's destiny to know this
simple solution on frequent occasions at the right time,
at the very first moment, to state it, but not to be heard
until too late, when everyone understood it, sometimes very
quickly. A few examples: at the end of 1915 Germany had
won its greatest military victories and England had not yet
introduced universal conscription. This—as we know today
—was the only moment in which Germany might have made
peace, but only if she agreed not to annex a single square
foot of territory. In letters and in conversations with those
he met—for at that time public discussion of war aims was
still forbidden—Max Weber tried to gain support for his
opinion. But the rulers of Germany wanted results from
the war and called the peace suggested by Weber a "peace
of renunciation." Shortly thereafter this opportunity was
lost forever.

Between 1916 when the *Lusitania* was sunk and the
beginning of 1917 when the Germans launched the unrestricted submarine warfare which was to align America
with the enemies of Germany, Max Weber repeatedly fore-
told the consequences of America's entry into the war in
letters and memoranda. His demand that a decision in
the U-boat question be based on a precise analysis of the
situation, drawn up under personal responsibility, was

stated so clearly that any intelligent listener should have understood.

After the German offer of an armistice, when it became known that the Entente's condition for acceptance was complete German disarmament, Max Weber wrote (*Frankfurter Zeitung*, October, 1918) at a time when people were talking of a thousand other things: "If President Wilson were to permit the disarming of Germany, he would beyond a doubt be excluding himself from the ranks of those who will determine the peace conditions. His position as world arbiter is based solely on the fact that German military power is at least so great that it cannot be reduced to submission without the help of American troops. If this situation were modified, the intransigent elements in the other enemy camps would be in a position to push the President aside with polite thanks for the help he has thus far provided. His role would be at an end." The newspapers reported that this article had made a great impression in North America. And yet, though it was a very simple matter and easy to understand, in this case it was America in Wilson's person that did not act according to Weber's analysis. The result was that Wilson actually was thrust aside at Versailles and that the weight of American military power was not thrown into the balance.

Immediately after the offer of an armistice, on October 11, 1918, Max Weber wrote letters to all the high-placed persons accessible to him, stating his opinion that the Kaiser must abdicate. "If he goes now, without pressure from outside, he will go in honor . . . the position of the dynasty will be safeguarded. I frankly confess that I have observed his way of governing with strong distaste. But in the interest of the Empire, I cannot wish an Emperor to end *in dishonor*. . . ." As a monarchist Weber wanted the Kaiser to abdicate, because otherwise the dynasty, "which we wish nevertheless to preserve," would be discredited. If the Emperor should again fail in his duty by staying on, only to leave later on under compulsion, it would have repercussions on whole generations. Weber suggested how this must be made clear to the Kaiser. No confession of guilt was required, but the simple statement: Fate was against me; I abdicate, because I wish to make things easier for the German nation. The reaction to Weber's effort was half-hearted. "Thus far," he complained, "everyone has agreed with me, but no one has the courage to act accordingly." After that events moved quickly. The enemy demanded the abdication of the Kaiser, and he fled across the border to Holland.

When it became known that the enemy was going to insist on the surrender of our military leaders, Weber expressed the opinion that they should anticipate this demand and voluntarily offer to go on trial before a regular international court. Such an act of heroism, he said, would be a moral inspiration to the German nation; and moreover, it would greatly embarrass the enemy. He wrote to Ludendorff; the letter led to a personal interview with negative results.

LACK OF POLITICAL INFLUENCE

Max Weber's memoranda, articles, and letters contain advice, insights, arguments; but they were not acts. It may be asked whether his political clairvoyance, which was almost always corroborated by subsequent events, *really* reflected political ability.

His friends, it is true, believed, when he spoke to them, that this man was the leader the country needed. During the war and more and more fervently during the revolution, they repeatedly expressed the desire that he should do everything in his power to seize the helm.

He seemed ready. But he was ready only in case he were *called*. He did not reach out for power. He did not have the innate will to power of the political man, who wishes to rule because that is his life. Only in Germany's hardest moments did his readiness become a positive will. But even then he waited. Called informally to Berlin by friends, he did not go: "I will come to Berlin only if something is wanted of me, not merely to sit around and discuss."

Sometimes it seemed as if an unconscious instinct led him to arrange things in such a way that leadership would pass him by. But in 1919, for example, he was really willing to be elected to the National Assembly and suffered keenly when officials of the Democratic Party prevented his election. Once in 1917, it is true, when a friend asked him why he did nothing to encourage the government to make political use of him, he stated clearly that this was not his wish: In politics, he said, a man must be alert and sure of himself at every hour of the day and night; I cannot rely on myself; I make mistakes.

There is an additional factor, which may have been crucial: striking as was his insight into the simple necessity of the moment, his political attitude had one weakness. He failed to reckon with one thing: the blind passion and dullness of the masses—whether of the educated, the army officers, or the politicians—which in all acute crises hold actual power in a democracy where every action must be appraised with a view to the next elections and the present reactions of public opinion. Max Weber saw all this clearly. But he saw it as he saw scientific truths. Precisely in this respect he remained aloof from what he recognized to be right. In his sovereign insight, he lacked the naïveté, the

instinctive shrewdness, the unscrupulousness of the politician, but also the effectiveness of the popular leader who,
firmly rooted in the real forces of life, not only sees them
but inwardly identifies himself with them.

This alone can account for his proposal, fitting if
one were living in a heroic world, that the German leaders
should voluntarily give themselves up; he forgot for a moment that such things are hardly possible in the world as
it is. It also explains how from the start he could speak
publicly with contempt of the revolution; the consequence
was that when Max Weber was proposed for a position of
official leadership, the government of the time rejected him;
neither the republican nor the former monarchical government had any use for him. He himself understood all this.
In his article on "Politics as a Vocation," he described those
statesmanlike qualities which he possessed: passion, sense
of responsibility, sense of proportion; but he also recognized
that outward honesty is not compatible with political action; he saw that there is a political ethics, which follows
from the statesman's responsibility for the actual consequences of his action in the world as it is. A passion for
truth, a hatred of pettiness and low cunning, always stood
in his way. A clear thinker, he knew what had to be done,
but his ethical sentiment made him unwilling to lie, to
dissemble, to cultivate the illusions, the veils over reality,
that the masses require. He was right in a sense that goes
much deeper than any mere nervous weakness when he
said: I make mistakes.

THE LOST OPPORTUNITY
Nevertheless quite a few of us wondered: what would have
happened if Max Weber had assumed leadership in Germany? A frequent answer was: it would have been dis-

astrous; he was too self-willed, to work with him one had
to obey him; he lacked flexibility, he could not adapt himself to new situations; he was without social grace, his
certainty of being right was crushing; at one time or another he always said too much. But in this form, all these
judgments are false.

Such a view of Max Weber's personal qualities was possible only in those who disliked him, because they did not
dare to stand up to him with their own conscience as rational beings. If they had done so, they would have learned
how the passion of Max Weber's temperament could be
both inflamed and subdued in communication—the communication in which men of integrity meet, understand
one another, trust one another, and arrive at an agreement.

Would his political activity have been disastrous?
With Max Weber in the leadership a forthright policy
would have been possible. The German people would have
been faced with the alternatives: either to rise to the truth,
to stop deluding themselves about what was necessary and
dare to act accordingly—or else, if they insisted on closing
their eyes to reality, to destroy Max Weber himself. That
is what would have happened before the war, when, if Max
Weber had had his way, the bourgeoisie and the workers
would have combated the "system" in behalf of authentic
political leadership and imposed limitations on the monarchy for the sake of a strong parliament. If such a movement had materialized, he might soon have found himself
in jail. Max Weber's illness excluded this possibility. During the war, he would have told the people the truth and
asked them to content themselves with what was obtainable. It is possible that if Max Weber had attempted to lead
in earnest, he would quickly have been thrust aside.

But it was the period of revolution that showed Max

Weber's true mettle. These were events without aftermath, hence without historical significance, but for those who were involved in them at the time, they possessed, even in their minor details, a power of symbolic revelation. Let me give two examples:

At a mass meeting attended chiefly by workers in the days of the Workers' and Soldiers' Councils, Max Weber outlined the illusions in which the socialists were indulging, explained what was possible and what was not, presented the true facts, and mercilessly destroyed the fantastic delusions of the proletariat, which believed that it had actually acceded to power. Max Weber was no more willing to flatter the *demos* than he had been willing to flatter the monarchy. His delivery was calm, to the point, powerful, and he himself so buoyed up by the spirit which had taken hold of him that after stormy interruptions the entire audience finally succumbed to the true "demagogy" of a sincere man; for a moment it seemed as if he would succeed in carrying these people along with him. That was too good to be true. It was only a moment; for in the long run the masses are guided by cruder motives than by what once in a long while, for a vanishing moment, flashes into their understanding.

When Germany was faced with the peace terms that were accepted in Versailles, Max Weber explained the situation in a mass meeting of students. Germany was no longer a world power. The German people were expected to swallow every humiliation, including an admission of war guilt. In a position of weakness, nothing could be done. Only honor could be saved, and from the seed of heroic defeat there would perhaps arise a new future which that generation would not live to see. Max Weber interrupted his exposition of the facts to declare: If we reject the enemy's terms and they occupy the country, you know what to do; we know from the methods of the Russian Revolution of 1905 what even weakness can accomplish. In that event we must abandon all hope; prison and court-martial will be our fate. And he went on: But as long as Germany is down, let us act accordingly; let us cease to display the insignia of pride beseeming a proud people at a time when they have become a mere front and self-deception; no more colors; anyone who wears *couleurs* * when Germany is down in defeat is a dog.—No one replied; there was a silence as if no one had understood. The following day members of the student corporations marched back and forth outside Max Weber's house, wearing their *couleurs* in protest. As senior member of a corporation, Weber sent back his ribbon.

Again Max Weber was without a following. It was as though he did not exist. He did not even try to influence the course of events. Never again did he refer to his readiness to lead a campaign of sabotage against the enemy and to face certain death.

Where the practical work of experts was required, as in framing the new Constitution, he played a part. He was responsible for the strong position of the Reichs-President, provided for in the Constitution. This was probably his only action of outstanding historical importance. Through it, he introduced into the Constitution a principle that might have provided a foundation for a new democratic authority and genuine leadership in Germany.

But the drafting of a constitution is not political action, though it makes political action possible. Here Max Weber's profound insight found full expression. But politi-

---

* *"Couleur"* refers to the uniforms of German student organizations.

cal action itself was at an end for him, even before he had
really attempted it. As he had done so often, he went back
to his scholarly tasks and in 1920 resigned from the Democratic Party; on the question of socialization, this party
had made compromises with Marxism, which struck Weber
as inadmissible: "A practical politician must make compromises, but a scholar is not justified in covering them."
At the time of his death in 1920, he had definitively abandoned politics and was devoting himself wholly to his scientific work.

THE ENDURING IMPORT OF MAX WEBER'S POLITICAL THINKING
In retrospect, Max Weber seems to have represented the
genius of the German people; as such he saw, suffered, and
advised, but was powerless and did not govern, a task left
to the incompetent. The disregarded insights of those days
have today become self-evident truths. There are many
who, in reading his works today, are tempted to claim him
for their own partisan aims or, because he followed no
party line, accuse him of political inconsistency. Democrats, nationalists, socialists all seem to find weapons in his
writings. But each one should ask whether, in his own
political thought and action, he is faithful to Max Weber's
true demands, which endure independently of parties,
changing situations, and special political interests.

For Weber, political life centered round the fact of
power (*Machtpragma*). Politics is struggle; struggle demands a leader who cannot, like the official whose honor
consists in conscientious execution of what higher authority
and the law demand, delegate responsibility to someone
else. A political leader must himself bear the responsibility.
But since he acts in the world and since power is his specific instrument, he cannot act according to an absolute

moral law without considering the consequences, trusting to God for success. Such procedure would reflect an ethical attitude, but it would be irresponsible. Since his field of action is the world, he must take the existing powers into consideration and act accordingly. Anyone who engages in politics "must deal with the diabolical forces that are present in every exercise of power." Even if one's goal is the establishment of justice on earth, the *apparatus of a human following* is needed. Such an apparatus cannot function unless it appeals to the passions of hatred and revenge, to "resentment and the need for pseudoethical justification"; it cannot function without "adventure, victory, power, and benefices." "The party leader depends for success entirely on this apparatus. Consequently he is dependent on its— not his own—motives. . . . Consequently, what he actually achieves under such conditions is not up to him, it is imposed on him by the base but ethically predominant motives that determine the action of his followers." What makes a true politician is "trained ruthlessness in appraising the realities of life, the power to endure them, and inwardly to face up to them." He does not hold the stupidity and meanness of the world—which he knows and accepts in advance—responsible, but himself. He has the "firmness of heart, which can persevere even when all his hopes are shattered," and in every situation he is able to carry on.

Others, however, must learn to understand the necessity that determines the statesman's actions. Weber makes clear the essential distinction between a civil servant and a statesman: from the one, administration without bias, passion, or prejudice is required, from the other, struggle; from the one, self-effacing obedience, from the other, accountability only to himself. "Civil servants with high ethical standards are particularly poor statesmen, irresponsible in the political sense of the term, and therefore ethically inferior." Germany was governed by civil servants, that was the drawback of the system. That is why Weber expressed indignation over "the utterly petit-bourgeois hostility of all parties to leadership," and still more so over the false leaders, the heroes of the podium with their declamations, "the vain and narrow-minded upstarts of the moment," who serve no cause and are interested only in the effect they are producing.

For he demands something more than understanding of the power-*pragma;* the statesman's will to power must have some substantial content. "The most impressive political triumphs are tainted with mortal futility" where there is no *faith*. In political life, according to Max Weber, faith implies a determination to attain practical day-to-day aims, but without losing sight of the human beings involved, not of their material welfare only, but also of their human dignity. Such faith can be effective only if the human will to power accepts self-imposed restrictions.

Thus it would be an easy evasion to interpret the political sense as an enthusiasm for undefined power as such and as an irrational glorification of the nation as a mere fact. Both lasting political success and the human excellence that develop in a successful state require integrity on the part of the statesman. At all times Weber condemned the purveyors of illusions: those who made false promises and fomented artificial passion during the war and the revolution, who veiled the facts, and nourished a spurious faith that is mere wishful thinking. He condemned the misuse of national sentiment to promote class interests, to perpetuate political stupidity, and to rationalize the motives of political partisanship; he condemned those who "degraded the name of the fatherland to the level of a demagogic party trade-mark"; and he condemned the shamelessness of those who in their political arguments say the opposite today of what they said yesterday. And for the same reason he ultimately condemned self-righteousness in favor of simple legality. When Count Arco was pardoned after murdering Eisner, Max Weber said to the students: "You applauded Count Arco because, and with this I agree, his behavior in court was chivalrous and in every sense manly. His act was prompted by the conviction that Kurt Eisner brought disgrace after disgrace upon Germany. I share that opinion. Nevertheless it is a dangerous weakness to pardon him as long as the law is on the statute books, and if I had been minister, I would have had him shot . . . political murder will become epidemic."

An eye for the reality of power, a faith that is willing to bear responsibility, integrity—these are prerequisites for political thinking, but they all require *professional competence:* Though essentially different from the public official, the statesman, the true leader, is to the mere demagogue as a trained official, specialized in his department, is to the dilettante. The statesman's knowledge is not specialized in the pejorative sense, but in addition to his native gift he must develop detachment, the "faculty of contemplating realities with serenity and composure." Vanity, the mortal enemy of devotion to actual work, is the source of all irresponsibility and incompetence, because of the tendency it creates to put oneself in the limelight as much as possible. Political competence can be acquired only in constant struggle against vanity—a trait common to all men and less detrimental in every other domain. Emotional politics, the politics of hatred, prevents the statesman from taking an objective view of himself and ruins everything he does, even to the tone of his speeches, which lose their

political effect. Over the years, Weber, in conformity with
this view, was infuriated by all the fuss and bother about
the colonies, by the tone taken in speeches and notes during
the war, by all the overbearing talk about power, by saber-
rattling, confessions of guilt, and professions of self-righteousness. Only a statesman disciplined in this respect can
master with professional competence the infinitely diversified concrete knowledge which is demanded of him.

Weber demanded and embodied an authentic faith,
without illusions, in his own people and an ability to tell
the truth even if it is unpalatable, provided it is politically
relevant. Such an ability has nothing in common with a
demagogic flaunting of truthfulness which, in self-contra-
diction, flatters the crowd, tramples the weak, indulges in
defying and insulting people, or in the venting of hatred.
Max Weber believed in German political thinking, not in
nationalistic ranting. Amid all the political tensions of
his career, his ultimate criterion of success remained unchanged: the physical and moral elevation of the German
people. "In order to re-establish Germany in its old glory
I would assuredly ally myself with any power on earth and
with the devil himself, but not with the power of stupidity."

The mysterious dividing line, where the conscious
ethic of responsibility seems to call ethical belief into question, though ultimately the former can exist only through
the latter, discloses antinomies, or ethical paradoxes. In
elucidating these paradoxes Weber was very hard on those
who naïvely suppose that mere theoretical justice can show
them the one correct answer.

But what is the ultimate goal? He gives us no clearly
defined answer. Human dignity and Germany's position in
world affairs were what he was concerned with, not one
without the other. To him this meant that future genera-

tions would consider us as their ancestors, not necessarily
in the sense of race and lineage, but as we think of the
Greeks, thanks to whom we are what we are.

MAX WEBER'S GENERAL POLITICAL APPROACH

In the following, I shall present Max Weber's general political approach, which remained unchanged—and is valid
even today—although after Germany's defeat in 1918 his
concrete proposals for German policy and conduct in international affairs changed radically.

From the first moment, Max Weber's political thinking concerned itself with what was to come. What could
now be the goal? What was within the realm of the possible? As ever, he demanded first and foremost honesty in
facing the new situation. Each individual and the people
are duty-bound to "the self-discipline of truthfulness."

Truthfulness demands recognition of the fact that Germany's role as a global power is irrevocably past. This insight signifies that any effort to change this situation can
result only in an irresponsible gamble (an attitude that
Max Weber discerned even toward the end of the First
World War). For the moment, such an attitude might
create an illusion, but it can lead to nothing but a new,
more severe catastrophe.

Max Weber's response to the defeat of the German
Empire was of the understanding, not of the will. The will
subordinated itself to the understanding. But in considering the conditions of the moment, he trusted in a German
future, provided that it was entered into in a spirit of
truthfulness, without wishful thinking.

The given element was the German nation. The German people lives on. When the state was powerless in 1918–
19, Max Weber restated his allegiance to the people.

Reason in political thinking has as its prerequisite objective knowledge. But what of the spirit by which it is guided? We have the record of a conversation between Max Weber and Schumpeter,[1] which may serve as a symbol for something that could otherwise not be conveyed in such abbreviated form. Both had met in a Vienna coffeehouse, in the presence of Ludo Moritz Hartmann and Somary. Schumpeter remarked how pleased he was with the Russian Revolution. Socialism was now no longer a discussion on paper, but had to prove its viability. Max Weber responded in great agitation: Communism, at this stage in Russian development, was virtually a crime, the road would lead over unparalleled human misery and end in a terrible catastrophe. "Quite likely," Schumpeter answered, "but what a fine laboratory." "A laboratory filled with mounds of corpses," Weber answered heatedly. "The same can be said of every dissecting room," Schumpeter replied. Every attempt to divert them failed. Weber became increasingly violent and loud, Schumpeter increasingly sarcastic and muted. The other guests listened with curiosity, until Weber jumped up, shouting, "I can't stand any more of this," and rushed out, followed by Hartmann, who brought him his hat. Schumpeter, left behind, said with a smile: "How can a man shout like that in a coffeehouse?" Here, the question arises: In what spirit does one pursue value-free, scientific objectivity? This question cannot be decided by any scientific knowledge. My heart goes out to Max Weber and his magnificent "tactlessness"—though he himself used to deplore such incidents afterwards—as against heartless intellectualism. Here was a scientist who never for one moment forgot his human responsibilities, who was

---

[1] Josef Alois Schumpeter, 1883–1950, Austrian economist, author of *Kapitalismus, Sozialismus und Demokratie*. The conversation is recorded in Felix Somary, *Erinnerungen*, pp. 171 ff.

never guilty of "scientific indifference," that caricature of
a serenity grounded in transcendence. It has been said of
Max Weber that his exclusion of value judgments and his
objectivism paralyzed spirit, will, and action. The contrary
is true.

Whatever goals are pursued in politics, politics itself,
when it is great and serious, is founded on responsibility.
Max Weber's distinction between the ethics of principle
and the ethics of responsibility, his demand for the ethics
of responsibility in political leadership, does not imply the
endorsement of unprincipled political thinking and action.
The ethics of responsibility includes belief in accountability
for the consequences of one's actions, readiness for any
kind of sacrifice, though not for a sacrifice that would destroy the meaning of politics itself. "It is an infinitely affect-
ing experience when a mature person—no matter whether
old or young in years—senses this responsibility for the consequences really and with his entire being and, acting from
ethical responsibility, says at a given point: 'Here I stand;
I can do no other.' . . . Any one of us who is not inwardly
dead may someday find himself in this position. In this
sense the ethics of principle and the ethics of responsibility
are not absolute opposites but complementary; together
they make the real man."

Max Weber did not accuse the world, or human nature,
or the German people. He despised such accusations, in
which the accusers with their summary, total judgment fall
into self-righteousness and the delusion that, if one had
only listened to them, everything would be right. He set
up the image of the great statesman who has the strength
to stand up for his cause against the opposition of the
world, the strength "to bore through hard boards with passionate patience and a sure eye."

As a politician, Max Weber saw through the politics

of *Gemuetlichkeit* with its undercurrent of anxiety. The self-satisfaction of those who considered themselves cleverer than he was and yet admired him, if with a touch of pity, leads politically to disaster. It fosters a self-perpetuating busybodiness whose routine is not inspired by the substantial politics of high responsibility. It is willfully blind to the real threats which suddenly bring disaster. It paralyzes the readiness to react with the courage of truth. In the course of much talk, truth is touched upon, but in so blunted a fashion that nothing is taken really seriously. Truth is robbed of its sharpness and consequently denatured. The minimizing of all things dissolves human seriousness. Nobility and rank disappear and with them the capacity for salvation.

Nobody was more realistic than Max Weber. But he distinguished between a reality that is inescapable and a reality that is the expression of ideas, opinions, and wills which it is possible to influence and transform. Unrestricted submarine warfare, which would predictably result in America's entry into the war, was not a necessity. Wilson's armistice demand for the complete disarmament of Germany—a demand which undermined Wilson's position of international power and caused the Treaty of Versailles to be concluded without him—was not a necessity. In this as in other cases, Max Weber saw what would happen and spoke out well in advance. But political education implies a willingness to modify one's manner of thinking—and the Germans showed no such willingness.

Max Weber has been termed unrealistic in a decisive point: he demanded too much of human beings and was bound to fail because he asked men for what they could not give. To this we answer: as long as our thoughts and drives are not purified by a great urge for truth, we shall remain in a condition which, in the foreseeable future, must lead humanity to destruction. If Max Weber's demands were excessive, the human situation was to blame, not his lack of realism.

The Marxist argument to the effect that Max Weber was an exponent of the bourgeoisie and that his thinking was therefore necessarily wrong, need only be mentioned in passing, since it takes no account of his actual opinions. Wherever political action was concerned with class issues, Max Weber was conscious of belonging to the bourgeois class of his day. For him, this did not mean unconditional participation, for he did not regard class distinctions as an absolute. The Marxist argument has real and destructive effect in a situation where brutal, actual power is wielded by Marxists; intellectually it has no substance, and to a thinking person it is ludicrous. The answer, in Max Weber's own terms, would be: "You cannot talk with religious fanatics." But in fact he did talk with them. The principle of his being was: people should be able to talk with each other, under any circumstances. Even to clarify differences it is necessary to talk. Those who remain open, who allow their own propositions and actions to be questioned, have a better chance of arriving at the truth. Those who close themselves off create the intellectual climate that leads to violence. As long as it is possible to talk without restraint, the answer to the Marxist objection is an invitation to an exploratory dialogue in which both sides are asked to state their assumptions and to analyze their content.

A revolting accusation, completely contrary to the character of Max Weber's political thinking, is that he paved the way for the Germany of Hitler. His sociological concepts (such as charismatic leadership and domination) and his political motives grounded in the nationalism and imperialism of his day, his realistic insights into the significance of power and violence in politics, have been said to be in the line of Nazism. It has been said that his distinction between the ethics of responsibility and the ethics of principle leads to the abdication of all principle in favor of violence and power.

But to see the devil and to recognize him for what he is, is not to emulate him. Did Max Weber advocate that power and violence be sovereign absolutes? Certainly not. In an essay on the meaning of the exclusion of value judgments, he writes: "In the sphere of value judgments, it might, quite conceivably, be meaningful and defensible to welcome an extremely powerful state as a coercive instrument against opposition, yet deny the state any intrinsic value, regarding it merely as a technical aid by which to realize the very different values which lend the state dignity, but only provided it makes no attempt to cast off its auxiliary status." This sentence, in which Max Weber speaks of a possibility, means that in the real world to exist is to have power and to use it when necessary as a safeguard. The state is a necessity. Max Weber did not love it, indeed he saw it as a puzzling monster. The state as a technical aid, however, lives by the political responsibility of all its members. It runs afoul when statesmanship gives way to self-perpetuating administration in accordance with conventional rules. If power and the technical instruments of violence break loose and become independent entities, the state is destroyed. Without the will to freedom in the people who sustain it, the state perishes.

Max Weber's sociological categories may have misled those who did not resolutely distinguish insight from will. His sociological concept of "charismatic leadership" was

not meant as a value judgment. It is in every case a historical event which is brought about by men. One can
neither justify nor condemn it by placing it in a sociological category. It may be strangely surprising to find, within
the same sociological category, Moses, Pericles, and Caesar
side by side with Knipperdolling and Hitler. Such a judgment, however, does not derive from sociological insight,
but from political will and discernment. When, in 1918,
Max Weber conceived of a democracy with a strong leader,
he saw that there were no leaders. Leaders can develop only
on a political proving ground, which today is provided only
by a genuine democracy. They cannot appear spontane-
ously when the need for them arises. Max Weber might
have said with Nietzsche: "The necessity for such leaders,
the dreadful danger that they may not appear, or that they
may warp or degenerate—these are our real anxieties and
grounds for gloom."

Max Weber did not experience what in the years after
his death became reality nor did he perceive the first signs
of it: the principle of totalitarian domination in the age of
technology, both in Germany and in Russia. Totalitarian
domination is the negative mirror image of what Max
Weber had in mind when he spoke of the difficult path that
leads to the realization of political greatness. Totalitarian
domination means the end of politics as Max Weber conceived it. He lived in the continuum of political freedom
that began with the Greeks.

Would Max Weber, for nationalistic reasons, have
given his allegiance to *any* German state? It would appear
so, if we consider that, according to him, what matters is
not the constitution or the ruling class of the moment, but
whether the political system allows men of supreme political ability to come to the fore, and whether it makes pos-

sible social justice and freedom. He combated the state
under Wilhelm II because it hindered the rise of able
statesmen in free democratic struggle and consequently
exposed the nation to the gravest danger. But this state,
tacitly and without explicit discussion, could still be said
to hold its authority in tenure from the reality of the
nation.

But what would have happened if Max Weber had
encountered a German state which had totally repudiated
its fealty to the nation? What would he have thought of
the Saar Plebiscite in 1933?

To me it seems that Max Weber's proposition—"no
matter which constitution, our first thought should be for
the German state, regardless of what kind; the constitution
follows after"—had lost its validity. This "state" no longer
held anything in tenure from the German nation. Now the
imperative was to free the German nation and redeem its
dignity. The plebiscite was a battle in this struggle for
liberation. It might have provided a mouthpiece for the
entire violated German nation. That is why, at the time,
I thought that Max Weber would have been in political
agreement with the small minority in the Saarland which
refused to be incorporated into an un-German Empire
ruled by a gang of murderers and their criminal and ignorant followers. But these are mere constructions based on
a knowledge of Max Weber's thinking. He did not live
to see the era of National Socialism. It is conceivable that
it might not have come to power if Max Weber, throughout the years to 1933, had been there to raise his voice.
But this is an unlikely supposition. The Germans did not
listen to him. Even today his political thinking finds scant
echo.

How would Max Weber have reacted had he witnessed

National Socialism? His despair of the Germans would certainly have reached unprecedented depths. But what about his political thought and action? A state which did not hold its authority in tenure from the nation was not a state to which, as a German, he could give allegiance. For this state destroyed the nation step by step and prepared its end.

Would Max Weber have despaired of the German nation altogether? Even though her face was incomparably more disfigured in 1933–1945 than it had been in 1918, even though the basest elements from the abyss had taken hold of the state and seized the technological equipment of an able people, even though what was still genuinely German was being killed or reduced to silence, did not something live on that remained German? Would Max Weber have allowed himself to be destroyed as a sacrifice for what is German? I do not believe so. We cannot know. Perhaps he would have remained silent. But of one thing I feel sure: to despair of the Germans altogether, totally and forever, would not have been possible for Max Weber.

When politics, understood as the politics of free people reacting to the course of their destiny, comes to an end, what then? Then the individual, deprived of his political dignity, may still be allowed, within the existential sphere left to him, to realize what is exposed at any moment to ruin from without: the intimacy of private existence in human relationships between individuals, the knowledge of things, inner truthfulness, fortitude amid destruction. Politics is destiny, and continues to be so even when this destiny signifies the end of politics, but politics is not the ultimate end for man as man.

The Scientist

Max Weber gained mastery over enormous fields of knowledge. He commanded the most divergent disciplines and was thoroughly familiar with the methods of natural science no less than of the humanities. Trained in law, he also studied theology; he was at home in the historical reality of past and present, in China and India, in the East and West. But all this would merely show the unusual scope of his mind. What provided his scientific activity with its axis was that *man* was at the center of his preoccupations, not man as an empty abstraction, but man as a concrete reality in historically changing society. Regardless of whether he was investigating the psychophysics of industrial labor or the rational content of theological dogmas, or studying the role of the city in the various civilizations, the object of his questioning was always men, whose development is determined by knowable conditions and whose actions result in something very different from what they had intended. Instead of undertaking the hopeless attempt to gain a truly valid insight into the one purpose underlying all happening, or to discover the law governing all things, or to fathom the totality of being, he worked with the ascertainable purposes conceived by real men, investigating their causes and consequences, which can only be known relatively, in particular contexts. Consequently, his scientific effort seems to be endlessly dispersed, although all of it is related to the one idea, the realization of which remains our unending task. And for the same reason, his scientific work cannot be adequately characterized by a description of his findings or an exposition of his general conception; we can only gain an idea of it by observing it in operation.

EXAMPLES OF WEBER'S INSIGHTS

Two examples may give us an idea of the special nature of Max Weber's insights into the destinies of mankind:

1. Since Montesquieu and Gibbon, the decline of the ancient world has been an object of wonder and of investigation. Max Weber saw the demonstrable unsoundness of the idea that it had been brought about by moral corruption and racial degeneration. He stressed another, very concrete factor and supported his contention by convincing arguments. Toward the end of the Roman republic, ancient culture became capitalistic, based on plantations operated by slaves, the supply of which had to be constantly renewed. Previously, the slaves had been maintained in patriarchal units, that is, they had families and reproduced. Now they were treated as capital, housed in barracks, and driven to work in chains by overseers. Their ranks had to be replenished by new acquisitions. This form of economy operated successfully down to the wars of Trajan, as long as large-scale wars continued to throw slaves on the market. But with the pacification of the Empire, the supply of slaves ceased and a shortage developed. This form of economy had to be abandoned. The slaves were again permitted to reproduce and raise families. They ceased to live in barracks and became husbandmen, bound to the soil, but again interested in their own livelihood. Thus the superstructure of the capitalist economy became steadily more reduced. But since this capitalist organization had come to sustain the Roman state, the army, and the whole economic life of the *orbis terrarum,* the return to a natural system

meant, in economic terms a transition to the Middle Ages, since commercial ties between the various regions were broken off, in military terms the disintegration of the Roman army organization, based on wages, and in political terms the impossibility of maintaining the unity of the Empire. This was the source of the increasing defenselessness of the Empire beginning in the third century.

In putting forward these facts, Max Weber did not mean to provide a complete explanation of the decline of the ancient world, but only to bring to light *one* demonstrable cause.

2. Another example leads us to what became Weber's central preoccupation. The capitalist spirit, which is the foundation of our life today, had never before existed in its present form. True, there has always been ruthless greed, lust for gold; there have also, in the past, been capitalist undertakings, that is, enterprises in which large fortunes were invested and large profits made. But nowhere was there anything like today: precise calculation of anticipated costs and profits, highly developed technology, industries which, existing and perpetuating themselves independently of individuals, satisfy most of the masses' vital needs.

Before this could become possible, several requirements had to be met: 1) the possibility of computing all costs, e.g. of foreseeing, on the basis of labor contracts, how much would have to be spent on wages (as opposed to the incalculable costs of slave labor); 2) the possibility of foreseeing legal decisions—this required a formal jurisprudence, as opposed to irrational, incalculable justice depending on the good will of a judge; 3) a rational state order, governed not by any party or arbitrary despotism, but by a rational and knowable law. Disappearance of slavery, formal jurisprudence, legal state order: all these factors tend to rationalize existence and to make it calculable.

But these factors would not have sufficed to give rise to a conception of labor that furthered the development of capitalism. Weber finds another new element, which he regards as decisive: the attitude of the worker who, instead of entering into a personal relationship with his employer, prefers to work for an impersonal enterprise, performing, in return for wages, an amount of work defined by contract, devoting his working hours entirely to his job, but otherwise free, and the closely related attitude of the entrepreneur, who consumes his energies building up his factory, reinvests his profits in order to expand and consolidate his enterprise, who furthers his interests but never really succeeds in enjoying his profits. From the standpoint of pleasure and enjoyment of life, both actually work to no purpose; they both perform according to an occupational ethic.

Today this spirit, usually embodied in the specialist, or taking on the form of an empty, exhausting, constantly calculating struggle for success, still carries the connotation of an occupational ethic. The question is: what is the origin of this spirit, of this impulse, which appears for the first time in this form in the world? Its origin is religious, although the religious impulse has been absorbed in today's purely secular conceptions. The notion of a vocational ideal has its origin in Luther. The particular form which was first to bring into being these striking consequences is to be sought in Calvinism. The religious doctrine here was: Man should not, as monks do, retreat from the world in an asceticism practiced in uncharitable inactivity; God wants to be glorified by active asceticism *in* the world. Consequently, man should work for others; the way to realize

God's will in the world is through useful works. The ultimate aim of work is not success or enjoyment of profits.
Work should be a form of asceticism in the world. God
predestined all men to a state of either eternal grace or
eternal condemnation. This no one can alter. Still, one can
look for indications of the state to which one has been predestined by God's unfathomable decree, but only indications; one can never be sure, one's destiny must always remain in doubt. One such indication is provided by success
in one's activities in the world: thus the aim of the tireless
planning and labor of employer and worker is to provide
not gain or worldly pleasure, but an indication that one is
predestined to a state of grace. If I were to start enjoying
my gains instead of using them to increase my success and
hence to glorify God in the world, this would indicate a
state of damnation. But even if I achieve the most magnificent success, my participation in a state of grace remains
in doubt, and this drives me indefatigably onward. This
religious attitude, which became widespread, was an incomparable spur to rational, calculated effort. It gave rise to an
economic system which is at once worldly and ascetic. Now
that the asceticism has lost its meaning, a purely secular
form of this attitude, having entered into combination with
new motivations, lives on like a ghost.

More complex and more convincing than this schematic exposition is the analysis of the relationship between
religion and capitalism in Max Weber's most complete
scientific work, *The Protestant Ethic and the Spirit of Capitalism.* But if we ask whether Max Weber believed that he
had found *the* cause of modern capitalism, his answer is:
not at all. By means of empirical research and scrupulous
interpretation, he merely disclosed the conditions necessary for the development of capitalism and then indicated

a positive factor which, clandestinely, as it were, brought forth consequences that had occurred to no one. These investigations broaden our horizon by elucidating a context that was hidden and that could operate only because it was hidden; and they help us to understand the husk that was left after the original substance had vanished.

Max Weber took a general interest in the distinguishing features of Western civilization and in the question of why these things happened here and nowhere else. Rational science (the Greeks), liberation from magic (the Jews), the cities with their local autonomy, the professional politicians and demagogues, constitutional government, the rational bureaucratic state, technological development, etc., are aspects of the fundamental problem which inspired Weber's investigation of the Protestant ethic. Formulated in economic terms, the problem is: *Why do we have capitalism in the Occident?* Why only here, when possibilities were present almost everywhere else? An essential feature of capitalism is rationalism: exact calculation, reckoning of all kinds. There has been rationalism all over the world, but only in the West has it been unlimited. Accordingly, the wider, more comprehensive question concerns the *origin* and *consequences* of the *rationalization* of human thought. Universal history, as Max Weber saw it, is an attempt to answer these questions.

THE UNIVERSAL HISTORIAN

Max Weber investigated because the knowledge he looked for was of deep concern to him. Firmly rooted in the present, he sought knowledge as a statesman or potential statesman. Consequently, he asked the political question: why is the German government leading us downhill? And: what are our real political aims? But the nation was only one point of departure for Max Weber's sociological curiosity. He was concerned with the state of the world as a whole. To understand this, we require a universal history; and to understand any historical event, we require conversely a profound understanding of our own present. It was precisely his concentration on the present as his own historical existence that made Max Weber a universal historian. His political frustration left his energies free for the satisfaction of his equally passionate intellectual curiosity. In this he was aided by his lifelong passion for history, which enabled him to amass an extraordinary knowledge of the most divergent epochs and civilizations.

As a universal historian he was not primarily concerned with the grandiose images of past epochs and civilizations, with the drama of history. To him images were only a means. Although he had great narrative power, narrative plays only a small part in his works. Anyone who takes them up in the hope of finding easy stories and descriptions or figures in the round will be disappointed. He will have difficulty threading his way through the tangle of names and allusions. Max Weber presupposes a knowledge of history in his readers. But measured by the penetration and concreteness of this historical understanding, most of the narratives and descriptions to be found in historical works seem vague and uncertain, as though the historian were concerned more with conveying an atmosphere than with imparting facts.

As a universal historian, Max Weber did not try to encompass the whole of the human world. He knew that the totality is questionable, or in any event endless and inexhaustible. Because he was interested in tangible facts, he recognized only relative totalities, and did not look for a construction that would embrace the whole of human affairs. Measured by Weber's universal history, the richest total philosophies of history seem threadbare, despite the seduction exerted by their easy grandeur.

Nor did Max Weber become a collector of historical data. He did not try to provide a compendium of all our historical knowledge. Measured by the intensity with which Weber explored his varied perspectives, such encyclopedias seem diffuse.

Further, he did not allow himself to dwell on striking figures or obvious relationships. His ultimate goal was not the *cultural* satisfaction derived from contemplating great thinkers as such. Weber's insights were inseparable from his sense of commitment, from his belief that the meaning of human existence is determined in the world. Beside them, such culture gives the impression of a detached, aesthetic contemplation of greatness—a contemplation that reflects passively courageous, skeptical despair.

Accordingly, Max Weber the universal historian is not a narrator like Ranke, nor a philosopher of history like Hegel, nor a collector of data like Schmoller, nor a contemplator of great figures like Burckhardt, but a sociologist. Each in its place, narrative, construction, collection, vision serve him as means. Because he takes none of these as his goal and lets none of them close him in, the world of human affairs is fully opened to his inquiry into the causes. His sociology is universal history because, engaged in a process that can never be completed, he rises to the *radical questions* in order to penetrate the great decisions, the root causes in the development of human affairs. He strove to understand how, on the basis of definable factors, human existence has become what it is. He strove for knowledge, but at the same time and in every instance to lay bare the limits of our knowledge. Despite his knowledge, which others no doubt took for a definitive penetration of things, he never lost his deference for reality, which is never known as such, but only in certain respects.

THE METHOD (Possibility, Comparison, Ideal Type)

For Max Weber history was a means by which to achieve a clear consciousness of present reality and present aims. Accordingly, he approached each period of the past as a contemporary. The essential feature of this *sense of the present* was that he did not see the present as if it were already history and as if all contemporary events had been necessarily determined—one who sees it in this light does not live in the present at all but imagines himself to be a spectator of something that is always in the past. But for him the past was always another present, and this was what made it real—one who regards history as mere past cannot help misrepresenting it in terms of his own present. It was only in this way that Weber was enabled to arrive at a clear picture, both historical and actual, of the decisions that were really made.

He himself defined the method that is essential to such an approach: in order to grasp the reality, we must see the *possibilities*. In the present, a formulation of the possibilities is the area in which I gain certainty concerning what I decide; without possibility, I have no freedom; without a vision of the possibilities, I act blindly; only a knowledge of the possibilities enables me to know what I am actually doing. Analogously, he employs the category of "objective possibility" in his historical appraisal of *past situations*. The historian considers a situation. His knowledge enables him to construct the possibilities of the day. By these constructions he first measures the possibilities of which the protagonists of the day were *aware*. And then, by the possibilities, he measures what really *happened,* in order to ask: for what *specific* reason did a particular possibility among several materialize? The historian turns happening back into possibility in order to find the critical factor in the decision which brought it about. Drawing on the logical investigations of others, Max Weber called the cause he found for the event which actually took place the adequate cause. This does not mean that what happened is regarded as an absolutely necessary consequence following from strict laws, but rather that, on the basis of certain regularities we have observed, we can understand why it happened as it did, because, if we ourselves had been involved, we should have expected it to happen.

One of the ways of discovering possibilities is *comparison.* As a universal historian, Max Weber constantly brings quite disparate events into relation with each other. When he compares developments in China, India, and the West, it is not in order to find historical laws or sociological types as abstract identities or similarities. Rather, he takes similarities as a means of arriving at a clearer understanding of the actual differences. In similar historical situations, similar developments are possible. But in the course of time opposite or different developments occur. By studying similar developments and using them as a contrasting background, we can discover the origin of each particular which is in turn conceived as one among a number of possibilities. In this way Max Weber arrived at the clearest understanding of what happened in each case. This he could do only in the light of universal history. There is a correlation between universal history and an exact understanding of concrete contexts. That is why in Max Weber's sociological analyses the method he applies over and over again is to draw comparisons, to circumscribe the possi-

bilities, and in this way to bring out the factors which may
in any sense have been determinant. Whether he speaks of
the origins of Jewish Prophecy and of the significance of
Judaism for world history, of the absence of progress in
India, of the significance of the battles of Marathon and
Salamis, it is always the simple pivotal point that is high-
lighted by the rich and many-sided empirical research.

In order to compare human contexts, I must subsume
them under concepts which denote their meaning—either
the meaning imputed to them by the participants, or their
potential bearing on other developments, or an objective
meaning. Reality is an endless fabric of meaningful and
meaningless factors. In order to apprehend it, we require
constructed concepts which, developed with an inner logic,
serve only as standards of reality: we then proceed to inquire to what degree reality conforms to them. Weber calls
these constructed concepts *ideal types.* To his mind they
are not reality itself, but technical instruments of investigation by which to approach reality. They do not denote
classes of phenomena, they are formal patterns, by means
of which we measure reality, in order, in so far as it conforms to them, to gain a pregnant formulation of it, and
in order to bring out clearly the elements that do not conform to them. They are not the goal of investigation, not
the laws of process, but means by which to gain the clearest
awareness of the specific characteristics of the human reality in question. The wealth of Weber's insights rests on the
construction of such ideal types, which prove to be fruitful for the concrete knowledge of reality; examples are the
traditional, charismatic, bureaucratic types of government,
the types of church and sect, the types of city, etc. These
concepts must be developed with precision; there are sharp

dividing lines between them; but reality is fluid, in it one
type blends into another.

THE DISTINCTIONS

The uncritical mind suffers from an ineradicable tendency
to look for a truth that can be recognized as universally
valid and taken for the definitive whole, by which I shall
know what is good, what I should do, and what reality
itself is. In his critical quest for knowledge, Max Weber
opposes this monistic impulse. He strove for cogent empirical knowledge and as a scientist observed distinctions on
which he insisted in the interest both of true knowledge
and of true philosophy. He insisted on genuine observance
of the distinction between empirical knowledge and value
judgment; between the particular knowledge that is always
one-sided and all conceptions of the totality; between empirical reality and the essence of Being.

a) Max Weber never wearied of repeating that no empirical investigation can provide a foundation on which to
determine what has value and what I ought to do. Where
an aim is presupposed, empirical knowledge can, to be
sure, indicate what means will help to achieve it and what
means will detract from it; and it can determine the secondary effects of an action detrimental to other values. But
empirical knowledge can never prove that the value and
purpose themselves are universally valid. On the contrary,
both our empirical knowledge and our determination to
adhere to our values and choices gain in clarity when
neither is allowed to encroach upon the other. Science
must be free from value judgments: this means that the
scientist must disregard his own preferences and examine
the phenomenon clearly, from all sides, taking no more

consideration of welcome facts than of inconvenient ones. My scientific duty to see the truth of the facts, and my practical duty to stand up for my own ideals, are different in nature. This does not mean that one can be fulfilled without the other. Weber merely insists that they must not be confused; only by keeping them separate are we enabled to fulfill them both. Scientific objectivity has nothing to do with a lack of moral principles. But to mix them destroys both objectivity and moral principles. In Max Weber's opinion, to speak with apparent objectivity while seemingly deriving a universally valid value judgment from the material is pusillanimity, characteristic of those who on the one hand cannot dispense with value judgments and on the other hand try to disclaim responsibility for their judgments. A sober questioning of reality is possible only if I take my distance from the object and from myself. But the value judgments which are suspended in scientific inquiry are in turn essential conditions of this inquiry, because they make us aware of hidden value judgments.

The freedom of science from values does not then mean for Weber that we should not make value judgments in practice, but quite the opposite; only by elucidating passionate preferences and by disciplining our will can we attain to genuine objectivity in scientific research. Nor does he mean that value judgments, whether actually made or possible, should not be an object of investigation. On the contrary, he regards them as the essential object of inquiry into human affairs; but he holds that, when it comes to examining their meaning, origins, and consequences, freedom from value provides the sober outlook indispensable to an accurate view of them. Finally, he does not imply that the choice of problems to investigate does not rest on value judgments; rather, a value judgment concerning

what is of interest to me is indispensable for true passion
in scientific research.

b) Max Weber recognized that all investigation is particular and that the *whole* is closed to us. If I were able
to know a universal in human affairs, either in the form of
universal, always identical natural laws, or as the totality, or
as a definite and unmistakable principle of development, I
could derive particular events from it as necessary consequences. But I actually gain knowledge, in relative perspectives, of rules and laws which apply merely to aspects of
reality, and I gain knowledge only of relative totalities,
never of *the* totality. Every reality is individual, endless, inexhaustible; the laws that apply to it are not such that we
can infer reality from them. Nor can we speak of a universal
primordial state, either cosmic or human, untroubled by
historical contingency, and say that historical individuation
developed out of such a state. Reality is at all times equally
individual, historical, and endlessly diverse. Thus there is
no universal either in a conceptual or a temporal sense,
there is no principle, no substance, no original human situation or original essence, no existence that has not yet been
individually determined, from which reality can be derived.
This was Max Weber's perspective when he said: "Endlessly
the stream of immeasurable happening rolls on toward eternity." Consequently man can only penetrate reality by empirical science, not deduce it and apprehend it as a whole.
The consequences of this insight are on the one hand a
rigorous view of empirical reality and on the other hand
the rejection of all metaphysical infringements on empirical knowledge.

Empirical reality must be definitely demonstrable: in
human action it is only the purpose intended by the men
involved (as distinguished from a supposed objective, his-

torical purpose, unknown to them); it is, further, the purpose intended by individuals and by many individuals (whereas totalities in the sense of human groups exerting an unconscious action are not empirically ascertainable); only the action of individuals is empirically real. It is not the business of empirical sociology to create conceptions of totalities; it investigates their functional significance as conceptions that influence human behavior. It does not absolutize them, nor does it deny their reality in so far as there is other evidence for it (though this reality can never be universally valid), nor does it decree that they must not be used in action. The individualist method of empirical sociology does not imply an individualist evaluation any more than the rationalistic character of its concepts implies belief in the predominance of rational motivations in human action. Empirical inquiry must inevitably reject the belief that the state, the Church, marriage, etc., are substances, but it does not question the existence of such conceptions as contents of faith; on the contrary, it investigates them as such, in their objective character as conceptions held by men and motivations of human conduct. Thus for sociology such beliefs, considered as meanings and purposes willed by real men, become transformed into objects of rational inquiry; the state, for example, is "solely a possibility that an action based in a demonstrable way on the conception of the state took place or is taking place or will take place. . . . No other clear meaning can be attributed to the statement that a state still exists."

Consequently Max Weber, as an empirical sociologist, is opposed to metaphysical concepts such as "spirit of the people" (*Volksgeist*), ideas as active forces, to the notion of necessary development, to the materialist view of history as a clear and unequivocal determination of the course of history. In his opinion no view of the totality of human history, no construction of world history is permissible. He persists in an endless methodic penetration by empirical investigation. He does not shape a neatly rounded whole. If he had had a system, it could only have been a system of methods and concepts *ad hoc*. But even such a system of concepts is not a meaningful goal. "The points of departure in the Arts will always remain variable as long as a Chinese sclerosis of cultural life has not destroyed man's habit of asking new questions of life, which will forever remain unalterably inexhaustible."

The relativity of all concepts that lend themselves to the investigation of empirical reality implies that every approach is one-sided, but that the possible perspectives are innumerable; in every case we have a combination of concrete and abstract elements. Supposed insights into the totality as the over-all historical reality, as the central reality on which everything else depends, are taken up by Weber, but only as ideal, typical constructions, which are possible and which are tested for the extent to which they further the concrete knowledge of actual facts. Thus he took up the Marxist constructions, rejecting their claim to total and absolute validity; on the same plane, he attempted to disclose the fundamental character of religious factors and their real though limited importance for economic and social history, and to show why what many regarded as mere superstructures could, in his opinion, be of primary causal importance in the light of empirical investigation.

Testing all concepts and constructions by the criterion —to what extent do they raise questions which lead to important results in empirical inquiry?—Max Weber was able to use them and thus to study every complex set of facts from every point of view. Precisely because he admitted of no completion in the field of knowledge, because he accorded scientific value to no total view, recognized no knowledge of the "authentic" factors of development, he was able to acquire the free perspectives and orientations which are the essence of unbiased investigation. To his mind, it is true, no human world could be wholly explained, each one remains an infinite problem, but for that very reason he obtained definite, reliable knowledge, and was able to avoid the widespread delusions that come of visions of totality or of underlying forces; he was able to avoid all absolutes based on one-sided views. In considering radically one-sided conceptions, all of which represent aspects of knowledge, he was able, through his awareness of their one-sidedness, to avoid being dominated by them and on the contrary to dominate them.

c) Because Max Weber as an empirical scientist favored concrete knowledge over total views, the particular over the general, precise investigation over mere theoretical reflection, penetrating inquiry over panoramic vistas and handy labels, causal analysis over imagery, intellectual construction over mere description; because he favored tangible empirical factors over substantial entities, he remained *within the realm of empirical reality, detached from the core of things* (in another context this determination to remain within the bounds of the knowable becomes a condition for the love of true Being). Because he was so close to reality, he did not claim to know the essences of things. He never supposed that he had fathomed the ultimate foundation of reality. In the context which he investigated most thoroughly on the basis of the empirical material—the relation of modern capitalism to Protestant ethics—he singled out one causal factor, but said firmly: this only demonstrates the presence of *one* cause; it is not proved whether its quantitative significance is great or small; I believe it to be great. Because being cannot as such become an object of empirical investigation, Weber takes up *every* mode of empirical reality, losing himself in none, examining each one for its causal significance. Natural conditions, technical instruments, historical situations, the ideas and purposes pursued by men, religious conceptions and their consequences, the role of political power—all these became for him empirical objects of relative importance. But he is all the more inevitably confronted, in his empirical investigation, with the fundamental realities which he must take as his point of departure, as unexplained presuppositions.

THE SCIENCE OF SOCIOLOGY

Max Weber's scientific work is the purest application of modern realistic thinking—which has achieved indubitable certainty only in the natural sciences and in mathematics—to the whole of human existence. He called this science sociology, so identifying it with the efforts that went under this name, although he owed no more to them than to the historical sciences, the philosophy of history, and jurisprudence. Nevertheless sociology as an empirical science could not include everything; he confined it to the study of the subjective meaning of human action in so far as this action takes account of the behavior of others. How with his vast knowledge he tilled this field cannot be described in brief; the most concrete and limited of his investigations serves the never-ending progress of human insight into what men have done or may do.

Officially Max Weber was an economist. He was opposed to the establishment of professorships in sociology. For he was well aware that this science draws heavily on other special sciences and requires a considerable critical sense. "Most of what goes by the name of sociology is a fraud," he said in the valedictory lecture delivered at Heidelberg University.

NONKNOWLEDGE IN KNOWLEDGE

There are two sides to Max Weber's scientific work. If either is disregarded, the other cannot be understood.

Universal empiricism is the striving to know everything that can be known. Wherever something can be proved the empiricist steps in. For him everything takes place in accordance with compelling logic and intelligible laws of causality. Everything?

Only what is knowable—"everything" only in so far as everything and the knowable are identical. Everything that can be known becomes subject to the relative character of our knowledge. But our knowledge encounters *limits*. Max Weber's science is inseparable from our awareness of what is not known. To begin with, everything that is individual is infinite and hence inexhaustible. In the second place, historical phenomena, because of their uniqueness, can never be fully interpreted. Finally, an origin is always in some way presupposed: the first conceptions of a religion cannot be understood genetically despite all our knowledge of the constellations and situations without which they would not have come into being.

In Max Weber's works the empirical science which "disenchants the world" seems to prevail almost exclusively. This gives rise to *misunderstandings*. This enormous knowledge transposed into science is mistakenly interpreted as a knowledge of human existence *as such*; some are foolishly delighted with it, whereas others reject it.

Thus he has been accused of having no mind for re-

ligion, for Indian philosophy, for the world of peasants and
landowners, for the integrity and substantiality of the
state, etc. But all these accusations are based on a confusion of universally valid knowledge *of* something with the
being that is *in* something and expresses itself through our
reflection on meaning. Once known, an original impulse is
no longer itself, but becomes a relative cognitive content.
Max Weber purified knowledge by confining it to empirical knowledge, not in order to restrict our thinking to this
kind of knowledge, but in order to clarify and to make
really possible the other modes of knowledge with their
different meanings and their always historical, never universally valid foundations. Integrity forbade him to make
concessions to those who promote their interests by refusing to acknowledge facts and by representing their
cause as a matter of knowable universal interest. Nor would
he make concessions to the nostalgic negations of unbeliev-
ers, who in knowledge try to recover the possession that they
have lost in faith: it is characteristic that true believers take
no umbrage at Max Weber's analytical sociology of religion,
that genuine practitioners of power politics have no objection to his cool, empirical observations. Recognition of
the fact that knowledge is relative only enhances the purity
of faith.

Another criticism is that Weber amassed too much
knowledge, that living human beings cannot master this
enormous mass of material. Knowledge, the argument goes
on, becomes meaningless; it serves no purpose, because it
recognizes no substance and loses itself in the endless; Max
Weber has gone as far as possible in this direction and his
method is no longer applicable. But in such an argument
the infinity of empty intellectualism is confused with the
infinity of the meaningful scientific process.

Finally, it is maintained that Max Weber failed as a scientist. He did indeed fail, but his was the authentic failure which lies in the very nature of true science. Inauthentic is the failure that resides in the intellectualism of random ideas and over-all schemas, which for a time confer a seeming intellectual satisfaction, but in the end leave nothing behind but the meaninglessness that lay concealed within them from the start. Inauthentic is the failure of those who, merely because they cannot master the infinity of knowledge, renounce the possibility of knowing. Inauthentic is the failure of those who, because they have mistakenly sought to capture being itself by knowledge, are disillusioned and forsake the way of knowledge altogether. Those who incur inauthentic failure maintain that nothing can be known and abandon the effort. Max Weber's failure consisted in taking a positive view of authentic nonknowledge, in approaching it by means of boundless, concrete, and clearly defined empirical knowledge, and in so opening up the possibility of an authentic being, which is not an object of knowledge. The more comprehensive the knowledge, the more deeply its failure leads into being; that is why Max Weber's projects were so gigantic that he could never complete them, why his works, despite their great scope, are enormous fragments, the unfinished buildings of a Titan. In sociology Max Weber rejected even the most disguised forms of metaphysics; his scientific attitude was almost ascetic. In this way he kept open the possibility of an authentic failure and declined the inauthentic satisfaction of a science that is untrue to itself. He refused to make easy by supposed knowledge what can succeed only through true faith. The relativity of knowledge seems to push us into a bottomless void, but only such a fall enables us, by an authentic and original act rooted in the will and faith of our historical present, to clear the way for truth and reason. It is the broadest horizon that allows free development.

Though Max Weber's scientific effort exceeded human strength, it was not an end in itself. It was the function of an Existenz, which it served. Sociology is only an offshoot of his deeper self, which he kept hidden and which can be glimpsed only indirectly: Max Weber the philosopher.

The Philosopher

Max Weber developed no philosophical system. It would be impossible to expound his philosophy as a doctrine. He declined to be called a philosopher. But to us he is the true philosopher of the time in which he lived. Because philosophy is not a gradually progressing science, which recognizes a timeless truth, each philosophy must achieve its reality as a historical existence rooted in the absolute and oriented toward transcendence. Max Weber taught no philosophy; he was a philosophy.

HIS IMPLICIT PHILOSOPHICAL POSITIONS

Only incidentally to his scientific activity did Max Weber, on the strength of his critical conscience, which could not accept the idea that his scientific investigation might be groundless, make explicit philosophical statements: on the *meaning of science,* on *possible ultimate perspectives,* on *what he was not aiming at in his scientific work.*

He looked on science as the cogent empirical and logical insight which progresses indefinitely and is never completed. The scientist, he said, works in order to be superseded; he can have the satisfaction of discovering something which is henceforth certain and definitive; but this knowledge is an island in the endless stream of the knowable. Science can never know the essence of reality but can only disclose facts and relationships in the course of its never-to-be-concluded progression; it can never tell us what we must absolutely do, but only indicate the means of carrying out a presupposed aim. Science may at one time have been regarded as the way to true being, to true art, true nature, the true God, and true happiness, but today no one holds such a belief. Science has disenchanted the world. It always assumes that its disciplines derive their importance from other sources—medicine, for example, from the practical consideration that human life must be preserved and suffering diminished; astronomy from the theoretical assumption that the laws of cosmic process are worth knowing. Science itself can never prove that science has meaning.

With this view Max Weber drew the necessary inference from the actual course of science. He quotes Plato, recalling the attitude expressed in the parable of the cave (at the beginning of the seventh book of the *Republic*). Men in this life are imprisoned in a cave, fettered in such a way that their eyes are turned toward the inner rock; they see only shadows of being, that fall on the cave wall; but when one of them shakes off his fetters, he can turn and see the sun. "He is a philosopher; the sun is the truth of science, which alone does not grasp after illusions and shadows, but after true Being." Today none of this is believed; what Plato expected of science is precisely what it does not give.

In that case, Tolstoi concluded, science is meaningless: "It is meaningless, because it gives no answer to the one question that is important for us: What should we do? how

should we live?" And also because through it death becomes meaningless; death should not be, because science
can never be concluded, and according to its immanent
meaning, a life devoted to it should have no end.

But Max Weber, who in opposition to Plato—or at
least to the interpretation of his philosophy as science—
fully agrees that science has no answer to Tolstoi's questions of meaning, does not, like Tolstoi, deny the meaning
of science. Diverging from both Plato and Tolstoi, this is
his reply to the question of the meaning of science: Universally valid knowledge of the empirically real and of the
logically compelling is indispensable to a man of independence and integrity; it implies devotion to a cause that is
espoused without self-interest; science teaches us to see inconvenient facts; man proves himself by showing what he
can bear to know. Science gives *clarity*. It discloses given
facts on which my action depends and gives awareness of
the rational *standpoint* from which action meaningfully
follows. It possesses its characteristic compelling truth only
if it is free from prophecy. We are free to believe a prophet
or not to believe him; scientific insight is compelling for
every man, or else it is not scientific insight.

The most stimulating of scientific possibilities is the
question of ultimate perspectives. In his *rational elucidation* of the perspectives from which my action or the action
of others meaningfully follows, Max Weber starts from
"the one fundamental fact, that so long as life remains
immanent and is interpreted in its own terms, it knows
only of an unceasing struggle of these gods with one another. Or speaking directly, the ultimately possible attitudes toward life are irreconcilable, and hence their struggle can never be brought to a final conclusion. Thus it is
necessary to make a decisive choice" (*Science as a Vocation*,

Oxford University Press, p. 152). "As Hellenic man at times sacrificed to Aphrodite and at other times to Apollo, and, above all, as everybody sacrificed to the gods of the city, so do we still nowadays, only the bearing of man has been disenchanted and denuded of its mystical but inwardly genuine plasticity. Fate, and certainly not 'science,' holds sway over these gods and their struggles" (ibid., p. 148).

To gain clarity concerning the ultimate attitudes toward life which give rise to this never-ending conflict and so lend all human existence a tragic character, to enable man to consider the ultimate meaning of his own actions, is the task of science: but of what science? "The discipline of philosophy and the essentially philosophical reflections of the specialized disciplines attempt to do this."

But it would be a misunderstanding to maintain that Max Weber simply identified philosophy with this science. Where he discusses the ultimate conflicts at greatest length, in order to use them as ideal types for the scientific elucidation of the sociology of religion, we see how political, erotic, intellectual, and religious laws oppose and exclude one another. But he expressly reduces all this to the relative importance of a possibility: these "intellectually constructed types of conflict between the orders of life mean only that in this context these inner conflicts are possible and adequate, not that there is no standpoint from which they might not be regarded as nullified."

Thus the notion of an unresolvable conflict between possibilities is an ultimate for every scientific view of the world, but it is not the last word for all awareness of being. What is rationally ultimate from one point of view is not so in an absolute sense. Max Weber speaks as a sociologist; only incidentally does he limit the relevance of his sociological statements.

Thus it is not Max Weber's view that by reflecting on the ultimate perspectives we can develop a schema, comprising a definite and unchanging number of value systems which, when I decide between them, show me where I stand philosophically. To him all constructions were relative orientations, steps after which the way to further clarification still lies open. For because they are universal, they are never adequate to the reality of action in any situation. Weber had a secret—and sometimes overt—contempt for philosophical generalities. "So-called ultimate positions? They result in idle talk, nothing else. And in particular: after long experience it has become my fundamental conviction that only by testing our own supposedly ultimate positions by our attitudes concerning sharply defined and very concrete problems can we attain clarity concerning our real aims." Here philosophy is immersed in life; in concrete situations it becomes the lucidity of life achieving self-awareness. But precisely at this point Max Weber stops reflecting about philosophy. Only seldom does he break off his analysis by speaking of limits.

In the same light, he strove in his sociological investigations only to disclose empirical facts and causes, but not to express what they might mean in terms of metaphysics. He had a profound feeling for the cipher language of things; he recognized the profundity with which Hegel and Burckhardt spoke of ciphers; but he did not set himself this task in his scientific work. "It is true that the course of human destiny is deeply moving to one who has surveyed a segment of it. But he will do well to keep his little personal commentaries to himself—just as we shall do well not to impart our impressions of the ocean and the mountains."

Max Weber did not philosophize in the strict sense; his

philosophy is to be sought in his acts as a politician, as a scientist, and as a man. It is real philosophy before interpretation, not the cogitated, unreal philosophy which can seemingly be present in mere thinking.

Max Weber as a Man

Max Weber was a *contradictory personality*. On the one hand, the commanding figure with his grand gestures and bewitching eloquence—on the other, the anonymity of his almost obscure existence. On the one hand, the grace of his movements, his warmth of heart, the childlike simplicity of his purely human interests—on the other, the stern, uncompromising seeker after truth, which at times so overpowered him as to make him curse God.

On the one hand, a passion for knowledge for which no pains were too great—on the other, indifference toward all his achievements.

On the one hand, constant concern with the seeming externals of scientific research—on the other, his deep roots in the authentic truth of Being.

On the one hand, unswerving devotion to methodic investigation—on the other, the conviction that all our knowledge is relative.

On the one hand, a ruthless break with those whose morals disappointed him—on the other, endless kindness and forgiveness of wrongs.

On the one hand, unrestricted struggle against an adversary—on the other, a chivalrous readiness for conciliation once victory seemed assured.

His agitation in the face of the evil which he saw coming over a period of twenty years—and his perfect serenity in the catastrophe of 1918.

His capacity for happiness in the present, the lofty serenity of his life—and his boundless, searing anger.

His uncompromising insistence on the ethical imperative as the law of the day—and his lucid awareness of the demons of the night.

Such contradictions are characteristic of this man as a man; but their persistent dominance seems to reflect his era. Max Weber did not take an attitude of opposition or superiority to his era. But this era was undergoing intolerable tensions. Amid his brilliant outward triumphs, his magnificent technical achievements, man could no longer find himself. He had become the slave of a mechanism which he had ceased even to understand. Steadily advancing in concrete achievement, this world with all its knowledge was ultimately without truth. In such an era greatness could not crystallize into a harmonious personality, a reflection of a harmonious world around it. The times cried out for personality, but they had no use for the greatest they possessed. The consistency with which they excluded Max Weber reveals something about the times themselves, something which no longer makes us indignant. The contradiction in Max Weber between world and Existenz made him, to be sure, characteristic of his era, for this contradiction was its very essence, but not in such a way as to permit the era to recognize itself in him. Unaware of its own inner disunity, it was devoted to self-seeking, wealth, and success; it suffered only in particular cases what Max Weber experienced and understood profoundly. He lived in the only way possible for a man of integrity in those times: breaking through all illusory forms, he disclosed the foundations of human Existenz. The destiny of the era, the destiny of Germany, became reality in a man who did not keep on the side lines but who himself was this destiny and helped to enact it. In torment and hope he was, as it were, the heart of Europe, which was on the point of losing its spiritual and human life.

To other men Max Weber was an orientation and a standard, not a model. On the dividing line between epochs, a man can arouse others, he cannot mold them. His integrity commanded him, the strongest among the men of his time, to reject all followers, in contrast to all the weaker men who set themselves up as leaders and struck prophetic attitudes. It would have been easy for him to create a following for himself, which was what many others did. But he met all men as equal to equal, stifling every kind of imitation and discipleship in the bud.

Max Weber seemed to stand between a passing and a rising era. He sometimes felt himself to be an epigone, yet he already lived in an age that had not yet dawned. But in the present humanity was to him a certainty, though without objective validity, without world stature, without monumentality: "It is the fate of our times, with their characteristic rationalization and intellectualization, and in particular with their disenchantment of the world, that precisely the ultimate and most sublime values have receded from public life to take refuge in the brotherliness of immediate relations between individuals. It is . . . no accident that today, within the smallest groups, between man and man, *pianissimo,* something throbs, which has its counterpart in the prophetic pneuma which in other days passed like raging fire through the great communities and welded them together."

Though in *history* Max Weber saw reality with equal objectivity wherever he found it, a particular resonance is apparent where that reality held a special appeal for him. Especially in the extreme affliction of the war years, he was preoccupied with the Jewish Prophets and their solitude. Looking at Michelangelo's ceiling in the Sistine Chapel, he felt the first signs of recovery from his illness. Rembrandt's picture in The Hague, *Saul and David,* was strangely close to him. The world of Aeschylus and of Shakespeare was congenial to him. He honored and respected the other world that has its summit in Goethe. He may well have felt an affinity with men who proved themselves in times of collapse. When someone praised Boethius for having preserved his philosophical certainty with Roman dignity and Greek wisdom amid the universal ruin of the sixth century, Max Weber assented with unusual warmth.

Condemned in a period of disintegration to leave his powers unused or to squander them, or so it seemed, to no consistent purpose, Max Weber chose to overcome negative attitudes, content, even when his strength failed him, that his head remained clear and his heart alive. This is the path of reason, to deal with a misfortune not by resigning ourselves or letting habit blunt our sensibilities, not by enduring it by virtue of our vitality or by forgetting and withdrawing into isolation, but by wholly suffering that misfortune and experiencing it with full clarity. Reason, the source of human being, is a colorless thing to contemplate. It cannot be characterized in itself, but only when subjected to the limitation and particularity of a character. Conceived in its perfection, it is nothing but an empty image, but seen in its reality, it is everything that constitutes the dignity of man. It is never complete in time, for it is merely man's path uphill. Its essence is to grow greater, not to be greater to begin with.

Man ascends through the quest for knowledge, he seeks scientific certainty and orientation in the realm of the possible, yet in such a way that it is not the mere understanding that determines, subordinates, concludes. Rather, in the extreme situations of life, it is reason, propelled by the impulse toward the essential, which guides the understanding. Max Weber's investigations reach out infinitely in all directions and derive unity by the essential which concerns man as man. Openness to things, even to the irrational and antirational, either with a view to mastering it and assimilating it or to recognizing it as the other, provided him with his wide scope, as did his closeness to every man he encountered, even the strangest. It was his reason that made him press forward to the limits in every sphere and to seek clarity in which to act with good will. Reason is freedom.

Freedom in himself and in those around him was for Max Weber the first of essentials. The carefulness with which he fostered such freedom in ever changing contexts, of communication, of debate, of questionless understanding, was the source of the trust he inspired. Freedom in the world cannot be defined as an intellectual attitude, as idealism, liberalism, or Germanism; it is humanity pure and simple. Many are those who do not even attempt it. It often languishes and is often betrayed. When it is met with, we experience it as a revelation of what is best in mankind, although as a possibility it is innate in every man.

Here lies the reason why Max Weber did not become a leader to those who wished to be subjected. The force of his reason awakened the force of reason in others. Weber did not influence men through authority, through superior knowledge and ability, through an obscure charisma—those would have been aesthetic charms—but by helping others to progress in self-awareness. He can never become the object of a cult, but only the exemplar of a rational man for all who wish to be rational and free, and to understand themselves. In a unique way he inspired courage, showing the way which, after him, man can and should follow.

Max Weber remained true to the ideas of the eighteenth century, which were later termed liberal: the possible freedom of the individual and all its implications; the inviolability of every man's personal sphere of existence, the rights of man, and human dignity. He gave the most urgent thought to the question of how, in a bureaucratized, mechanized, barbarized future, when the human masses on the plains of the Mississippi and Siberia would be rigorously confined to rigid estates and corporations as in a new Middle Ages, the individual might preserve his rationality and personality.

When we survey his epoch and our own, it becomes evident that at a time when men in general were succumbing to illusions and fanaticism, when irrationality was being consecrated by false prophets, deceived deceivers, and violent despots, Max Weber represented the undying presence of reason.

And in an age when reason was becoming intellectualized or degenerating into a mere thinking technique, into ungrounded knowledge and sophistry, which can only undermine and destroy, Max Weber was the incarnation of man; his humanity was the historical manifestation of reason.

Reason is impersonal; it becomes *human* through its movement in time. In historical situations it inspires solidarity among men, the struggle for justice, the tolerance that knows where to stop, the courage to support or to oppose a cause at the risk of one's life. To show Weber's humane reason in action, one could go on endlessly, relating what he did, how he reacted, how he judged, and what he loved. Although he espoused no "great cause" in the world, although he did not take a leading part in history, he did not keep aloof. With uncompromising passion, he devoted himself to matters which to others seemed unimportant. His ready helpfulness, his activity as his friends' advocate, his concern for the academic careers of others, for shared scientific investigations, his numerous vain attempts to exert a political influence—all this took up a large part of his life. At every moment he returned from the heights of his scientific endeavor to his present human situation among those whom he loved or respected. This was his center of gravity, regardless of whether the matters with which he concerned himself in it were great or small; for in the eyes of God it makes no difference whether a man rules the world or helps a friend in his lonely affliction, provided that in so doing he throws his whole self into the balance.

Max Weber was far removed from defiant indifference to the world; he did not allow his independence to become smug isolation. Without exaggerating the importance of his position in the academic community, he regarded it as a positive element in his life. That is why he was grieved —though he took it serenely—when, after illness had forced his retirement from active teaching, the faculty did not, as the government suggested, allow him to retain his membership and his voice in its councils; or when, during the war, a number of professors organized a political discussion club and he was not asked to participate. He was so far removed from vanity that he had no need to regard these little things with indifference.

It would be a mistake to suppose that this wholehearted German hated or despised any foreign nation. He took a deep and passionate interest in the destinies of other nations, especially of Russia and the Anglo-Saxon countries. During the war he showed a chivalrous concern for every prisoner who was accessible to him and did not hesitate to oppose the then prevailing nationalistic instincts, hatred and spy phobia. He never ceased to regard every man as a man, endowed with inalienable rights.

Max Weber's struggle was for justice. When a scholar became the butt of an unjust and insulting attack, when Max Weber's publisher was unjustly accused, when a gifted colleague was barred from an academic career, he never declined an appeal for help. He despised anti-Semitism. Although, to his mind, all political life centered on foreign policy and national power, his opinions in social questions were remarkably sound. Caught up in the social movement in the eighties and nineties, he never closed his eyes to the just claims of man as man. But there was no will to power in Max Weber's struggle. Though the will to power was a motive well known to him, he himself did not share it. He never exploited or sought to consolidate a personal victory. The idealized will to power that made such great statesmen as Caesar and Napoleon, Cromwell and Bismarck, admirable but virtually intolerable as human beings, was lacking in Max Weber.

Even his reason was without will to power. It imposed limits upon itself. For himself absolutely obedient to the ethical law of reason in the Kantian sense, he allowed his moral judgment to be tempered by the reality of the man he encountered. His moral judgment, to be sure, was uncompromising, but he never ceased to question it, demanding the absolute only of himself, and though merciless in exposing frauds, never set himself up as a judge of others.

Toward servility and meanness he showed a silent intolerance; only when a *cause* seemed to demand it was he
willing to take up arms against them.

Max Weber was convinced that a certain university
instructor had publicly lied and was a disgrace to the teaching profession. Others suspected this to be so, but were not
sensitive to the disgrace and felt no need to bring the facts
to light. Max Weber took the case to court. Even friends
said he was exceeding the limits of common sense. Agree-
ing with him but distressed, one friend compared his action
to Niagara Falls pouring into a washtub. Others considered
his behavior ludicrous and predicted that he would discredit himself. Consummately adroit in court, Max Weber
at once became the guiding spirit of the trial and succeeded
in proving the truth. Recalcitrant witnesses revealed their
knowledge against their will under his cross-examination.
The instructor was dismissed from the university. Then
everyone found the proceedings perfectly sensible and the
instructor's behavior scandalous.

This willingness to incur discredit, to rock the boat
even at the risk of making himself ridiculous in order to
save the substance of being when it is threatened, was the
expression of his sense of responsibility to the historical
present. What is true here and now must be done. To let
things slide, to shrug them off as small and unimportant
is to undermine the world from within. He stated in general terms what we must do: "go about our work and
meet the requirements of the day—both as men and in
our professions. And that is a very simple matter, provided
that every man find and obey the daemon who holds the
threads of his life."

Firmly grounded in himself, *he attached little importance to his personal prestige.* In a day when cultivated

men in general set great store by intellectual achievement, felt obliged to justify themselves by producing something of their own, and bolstered up their self-esteem by publishing books, Max Weber, a true creator in the realm of ideas, was quite indifferent toward his standing. At the time of his death little of his work was accessible to the public. His most important writings were tucked away in periodicals. From these and his posthumous papers Marianne Weber compiled a ten-volume edition of his works. Max Weber had no desire to write "books." He began to do so reluctantly toward the end of his life, when the task he had set himself seemed to demand it. Instinctively he chose a style of writing which made the man behind the writer unrecognizable. Here again he stood on the dividing line between two worlds: the one dying, in which nothing counted but objectivity, which he respected as an achievement in others, the other being born, in which objectivity is equated with technology and truth is seen as a mystery revealed. This accounts for his attitude of selfless serenity toward the scientific work in which he himself was so passionately immersed, an attitude expressed in the words: "What is not done by me will be done by others." Objectivity is replaceable; anonymity in its historical embodiment is being.

Max Weber's indifference toward his status is also discernible in his language. His style is rather disconcerting on first reading. Side by side with penetrating thought, exactness of definition, and careful organization, we find indifference to the linguistic form, composition, bulk, and proportions of his work.

Max Weber was not a careful stylist. His writing was the immediate expression of his intensive thought and perceptive power; he did not polish. As a result, his style is often colorless; but even then it conveys something that is characteristic of him alone.

Often we find repetitions, digressions, followed by a leap back to the subject, enumerations that are not absolutely necessary, involved sentences, incidental remarks.

Max Weber could not bear to reread even his manuscripts, much less his printed works: he took no pleasure in the published work, but proceeded with the task in which it was only a step.

Because Max Weber's mind was entirely on his subject and not at all on his expression, he succeeded in spite of himself in speaking a truly original language: his words make us feel the direct presence of a living mind. Because his writing was formless in a period when most writers tried to embellish their colorless content by laboring their form, the form he achieved carried the authenticity which is the adequate expression of really original thinking and of fulfilled humanity.

In his language as in everything else, Max Weber was overgenerous, undemanding, and open. He never posed, but showed himself at each moment for what he was as a man and as a thinker. He had the courage to lay himself bare, to express himself without artifice.

FAITH AND TRUTH

Max Weber was never willing to make common cause with militants of any faith; with such men, he held, it is impossible to talk. In their fanaticism they cling to unalterable ideas. He, on the contrary, championed the unrestricted rationality which in its never-ending movement comes to a limit which calls for a militant decision. Militants of faith cling to illusory schemes of total knowledge. Totality—relatively justified like all categories—dominates both the idols of reactionary thinking and the utopias of revolutionary thinking. Fanatics are those who believe they have an immediate intuition of absolute being (which implies that the absolute is immanent). They are confident that they are in harmony with this absolute, that what actually happens, whether governed by necessity or by man's will, is ultimately what should happen and never question the rightness of their beliefs. Such men have lost both their original relation to transcendence and their capacity for communication with others.

Max Weber stood his ground against all these illusions, perversions, temptations, against all intellectual absolutisms, and against the faithlessness of nihilism as well. He might well have lost heart and withdrawn into misanthropy. He was sustained by his faith, that simple, unknowing faith which, drawing on the deepest source, never ceased to accept life, seeking and finding something worthy of love in the midst of disaster, and capable of appreciating even what is absolutely alien. He was never weary of life, nor was life for its own sake ever the ultimate for him. The idea of dying in battle filled him with awe, since it gave meaning to something that otherwise men must all endure passively.

As the situation grew worse, his faith grew greater. As long as things seemed to go well, he was the merciless pessimist, trying to rescue what could be rescued; in time of disaster he was serene—all was not lost, something, some potentiality, would emerge again. This was not easy optimism, it was an indestructible faith and affirmation of the eternal struggle for essential being. In 1919, at the time of his valedictory lecture, German reality offered him no source of encouragement—on the surface, the situation looked utterly hopeless. He spoke of the German forests that continue as they are, neither remote monumental grandeur nor sentimental idyl, symbolizing what is best in the Germans, their capacity for preserving their individuality, for quiet reflection, for response to everything human. And as he had always done, in times good and bad, he reiterated his profession of faith: I thank God that I am a German.

With all his reflection, Max Weber was naïve. In his questioning and his thinking he went further than is normally possible for man. But he never regarded the results of his thoughts and investigations as anything more than means—they did not possess him, he possessed them—and was always something more than his intellectual achievement. His whole life was spent in the process of experience, search, and analysis; but all the particular aspects of his personality were transcended in the unity—which was no longer an object of knowledge—of his authentic selfhood. Although his faith left behind it no articulate, definitive content, it informed all his thought and experience.

If we wish nevertheless to formulate this faith, we may cite the mysterious words spoken on his deathbed: The true is the truth (*Das Wahre ist die Wahrheit*). To us these words are not a tautology, but a kind of magical incantation, expressing the truth of an Existenz, which recognizes every kind of knowledge, including the empirical, only as functions in a responsible process, the source and goal of which are not known, but are affirmed.

From the outset the quest for truth took the form of *struggle* for Max Weber. As a young man he learned in the atmosphere of Treitschke and Bismarck "that earnest, conscientious effort, unconcerned with results and in the sole interest of the truth, is held in low esteem." Later on, his struggle for truth was directed against those who strive for meaning and value in knowledge as knowledge, but who, precisely by so doing, confuse value judgment and knowledge, decision and insight; further, against those who strive for absolute knowledge and so become inauthentic, because all knowledge is valid only from a certain point of view and in a certain respect. He struggled against the rationalists, because they do not take a critical view of the laws of knowledge, and against the irrationalists, because they fail to recognize the role of knowledge as an irreplaceable means of grasping the truth; against philosophical dishonesty, which for the sake of harmony conceals the abysmal depths with conceptual schematisms; this "formal garden" style, as he called it, never ceased to arouse his anger. Consequently, Weber was attacked for his relativism, for his cold objectivity; he was attacked on the ground that freedom from value judgments is supposedly impossible and that a science characterized by freedom from value judgments gives no satisfaction. But behind Weber's demands stood a passion for truth, which by pursuing every mode of knowledge with clarity strives the more resolutely toward the point where knowledge is not gained through science, but by acting and producing in the world. This freedom from values has implications both for scientific purity and for authentic action. His sense of truth was remote from both the self-satisfied materialism of the liberals and their optimistic faith in science. To his mind the responsibility of the free individual was the inviolable condition of all values in the world. He rejected every form of violation of the freedom of conscience.

In an original way Max Weber's scientific work reveals an unconditional drive for truth. He did not interpret history in a personal manner, nor was history for him a remote object. He entered into it with eyes trained by the reality of his own present, but, as though present in both realms at once, saw it as another world. That is why for all their objectivity, his historical analyses concern us so profoundly. And this is also why we are never certain of exactly how they should be interpreted. Some believe that the secret motive of his investigations of Calvinism was his affinity with asceticism, others that it was hatred of modern mechanization. Apparent justification can be found for both theses, and both are false. If we approach Max Weber's treatment of Calvinism, of the Jewish Prophets, of the great demagogues, etc., with the mistaken assumption that Max Weber reveals himself by his glorification of these phenomena, we cannot but be startled by the equivocal light in which they appear. And the deeper Max Weber pursues his investigations, the stronger this impression becomes, so that in the end we are at a loss to say whether his evaluation is positive or negative. The very essence of human action seems to be manifested by the boundless justice and candor of this scientist, who does not weigh the right and the wrong, but without general evaluation discloses historical contexts with their origins, possibilities, and consequences in reality. Indirectly these investigations impart a deeply hidden evaluation of existence itself, which could only be falsified by explicit value judgments.

FAILURE

Max Weber was a great political writer and the founder of present-day sociology; he is recognized as a great scientist and as the author of extraordinary works; he was a good husband and friend, a man who knew happiness. Yet political action was denied him, his works remained gigantic fragments; for many years he suffered poor health, and he influenced only a small number of people in his lifetime.

These mere facts concerning Max Weber's failure in the externals of existence tell us nothing about the essence of his failure. There was about him an aura of failure in a deeper sense. His failure does not correspond to what he was unable to do, nor his success to what he was capable of accomplishing. His failure was a defeat that is akin to an active will, the true failure of a man in the historical existence that has been imposed on him:

In the *political* sphere an aspect of his being was never completely fulfilled, remained pure possibility. His political insight was that of Cassandra, who could convince no one and do nothing but suffer. He resembled Machiavelli or Mirabeau, who towered above all the other political thinkers of their time by their merciless realism, but remained without important influence; yet they failed for lack of the character which Max Weber possessed. He set himself the highest aim: to act politically without personal will to power, on the strength of a vocation. His failure was essential, because what he wanted was humanly true but in fact impossible of achievement.

In *science,* his work remained fragmentary; not because he lacked energy, but because he saw his task in terms of truth. He felt that he failed with his unlimited knowledge, precisely because it is the essence of knowledge to fail at the limits, in order to open up the way to deeper truth in action and in existence. He *aimed* at the point where failure becomes the truth. By its very nature science can never be completed; in science an extraordinary fragment is more than any completion, which is always illusory.

As a *philosophically-minded man,* he suffered the limits of finiteness; for all the reality of his action, he suffered outwardly from the lack of adequate scope and because he believed that his work lacked historical relevance: he sought objectivity, something whole and valid in the world, to which he could give himself in order to become authentically himself—and could not help but feel excluded from the wide stage of actuality and thrown back upon himself, like one who has been deprived of world and space. But he did not react to this failure as failure. He never weakened, he always, under all circumstances, devoted his whole being to whatever he felt to be his task. Only at the limit, where the commitment is complete, did his action, regardless of whether it affected greater or lesser fields of reality, disclose its relative and symbolic character. This was his true failure in the sense of a return to the authentic source.

Even though Max Weber failed on the objective plane, his failure is like an intimation of the truth, because the movement of his thought broke through the crust of objectivity, penetrating to those innermost depths of man which lie beyond personal happiness and loyalty to one's dear ones. On this ultimate plane of being Max Weber the man reflects the eternal presence of the authentic source.

What he was as a man cannot be expressed by subsuming him under any psychological, sociological, or historical type. Those who called him an outsider, a presumptuous subjectivist, a liberal, a nationalist, a democrat, who regarded him as a representative of the individualistic bourgeoisie by whom precisely he was thrust aside, and as the prototype of an age to which, as we have shown, he was precisely in opposition; or who stressed his asceticism, or his heroic skepticism, or finally, without reverence for true greatness and destiny, spoke of an escape into heroism, the sublimest form of shirking—they are all mistaken. In his own investigations and logical reflections, Weber himself combated this method of subsuming men and spiritual real-

ities under universal concepts, of classifying them according to their epoch or their place in the history of ideas, or
according to antinomies which appear to provide a sharp
characterization; he realized that this method is nothing
more than easy talk and confers no genuine insight, that
such labeling is mere intellectual barbarism. Least of all
can it be applied to Weber himself. Those who do so
imagine that they understand him at first sight and fail to
see his depths. Only by going beyond temporal embodi-
ments, by penetrating to the very source of human potentiality, can we gain a glimpse of what man is.

Equally on the wrong track are those who take him as
a guide and prototype. Seldom has a great man declined so
radically to be anything of the sort. What matters is that
we find ourselves with his help. He calls on us to seek the
truth for ourselves in communication as we advance through
time, not to look for a ready-made truth to accept and
admire. In failure he hands on the torch, freedom to freedom.

The race of men born into the world of Homer and the
Jewish Prophets did not die with Nietzsche. Its last great
representative so far has been Max Weber. He is our contemporary, for although in these times of headlong change
the specific realities of Weber's day have vanished in the
brief period since his death, the fundamental questions of
human existence and knowledge and the decisive tasks have
not. We no longer have a great man capable, as he was, of
helping us to find ourselves. He was the last. Consequently,
we can still orient our lives by him even now that he has
begun to recede slowly into history. To us who knew him
he is a living presence; to others he will always embody the
best, freest type of German, the authentic Germany.

In late antiquity, amid a leveled world that had lost

its faith, the individual looked to Stoic philosophy for support. For philosophy Socrates showed the way, because as a real man he had been, done, and suffered what philosophy for centuries thereafter sought to understand. In the world into which we are entering, in a time of mass accumulation and mass domination, of universal utilitarianism, crushing misery, and banal happiness, it will again be the task of the individual to seek his philosophical truth. No objectivity will teach him. Perhaps the open secret of a man such as Max Weber will speak to him and kindle him. If this happens, we may say: Those who understand failure and death can approach him. He will remain incomprehensible to those who, entranced by the beauties of the world which Max Weber also enjoyed in moments of serenity, forget death.